Somatoform Disorders

People with somatoform disorder (which used to be known as hysteria) present with a range of symptoms that may last for years and can not be traced to a specific physical cause. Such symptoms may include frequent headaches; back pain; abdominal cramping and pelvic pain; pain in the joints, legs and arms; chest or abdominal pain, and gastrointestinal problems, but classically present as medically unexplained neurological symptoms.

This book is an indepth, clinically oriented review of the somatoform disorders and related clinical presentations (such as chronic fatigue syndrome) with special reference to how they present in a medicolegal setting. It is aimed at both clinicians and lawyers who deal with injury claims where these disorders impact much more frequently than is generally recognised.

Michael Trimble is Professor of Behavioural Neurology at the Institute of Neurology in London and consultant physician to the National Hospital for Neurology and Neurosurgery. He has written widely in the interface between neurology and psychiatry, and has run a neuropsychiatry research group which has taken a special interest in patients who present with medically unexplained symptoms.

Somatoform Disorders

A Medicolegal Guide

Michael Trimble
Institute of Neurology

CAMBRIDGE
UNIVERSITY PRESS

CAMBRIDGE UNIVERSITY PRESS
Cambridge, New York, Melbourne, Madrid, Cape Town, Singapore,
São Paulo, Delhi, Dubai, Tokyo, Mexico City

Cambridge University Press
The Edinburgh Building, Cambridge CB2 8RU, UK

Published in the United States of America by Cambridge University Press, New York

www.cambridge.org
Information on this title: www.cambridge.org/9780521169257

First published 2004
Reprinted 2006
First paperback edition 2010

A catalogue record for this publication is available from the British Library

Library of Congress Cataloguing in Publication data
Trimble, Michael R.
Somatoform disorders: a medicolegal guide/Michael Trimble.
    p.   cm.
Includes bibliographical references and index.
ISBN 0 521 81108 2 (hardback)
1. Somatoform disorders.   2. Medicine, Psychosomatic.   3. Forensic psychiatry.   1. Title.
[DNLM: 1. Somatoform Disorders.   2. Forensic Psychiatry.   3. Hysteria. WM 170 T831s 2004]
RC552.S66T756   2004
614'.1 – dc21   2003055284

ISBN 978-0-521-81108-8 Hardback
ISBN 978-0-521-16925-7 Paperback

For Jenifer, now Dame – 22 years later

Contents

Preface	*page* ix	
Acknowledgements	xii	
1	Historical overview	1
2	Classification and the somatoform disorders	21
3	Clinical presentations	41
4	Malingering	84
5	Memory in a medicolegal context	109
6	Assessment, treatment and prognosis	140
7	Somatoform disorders in a medicolegal context	168
8	Mechanisms	197
9	Causation and the question of consciousness	220
	Appendix: Civil Procedure Rules Part 35 (www.lcd.gov.uk/civil/procrules)	243
	Index	247

Preface

Hysteria, we are often told, is an old-fashioned term for a disorder which has virtually disappeared. Certainly the term is old-fashioned, having been ingrained into medical practice for over 2000 years. Certainly it carries with it a considerable amount of intellectual and emotional baggage which, over the centuries, has rendered it a cumbersome subject to discuss. It has not however disappeared, in spite of the attempts of some to abolish it by renaming it, or others to suggest it is a merely culturally derived set of symptoms which peaked in incidence with the rise of oppressive Victorian male doctors delighting in the symptomatology in their pretty petulant female patients. In fact, patients who present to doctors with medically unexplained symptoms are as common now as they ever have been, although the more extravagant forms are certainly restricted in any large numbers to specialist centres. However, this was probably the case when, for example, the great Charcot collected together his coterie at the Salpêtrière in Paris towards the end of the nineteenth century.

Hysteria was renamed by committee, and now masquerades under such terms as somatoform disorder and somatisation disorder. The change of name reflects the fact that the patients with these chameleon symptoms come to the clinic for the comfort of a diagnosis, as long as the diagnosis is not that of hysteria!

The National Hospital for Neurology and Neurosurgery, or, as it was once more elegantly called, the National Hospital for Nervous Diseases, is one specialist centre which has attracted, particularly, the neurological variants of hysteria ever since it first opened. My predecessor, Eliot Slater, took a particular interest in these patients and his pronouncements on the subject are well known. Another predecessor, Harold Merskey, has also written extensively in this area.

It is then with considerable hesitation that I too have written on this subject. In part, this has been driven, as with my predecessors, by the very fact of the large number of patients that come to the hospital who in the past would have borne the diagnosis of hysteria or conversion disorder. In my experience these conditions are even more prevalent today than previously, and the diagnostic difficulties which they can present are still as complex as in earlier times. Arguments still abound (in non-medicolegal circles) about the nature and causes of symptomatology, about the organic and the non-organic, about the role of consciousness in the development of the symptoms, and the potential for therapeutic remediation.

There are several recently published books on the subject of hysteria, and this one is not an attempt to go over old ground. In 1981 I published a book entitled *Post-Traumatic Neurosis*, with a subtitle 'From railway spine to whiplash injury'. This book led me into the fascinating history of posttraumatic hysteria, and the nineteenth-century debates about the cause of symptoms following accidents, particularly railway accidents, and the role of compensation in either creating or maintaining the symptomatology. To some extent this book is an update of that earlier version, but now written with many more years of medicolegal experience in the kit bag.

I think the final motive for writing the book was the persistent interrogation by lawyers about the issue of consciousness: 'Doctor, are the symptoms conscious or not?' Further, I found that amongst the legal profession there was even more ignorance about hysteria, posttraumatic hysteria, somatoform disorders and somatisation, than amongst many medical practitioners, particularly referring here to non-psychiatrists.

The book then is intended to help and hopefully satisfy the needs of several groups. This of course is a difficult task. However, it is hoped that psychiatrists will enjoy the exploration of the history of the subject, and the discussion of the clinical presentations, especially at the fringes. It is hoped that these clinical chapters will also be of relevance to lawyers and those interested in the law who may in their professional work come across people with the medical problems discussed herein. More difficult has been the excursion into issues of causation and consciousness, and also the legal aspects of compensation for psychiatric injury. Here I have done my best to lay out the current position as I understand it, with the help of a number of legal colleagues, and to express it in a way which I hope is intelligible enough for non-legal practitioners who seek access to this kind of knowledge. I apologise in advance to those who may feel I have simplified the text in some areas, with the hope of explaining the complicated simply, and to others who feel that I have somehow missed the simple by making it too complicated.

Chapter 1 presents a historical overview: this goes over old ground, but with an emphasis on the development of the concept of posttraumatic hysteria. In Chapter 2 I have tried to outline the way that the term 'hysteria' has transmogrified to become somatoform and dissociative disorders, with variants on that theme.

Chapter 3 looks at some of these variants, a number of which readers may be surprised to find in the context of a book on somatoform disorders. However, in many of these settings we are dealing with patients who have medically unexplained symptoms. This naturally leads on to the consideration of malingering in Chapter 4. Malingering is central to many of the medicolegal arguments, and is a subject which, like many a troublesome child, should, according to many, be seen but not heard. Testing for malingering is notoriously difficult, but in medicolegal practice it is often suggested this is assisted with psychological testing, and this is discussed in Chapter 5. This chapter explores in some detail the whole area of memory in a medicolegal context. This issue of memory is reverted to later when, in Chapter 8, mechanisms are discussed (following on from the earlier theories outlined in Chapter 1), and in the final chapter on consciousness.

Chapter 6 deals with assessment and treatment and prognosis. There are not many studies in this area, but summarised here are also the results of studies which have looked at the issue of the role of compensation in the maintenance of symptoms and thus prognosis.

It is in Chapter 7 that I have tried to understand the intricacies of the legal process of claiming for psychiatric injury, and have put in a section on the new Civil Procedure Rules (CPRs). This is intended as a guide, but also has a plea. I have tried to outline some of the difficulties that experts have in following the terms of the CPR and also pointed out some of the anomalies. If I have come down somewhat harshly on lawyers here, it is because lawyers continue to come down harshly on experts in relationship to their failure or otherwise to obey the strictures of the new directives.

In the last chapter I discuss the issues surrounding causation and finally the question of consciousness. Those seeking a ready answer to the question outlined above, about whether the patient is conscious of his or her symptoms, may be disappointed with this exegesis, and I am sure there will be those who disagree with both the underlying philosophies presented and the conclusions, particularly on aspects of free will. However, the chapter does reveal the differences between the legal and the medical mind both in relationship to causation and to consciousness, both of which are central to the posttraumatic hysteria debate.

I have avoided the development of new terminology, with the exception of introducing the term 'lexigenic', to refer to the harmful effects of the legal process on patients' symptomatology. It is hoped that by introducing the term, more attention may be given to these factors in claimant assessment, and this may stimulate some much-needed work into this malign protean effect.

Acknowledgements

I should like to thank the following who have read sections of this book and offered very helpful comments, and with whom I have enjoyed discussions on these matters in the past, and hopefully will continue to do so in the future: Richard Brown, John Cutting, Michael Jones, Luke Kartsounis, Maurice Lipsedge, Christopher Mace, Graham Powell, John Smythies, Alan Sprince and Duncan Veasey.

I also want to thank Jackie Ashmenall, my personal assistant, who has helped with the preparation of this manuscript, and has tirelessly organised my medicolegal practice over the years.

Historical overview

The word hysteria . . . has so great and beautiful a history that it would be painful to give it up.

(Janet, 1901, p. 527)

Introduction

Hysteria is as old as the earliest medical texts. Originally it was a concept of the cause of symptoms, found exclusively in women, thought to be due to the wandering womb, which, being frustrated by lack of proper use, leaves its anatomical position and travels around the body causing pressure in anomalous places, and hence symptoms. Although there has been an academic debate about what the Egyptians and subsequently the Greeks were actually referring to when they discussed the wandering womb, early history reflects on two important points. First, symptoms such as are seen today were documented over 2000 years ago, across at least two different cultures, and second, that the postulated mechanism was gender-related.

Examples of the kind of symptoms that are to be described later in this book are noted in these texts, including convulsions and paralyses, and the classical globus hystericus, caused by pressure from the wandering uterus on the throat. Inscriptions from the temple of Aesculapius in Epidaurus record episodes of hysterical aphonia and blindness, and possibly the first recorded case of malingering:

Nikanor, a lame man. While he was sitting wide-awake, a boy snatched his crutch from him and ran away. But Nikanor got up, pursued him, and so was cured (Veith, 1965, p. 19).

The Middle Ages, with its neo-Platonic theological stranglehold on developing scientific thought, and thus on the medical sciences, conflated the manifestations that we would now view as hysteria with those of witchcraft. The latter first became a statutory crime in 1541, a date which heralded 200 years of witch-hunting and persecution. The detection of witches became paramount, and stigmata were identified. In particular, so-called witches, patches – areas of sensory anaesthesia – were recorded, but the muscular contortions and convulsions of the afflicted were well noted.

Edward Jorden (1569–1632), a physician of London and Bath, in 1603 wrote a treatise called *A Briefe Discourse of a Disease Called the Suffocation of the Mother*, essentially to counteract the prevailing mood, which was to attribute such symptoms to possession by some supernatural power. His view was that the so-thought stigmata of witchcraft were in fact signs of mental illness, thus reclaiming, for the first time since Hippocrates, the essentially medical, somatic nature of the phenomena.

His book was occasioned by a trial in 1602, in which a charwoman, Elizabeth Jackson, was accused of bewitching the 14-year-old Mary Glover. The latter had convulsions, episodes of loss of speech, periodic blindness, paralysis and loss of sensation of the left side of the body, aggressivity and personality changes. The trial was probably the first in recorded history in which a psychiatrist was called to give evidence, but even then, as today, the adversarial nature of the proceedings ensured that there was another psychiatrist present, also giving evidence, who fundamentally disagreed with the formulations of Dr Jorden.

Jorden recognised the polymorphous nature of the symptoms, their link to the female sex and the importance of 'perturbations of the mind' in the cause of the disorder.

A shift of emphasis

Mass hysteria, in which groups of people manifested mainly motor abnormalities, became well described in the Middle Ages, and culminated in the grand chorea epidemics of Europe. Outbreaks of St Vitus' dance, Tarantism, *convulsionnaires* and the like referred to groups of people, from half a dozen to several hundred, who would display exaggerated movements, dance and convulse until they dropped exhausted (Hecker, 1844). Many episodes were noted in relation to natural disasters, for example after the spread of the great plague, but other outbreaks came in closely knit social groups, often united by some strong religious belief. These outbreaks were similar in form to episodes of contemporary episodic epidemic hysteria, about which more is discussed later. However, these phenomena emphasised the imitative nature of many hysterical afflictions, and the powerful role of social and cultural pressures, and contagion in their pathogenesis.

Concepts of aetiology moved from the supernatural to the natural; the uterus remained popular, but several other shifts of emphasis occurred. The uterine theories slowly gave way to two interpenetrating themes, namely that the main organ involved in hysteria was the brain, and that somehow emotions were highly relevant. The sixteenth-century physician Paracelsus (1493–1541) used the term *chorea lascivia*, a disorder he opined which was provoked by ideas. The English neurologist

Thomas Willis (1621–75) was one of the first to espouse the central importance of the brain. He reflected that 'this passion comes not from the vapours rising into the head from the uterus or spleen, nor from a rapid flow of blood into the pulmonary vessels, but has its origin in the brain itself' (Dewhurst, 1980, p. 87). He was led to this conclusion, not only following postmortem examinations and by his clinical observations of the disorder in prepubertal and senile women, but by the irreconcilable fact that he observed hysteria in men!

The emphasis on the emotions was taken up by several writers, including Willis, but considerably advanced by Thomas Sydenham (1624–89). He said that, of all chronic medical conditions in his practice, next to infections hysteria was the commonest, afflicting one-sixth of patients. He recognised the condition of male hysteria, although referred to it as 'hypochondriasis', and he noted the polymorphous presentations, stating that 'few of the maladies of miserable mortality are not imitated by it' (Sydenham, 1850, p. 85). Not only did Sydenham suggest the chronic nature of the condition, but he also hinted at personality contributions. Patients were prone to irritability and anger outbursts; they were capricious and labile in their moods and affections. He firmly placed the origins of hysteria in the mind, referring to 'over-ordinate commotions of the mind', with a 'faulty disposition of the animal spirits' (p. 85).

The Italian physician Baglivi (1668–1707), in his classification of diseases, included hysteria under 'diseases of the mind', implicating the emotions even more directly than Willis or Sydenham in causing hysteria. He thought that emotional instability was an important factor in the chronicity of symptoms.

Associations with what we may now refer to as depression were noted in Burton's *The Anatomy of Melancholy* (1621), and the concept that the mind could influence the body, a precursor of twentieth-century psychosomatic concepts, was well accepted. The Scottish physician Sir Robert Whytt (1714–66), discoverer of reflex activity in the nervous system, and one who recognised that the mind could cause actions not appreciated by consciousness, discussed the newly invented term 'nervous'. Noting how physicians tended to use this term for all disorders they were ignorant of, he gave his own definition thus:

those disorders may, peculiarly, deserve the name of *nervous*, which, on account of an unusual delicacy, or unnatural state of the nerves, are produced by causes, which, in people of a sound constitution, would either have no such effects, or at least in a much less degree (Whytt, 1751, p. 102).

Of those that so suffered, there were three groups: the simply nervous, the hysteric and the hypochondriac. Hypochondriacs were patients who were seldom free of complaints. Passions of the mind acted through the brain to provoke sensory and motor alterations, symptoms which were various and chameleon-like. In a passage which antedated posttraumatic stress disorder (PTSD) by over 200 years he wrote:

Thus doleful or moving stories, horrible or unexpected sights, great grief, anger, terror and other passions, frequently occasion the most sudden and violent nervous symptoms (p. 206).

Another Scottish physician, George Cheyne (1671–1743), wrote on hysterical and hypochondriacal disorders, referring to them collectively as the English malady. Not surprisingly, the weather was incriminated in aetiology, as were the advances of civilisation. However, he drew distinctions between original and acquired nervous disorders. The former were people born with weak nerves; the latter have their disorder brought on by accidents or by their poor lifestyle, and intemperance. Accidents, for the first time, became clearly noted in this literature on hysteria, but did not necessarily act alone. In one of robust constitution, the debilitating effect of lifestyle, acting through the blood and defrauded juices, was also important. Cheyne outlined a dilemma which is ever-present today:

Nervous distempers especially are under some Kind of Disgrace and Imputation . . . so that often when I am consulted in a case, before I was acquainted with the Character and Temper of the Patient, and found it to be what is commonly call'd Nervous, I have been in the utmost Difficulty, when desir'd to define or name the Distemper, for fear of affronting them, or fixing a reproach on a family or Person. If I said it was the Vapours, Hysteric or Hypochondriacal Disorders, they thought I call'd them Mad or Fantastical: and if they were such as valued themselves, on fearing neither God nor Devil, I was in Hazard of a Drubbing for seeming to impeach their courage: and was thought as rude, as if I had given them the Lye, and even the very best has been, I myself was thought a fool, a weak and ignorant Coxcomb, and perhaps dismiss'd in Scorn (Cheyne, 1733).

The emphasis on underlying personality structure as important for an understanding of these disorders was further discussed by the German neuropsychiatrist Wilhelm Griesinger (1817–68). He noted the

peculiar hysterical disposition, viz., immoderate sensitiveness, especially to the slightest reproach, a tendency to refer everything to themselves, great irritability, great change of disposition on the least or even from no external motive (humours, caprices), and not the slightest reason can be given for the change; they often exhibit tender sympathy for other female individuals, peculiar eccentricities . . . This general state comprises many peculiarities of character, often of quite another kind, as a tendency to deception and prevarication, to all kinds of misdemeanours, jealousy, malice etc. (Griesinger, 1862, pp. 179–180).

Interestingly, Griesinger also commented on the history of the patients, noting the relevance of past episodes of sensory disturbances, paralyses, globus hystericus and the like.

Themes of either sexual frustration or sexual excess in hysteria, while tending to wane in the eighteenth century, and inherent in names such as the *hysteria libidinosa* (Boissier de Sauvages, 1706–67), or *furor uterinus*, continued to resurface. They were put into a somatic context by Griesinger, who thought that local diseases of the generative organs were linked to hysteria, a theme taken up in England by Thomas Laycock (1812–76), teacher of the neurologist Hughlings Jackson (1835–1911). His writings were aimed at trying to understand the reciprocal relationships between the body and mind, developing a biologically oriented scientific psychology. He believed that in hysteria the nervous system was implicated, that it was seen in the majority of cases in females of child-bearing age, and therefore the generative organs were involved in the pathogenesis. The condition often came on following grief, terror, fear or disappointment in love; these emotional events excited deranged actions in the generative system and thence the hysterical phenomena (Laycock, 1840).

Laycock's investigations took him to speculate into the nature of the mind, and on the role of consciousness in these phenomena. Following on from Whytt's studies of reflex activity, and Marshall Hall's (1790–1857) demonstration in animals of the spinal reflex arc, Laycock suggested that the cerebrum (cranial ganglia) was also a reflex centre like the spinal ganglia. From this he developed his law of the unconscious functional activity of the brain. This was several decades before the Freudian elaboration.

The general practitioner, later ophthalmologist, Robert Brudenell Carter (1828–1918) divided hysteria into two main forms – simple, which manifest essentially as hysterical seizures, and complicated. The latter, foreboding the later Briquet's form, 'generally involves much moral and intellectual, as well as physical derangement, and when it is fully established, the primary convulsion, the *fons et origo mali* is sometimes suffered to fall into obeyance . . . being arrested by the urgency of new maladies' (Carter, 1853, pp. 28–9). He implicated sexual emotions as causative, and shifted the whole debate away from pathology of the sexual organs to inhibited sexual passions.

This was, according to Veith (1965), the first theory of repression. Emotions led to physical disorders by somatic discharge; affects provoked the wide range of motor and sensory states seen in the condition. Interestingly, Carter also observed the factitious nature of the illness in many patients, and how they used leaches in the mouth to produce bleeding, bandages to cause limb swellings and the like. Although since the time of Sydenham, the chameleon-like nature of hysteria was recognised, and its simulative nature alluded to, this seems to be one of the first texts to raise the question of patients' motives and actions more directly.

Hysteria in nineteenth-century France

Thus, summarising the history of hysteria to the mid nineteenth century, several statements can be made. The condition hysteria had been recognised for centuries, and had been the source of much speculation regarding aetiology and pathogenesis. Certainly, it is not clear how many patients falling under this diagnosis given perhaps by Sydenham or one of his contemporaries were in reality suffering from unrecognised organic disorders, and many diagnostic and nosological confusions existed. However, trends and general statements can be noted. Causation shifted away from the uterus to the brain, and then to the mind. Psychosomatic concepts were readily accepted. Emotions, but especially sexual emotions, discharging through the somatic apparatus provoked the polymorphous, often bizarre symptomatology recognised as hysteria. The potential chronicity of the condition was also recognised, as was its occurrence in males. Certain types of people, that is, certain personality types, seemed more susceptible, and external exciting causes such as accidents could be relevant.

As the nineteenth century progressed, there was an explosion of interest in hysteria; the main writings came not from England, but from France. Not only did the sexual theme become revived, but also the concept of posttraumatic hysteria was crystallised.

Some of the early nineteenth century French physicians, such as Pinel (1745–1826), Landouzy (1818–64) and Dubois d'Amiens (1797–1873), reverted to uterine theories, challenging the concept of male hysteria. The relationship with hypochondriasis was again raked over. Hypochondriasis, as noted above, was used by Sydenham to refer to a form of male hysteria. Writing shortly after Willis, Sir Richard Blackmore (1653–1729), in his book *A Treatise of the Spleen and Vapours; or, Hypochondriacal and Hysterical Affections* (1725), regarded hypochondriasis and hysteria to be the same malady, differing only in degree of severity, and he hinted at underlying personality factors: 'fluctuation of judgement . . . reversing of opinions and resolutions, inconstancy, timidity, absence of mind, want of self-determining power, inattention, incogitancy, diffidence, suspicion, and an aptness to take well-meant things amiss' were cardinal features (Hunter and Mcalpine, 1963, p. 321).

Jean Pierre Falret (1794–1870) seems to have been the first to use hypochondriasis in this way in France, but the nervous, cerebral origins of hysteria found increasing support through Brachet (1909–88), Georget (1795–1828) and Pierre Briquet (1796–1881). Briquet was chief physician to the Paris Charité, and he readily admitted that he undertook to study hysteria as a matter of duty, on account of the frequency of cases that he reluctantly had to examine.

His book *Traité Clinique et Thérapeutique de l'Hystérie* (1859) reported on the results of personal examinations of nearly 450 patients, and stands as the nineteenth-century landmark in hysteria studies, having a considerable influence on Charcot and his school.

Briquet firmly rejected uterine theories, and described a series of cases in males. He outlined the multifarious symptoms, including the spasms, anaesthesias, convulsions, paralyses and contractures which by now had become familiar in descriptions of patients diagnosed as having hysteria. In one table he refers to the length of time that the symptoms lasted. Of 418 patients, 179 had the condition for between 6 months and 4 years, 81 between 5 and 10 years, and the rest lasted a longer time: in 59 patients the condition lasted longer than 20 years, while in 5 patients it spanned 55 years. These patients were polysymptomatic, 'des troubles permanents qui portent sur presque tous les organes' (Briquet, 1859, p. 519). Clearly forerunners of the later-christened Briquet's hysteria!

As to pathogenesis, he was clear that it was a condition of that portion of the brain which received sensations and affective impressions, and he described hysteria as a nervousness (neurosis) of the encephalon. However, he recognised many interacting factors. These included heredity, and emotional predisposition, impressionability and emotional lability. He cited several antecedents, including the excitement of accidents, and physical abuse. Incidentally, Briquet was critical of the term 'hysteria', but felt it should not be given up because it had been in use so long and everyone understood its meaning.

Charcot and his school

The hysteria mantle than fell to Charcot (1825–93), the doyen of mid to late nineteenth-century French neurology, and his school of successors, many of whom also wrote on the subject of hysteria. Working at the Salpêtrière, where he became chief of neurology in 1882, he observed in detail the clinical phenomenology of cases of hysteria. It was his view that hysteria should be viewed as any other neurological condition, and by sufficient and detailed observations it should be possible to define its cause and course, the former being sought in the brain. Hysteria major (*la grande hystérie*) was hysteria with convulsions (Charcot, 1889).

He documented the physical stigmata of hysteria in considerable detail. These included anaesthetic patches, often involving the whole of one side of the body, contraction of the visual fields, and, interestingly, ovarian tenderness – a reversion to the genital region! Hysteria in his clinic was rarely monosymptomatic, and often chronic.

It is known that Charcot's later theories of causation moved towards a more psychological approach. This was partly due to his work with hypnotism, but also because of his observations of traumatic hysteria. He tended to move away from the use of the term 'hysteria', and preferred the expression 'neurosis'.

With regards to hypnotism, he started to use this after experimenting with magnetism and electricity, as a way of influencing hysterical symptoms. By hypnotising patients he was able to demonstrate that the symptoms of hysteria could be produced, or resolved, but importantly, that in posttraumatic cases, identical symptoms to the posttraumatic symptoms could be reproduced. He therefore did not accept any fundamental difference between hysteria of traumatic and non-traumatic origin.

Charcot quoted with approval the work of the English surgeon Sir Benjamin Brodie (1783–1862), who had observed the disuse atrophy of the limbs of patients diagnosed with motor forms of hysteria, and that hysterical conditions could come on after only minor local insults (Brodie, 1837). He also readily quoted Russell Reynolds (1828–96), who had introduced the concept of psychical paralysis, in which states the paralysis is invoked by an idea (Reynolds, 1869). Through hypnosis one could call into existence an idea or group of ideas which may be connected with previous associations, but that remained free from the control of personal ideas or the ego, and which could become fixed. To quote Charcot directly:

A man predisposed to hysteria has received a blow to the shoulder. This slight traumatism or local shock has sufficed to produce in this nervous individual a sense of numbness extending over the whole of the limb, and a slight indication of paralysis. In consequence of this sensation the idea comes to the patient's mind that he might become paralysed; in one word through autosuggestion, the rudimentary paralysis becomes real (Charcot and Marie, 1892, p. 630).

Although it is often contended that Charcot never moved away from his neurological approach to understanding the symptoms of hysteria, the above comments are clearly a herald to the later-developed Freudian theories. They are also a reaffirmation of the importance he placed on suggestion in the evolving symptomatology.

By the time he was writing, Charcot was quite familiar with the concepts of nervous shock and traumatic hysteria, as had developed from the discussions about railway spine, discussed below, and which had appeared in the English medical literature a decade or two before. Similar cases, of posttraumatic hysteria, had been reported in France and Germany, and following many types of accidents, not just from the railways. Charcot reported many cases of hysteria provoked by an accident, and opined that the severity of the accident was less important than the patient's constitution. Further, he quoted cases in which fright or emotional shock, with no physical injury, also precipitated hysterical symptoms.

Of course, for Charcot and his school, it remained the nervous system which was abnormal in such cases, and his invocation of hereditary factors was related to the predominant place of degenerative theories of causation in nineteenth-century neurology. Thus, not all people would succumb to hysteria, or could be hypnotised; only those with certain nervous constitutions, which reflected hereditary and sometimes sinister moral degeneration.

Janet and dissociation

For many years the seminal contributions of Pierre Janet (1859–1947) to the hysteria debate were overridden by those of Freud, but in recent times, with a renewed interest in the phenomenon of dissociation, a revival of interest in Janet's views has occurred.

Janet initially studied philosophy, but started experimenting with hypnosis at Le Havre, and then studied medicine in Paris, spending time at the Salpêtrière, where he examined Charcot's patients. Charcot encouraged him to study experimental psychology, and patients with hysteria and neurasthenia became his main interest.

By careful analysis of the patients' symptoms and the content of their mental states, he developed a scheme that related to subconscious mental ideas, which themselves were related to traumatic events, and which could become replaced by symptoms. The mechanism was through a narrowing of the patients' consciousness, related to a weakening of psychological synthesis. Subconscious fixed ideas could be clarified through hypnosis (or by examining dreams), and their exposure provided a therapeutic avenue. Incidentally, Janet always claimed that psychoanalysis was an extension of his ideas, and that he discovered the method of cathartic cure.

Janet, like Charcot, also emphasised patients' predispositions, an elaboration of the degeneracy ideas. For him these abnormal tendencies were not only preponderant in hysteria, but were related to fundamental properties of the brain. Merskey comments as follows:

Janet was associated also with a tendency of the Parisian group to identify increasing numbers of traits which characterised the hysterical personality. Briquet (1859) only mentioned seven such traits, but Axenfeld (1864) identified 12, including affective features, with which he also mentioned sensitivity, vivid imagination, simulation and egocentricity or selfishness. Successive workers with Charcot identified 15 (Du Saulle, 1883), or 17 (Richer, 1885), and ultimately the numbers rise to Janet's 23 in 1907 (Merskey, 1995, p. 33).

Janet developed further the concept of symptoms being dependent on ideas, noting that suggestibility is important, but that there also existed 'a number of mental states anterior to suggestibility' (Janet, 1901, p. 227). Suggestion, in which there is 'complete and automatic development of an idea', takes place 'outside the will and personal perception of the subject' (Merskey, 1995, p. 251). These are subconscious acts. In the same way that ideas can become associated, so they can be dissociated, and dissociated ideas can have their own independent existence. There is a dissociation of mental unity, and 'at the moment of suggestion there is a shock, an emotion which destroys the feeble personal synthesis of the subject. The suggested idea remains isolated, more or less completely separated from the other ideas; it can then develop and suppress all else, or even foreign thoughts . . . a tendency to suggestion and subconscious acts is the sign of mental disease, but it is above all, the sign of hysteria' (Merskey, 1995, pp. 275–6). These fixed ideas grow, and install themselves in the mind, in a phrase of Charcot's, quoted by Janet, 'like parasites'. The links with the later-developed Freudian idea of repression is clear.

Some of Charcot's antagonists and successors took the concept of suggestion to a more extreme degree, insisting that hysteria was nothing but suggestion, and that, even worse, the great master himself actually suggested to patients the symptoms they should have. Everyone was more or less suggestible, more or less hysterical; there was no entity of hysteria at all.

The freudian approach

The story of how the Viennese neurologist Sigmund Freud (1856–1939) went to Paris for 5 months in 1885–6 to study with Charcot is well known. Although he still busied himself with neuropathology, he swiftly fell under Charcot's spell, and his interest in psychology crystallised. He returned to Vienna, and presented to the local society of physicians a case of traumatic hysteria in a male whom he had seen with Charcot. This was not well received. Although hysteria in males was by that time accepted, to equate male hysteria with traumatic neurosis was unacceptable. Freud then felt obliged to present a case of his own, which he did a month later:

A 29 year old man was knocked down in the street, and over the next two years had convulsions. He then developed hemi-anaesthesia and other stigmata of hysteria. The diagnosis was post-traumatic hysteria.

The reception of this presentation was also lukewarm! Withstanding this rejection, as Freud saw it, from the Austrian medical establishment, he then pursued his interest in hypnosis with Joseph Breuer (1842–1925). The story which led on to the development of psychoanalysis and his psychological elaborations of the structure of the human psyche is well known. Hysterical symptoms related to traumatic ideas, absent from consciousness, which could be uncovered by the analytic method. The unconscious mind, riven with conflicts, converted energies into physical symptoms, the latter resolving the psychic tension. To quote in full:

Our experiences have shown us, however, that the most various symptoms, which are ostensibly spontaneous and, as one might say, idiopathic products of hysteria, are just as strictly related to the precipitating trauma as the phenomena to which we have just alluded and which exhibit the connection quite clearly. The symptoms which we have been able to trace back to precipitating factors of this sort include neuralgias and anaesthesias of various kinds, many of which had persisted for years, contractures and paralyses, hysterical attacks and epileptoid convulsions, which every observer regards as true epilepsy, petit mal and disorders in the nature of tic, chronic vomiting and anorexia, carried to the pitch of rejection of all nourishment, various forms of disturbance of vision, constantly recurring visual hallucinations etc. The disproportion between the many years duration of the hysterical symptom and the single occurrence which provoked it is what we are accustomed invariably to find in traumatic neuroses. Quite frequently it is some event in childhood that sets up a more or less severe symptom which persists during the years that follow (Breuer and Freud, 1893, p. 88).

Often the connection between the trauma and the symptom was a symbolic one. While initially Freud attributed the childhood event to some actual sexual seduction, he later turned to a fantasised trauma, leading him on to his theories of the developmental phases of the human mind, with its tripartite division into id, ego and superego, the concepts of libidinal fixation, and the Oedipus complex. One consequence of all of this was to reaffirm a common link between the pathogenesis of common hysteria and traumatic hysteria. The memory of the trauma remains buried, but is still working pathogenetically, hence the famous remark, 'hysterics suffer mainly from reminiscences' (Breuer and Freud, 1893, p. 91). It was epigenetic, that is postnatal and developmental factors rather than any degenerative diathesis that were the key to understanding these patients.

Mechanisms invoked included pathological association, dissociation, suppression – later to become repression – and primary gain, through which unconscious conflicts are resolved by symptom formation. The latter were causal, as opposed to secondary gains, which were seen as maintaining the symptoms, bringing relief from some disagreeable social situation or relationship. Conversion, a term not used originally by Freud, but which was used in an original way by him, thus referred to the psychologically converted physical symptoms. By now, then, neurosis had become a psychoneurosis, and hysteria was a paradigm.

Posttraumatic hysteria in England and Germany

The idea that hysteria disappeared from medical eyes with the death of Charcot is totally dispelled by the profusion of cases of classical hysteria noted in soldiers who broke down during the First World War. Further, these clinical syndromes rather negated the developing Freudian theories, namely that all neuroses were at the heart related to sexual traumas.

Descriptions of posttraumatic neuroses arising in the setting of combat have a long and respectable history, which precedes the American *Diagnostic and Statistical Manual of Mental Disorders* (DSM-III; American Psychiatric Association, 1987) by centuries (Trimble, 1981). Medical scientific attention to these syndromes intensified during the Great War, when hundreds of thousands of soldiers presented with hysteria. The medical profession was faced with one huge dilemma, namely who was suffering from neurological and who had psychiatric disability and how to tell the difference. The authorities, on the other hand, were faced with a different dilemma, namely who was and who was not suffering from any disability, and who may be malingering. These dilemmas, as this book reveals, are still unresolved, or least in part, today.

There are several excellent accounts of shellshock in the literature, but much of the following comes from the elegant and absorbing treatise *A War of Nerves* by Ben

Shephard (2000), *Traumatic Pasts*, edited by Mark Micale and Paul Lerner (2001), and *Post-traumatic Neurosis* (Trimble, 1981).

The significant history of the posttraumatic neuroses really began with civilian accidents in the mid nineteenth century. This was a time of rapidly developing industrialisation, with the setting-up of large companies with corresponding work forces, and responsibilities to their customers. It was the time of the development and expansion of the railway system, and with trains came passengers, and with the system came accidents. Not surprisingly, the first major industrial corporations to become the target for lawsuits were the railway companies.

The Victorians viewed their age as one of rapid advancement on all technological and scientific fronts. In an era, like our own, of rapid progress and change, there are always those who can foresee in progress only danger and decline, and fears, often irrational, can easily be excited. Threats emerge from the unknown forces and hidden powers that the mystery of the modern brings with it: steam for then, nuclear power for now.

Although railways in some form or other had been in use for some 200 years, it was the nineteenth century that saw the development internationally of passenger railway systems. This came about with the invention of the steam engine, the use of iron for rails and an increasing pressure from the public to travel.

The railway was the very symbol of progress, but also of power and the poltergeist, suddenly inflicting injury and death on to unsuspecting victims in seemingly aleatory ways. Accidents were widely reported, grief became not private but a public affair, and the culture of victim creation had arrived.

In 1864 Parliament made railway companies legally responsible for the health and safety of their work force and passengers. Lawyers became involved, and with them medical experts.

At this time, the concept of concussion had become popular in neurology, initially used in conjunction with spinal injuries, hence the term 'concussion of the spine'; later the same ideas extended to concussion of the brain. In concussion, the minute but unobservable structure of the nervous tissue was thought to be damaged by a traumatic blow. These essentially were thought of as organic lesions of the central nervous matter, and could even occur following relatively trivial insults.

In the early 1860s the *Lancet* started a debate about the consequences of railway accidents and urged physicians to study the subject. John Eric Erichsen, Professor of Surgery at University College Hospital, London, did just that and crystallised his views in a book entitled *On Concussion of the Spine: nervous shock, and other obscure injuries of the nervous system* (1882). He wished to draw attention to spinal injuries which occurred in a civilian setting, often from slight trauma, and which were seen 'in none more frequently or with greater severity than in those which are sustained by persons who have been subjected to the violent shock of railway collision' (Trimble, 1981, p. 9).

Erichsen's concept reified into the condition railway spine, which then became referred to as Erichsen's disease. It was special to railway accidents, although it had an affinity with similar spinal trauma of other causes. The symptoms were diverse and varied in both severity and chronicity (Erichsen, 1882). Some patients recovered, but others progressed to the clinical pictures still seen today, and discussed in later chapters of this book.

Erichsen case 19

A 49 year old man was in a railway collision in 1864. He was dashed backwards and forwards, but seemed to suffer no immediate injury, and indeed helped free other passengers. The next day he felt shaken, and over the next few weeks he was anxious and depressed and complained of some back pain. Walking became compromised, muscle spasms occurred, he became forgetful and then his vision faded. Three months after the accident he developed contractures, first of the right hand, then of the left. His gait was peculiar, he walked with a stick. He could not bend his back, which was rigid, nor could he turn his head. Nine years later his condition remained unimproved. Diagnosis: concussion of the spine.

Erichsen opined that the cause of such syndromes was 'commotions of the spinal cord' due to molecular changes in its structure. Railway spine was born. Lawyers requested doctors to examine injured passengers, the latter became plaintiffs, were viewed as victims, and all three clutched for Erichsen's book.

Erichsen also recognised patients who developed various emotional symptoms after exposure to shock – commoner in females – which were due to terror. This he referred to as hysteria, which he suggested revealed unconscious exaggeration of symptoms, especially pain. However, in the case of railway-related hysteria he noted: 'This state will continue, indeed, as long as the mind is impressed by the prospect of impending litigation. When once that has been removed, recovery, provided there be no organic complication, will take place so rapidly as to lead to the suspicion that the whole of the sufferings were purposefully simulated, and that the patient was a malingerer' (Erichsen, 1882, p. 198).

Erichsen thus distinguished the organically based concussion of the spine from hysteria, and the latter he suggested hinted often at malingering. However, he acknowledged his ignorance about the mechanism of hysteria, and refuted the idea that it all related to malingering. In accidents he lamented: 'the complication of hysteria and real injury is one that is extremely difficult to unravel'.

Echoing the similar sentiments of some commentators of later generations with regards to PTSD, one author commented on Erichsen's book that litigants were 'appraised of clinical and pathological possibilities that were before undreamed of . . . Erichsen's little volume became a guide book that might lead the dishonest plaintiff, if he felt so disposed, to set out on a broad road of imposture and dissimulation with the expectation of getting a heavy verdict' (Trimble, 1981, p. 20).

The tone of litigation changed. In the nineteenth century and before, legal cases involving personal injury were mainly related to material injuries, loss of an arm and so forth, where loss was readily identifiable and quantifiable. With concussion of the spine, plaintiffs were seen at best as suffering from shock, and at worst from some form of molecular or vascular disorder of the spinal column. Such changes were invisible, and the damage from any injury virtually unquantifiable.

Similar views to those of Erichsen were held in Germany, particularly by Oppenheim (1858–1919), namely that traumatic neuroses were to be identified as separate disorders, and could be viewed somatically, reflecting underlying molecular pathology. As noted above, this position was not that of Charcot, and later Freud, who were identifying common mechanisms underlying the neuroses, and emphasising psychological rather than organic factors.

War neuroses

The First World War revived these debates, and put an end to the concept of concussion of the spine. As Fischer-Homberger (1971) commented: 'The German army would have dwindled to very little and Germany's financial resources would have been exhausted, if the doctrines of Oppenheim had continued to be followed' (p. 127). In other words, with the large numbers of soldiers falling ill, the inevitable compensation payments needed to satisfy the demand would have been vast if all the symptoms were deemed organically based.

The number of soldiers who had some form of nervous breakdown on the battlefield was horrendous. By December 1914, the British Army High Command had received reports that 7%–10% of officers and 3%–4% of other ranks were suffering such breakdowns, and it was later estimated that shellshock cases accounted for up to 40% of casualties from the front. Some 80 000 cases of shellshock cases were in army hospitals, and half of these ended up in UK institutions (Stone, 1985). This was surely an underestimate, not only because of the diagnostic uncertainty of many cases, with distinct neurological flavouring, but also because of the stigma attached to the diagnosis. Similar clinical pictures were seen in the French and German armies, and their respective languages contained equivalent words, such as *Granaterschütterung*.

At first shellshock, like railway spine, was thought to be organically based. Sir Frederick Mott (1853–1926) put forward views that the exploding shells caused commotion of the nervous cells and blood vessels, damaging spinal pathways (Mott, 1916). It soon became apparent, however, that symptoms of shellshock were found among those never exposed to exploding shells, and the issue of predisposition again became relevant. Who broke down was thought to be rather a matter of the person who fractured as opposed to the situation of the trauma. The organic view of these conditions was also rejected in Germany, and treatments more and more emphasised a pragmatic psychotherapeutic approach. Physicians such as Charles Myers (1873–1946), who introduced prompt treatments for cases near the front line, realised that the shellshock of war was clinically similar to the hysterias and neurasthenias of peacetime. Viewing similar cases in the Second World War, another psychiatrist with considerable war experience, Abraham Kardiner (1891–1981), came to similar conclusions (Kardiner and Spiegel, 1941).

As a result of study of these war-related neuroses, the aetiological position once more shifted. It became less a matter of sex, but more one of conflict, between fear and duty. The earlier Freudian psychology had given way to ego-psychology, and concepts of a failure of adaptation of an individual to changing environments. The ego fails in its adaptation to the situation and symptoms result. The concept of the trauma itself as aetiological began to fragment, and the notion of the importance of the meaning and experience of the trauma emerged.

The problem of the number of casualties with these conditions in the First World War became so great, and the contamination with malingering so obvious, that the authorities had to act. Many in high command thought the diagnosis of shellshock spurious, and it became associated with the derogation lack of moral fibre, cowardice and other epithets of failure. It is obvious that many soldiers wished to avoid the horror of the war, and to remove themselves from the immediacy of death, and that medical invalidity was one way out. Official committees and memoranda called out for the removal of the term 'shellshock', as did most physicians. 'I endorse this appeal to drop the term shell-shock, first because for the vast majority of cases to which it was applied it suggested a pathology which was utterly untrue, and secondly because to the patients themselves to whom it was applied it gave the impression that it meant that they had received a very mortal hurt, that they could not be expected to be well for a very long time to come' (Ross, 1941, p. 31). Ross pointed out the power of giving names to such states, and lamented that a variant, referred to as effort syndrome (disorderly action of the heart or DOH), had replaced shellshock, 'with quite devastating effects'.

The clinical pictures were varied, but typical. There were acute and chronic forms, but somatic symptoms were predominant. Convulsions, paralyses, contractures, anaesthesias, tics, choreas, loss of sight or hearing, stammering, neurasthenias, essentially the full house of symptoms seen over the centuries allied to the diagnosis of hysteria were recorded.

The end of the First World War did not see the end of the problem. First, many chronic cases remained, and they required not only ongoing care, but also pensions.

A school of thought developed that many such people would have adapted poorly to civilian life anyway, even if they had not been in the war, and the possibility of a pension perpetuated the problem. Again, to quote Ross:

> . . . the class of what are sometimes called traumatic neurosis. It is probably true that trauma never causes neurosis. Trauma may cause physical disability, but not neurosis unless some anxiety is added on. We do not have neurosis subsequent to hunting or skiing accidents. We have them very markedly after motor accidents and after accidents arising out of a workman's occupation, i.e. we have them after an accident where someone else is responsible and will have to pay, especially if that payment will be made not by an individual but by a company. Judges and juries might think twice before they compensated a man who has only been frightened, if the person who had to pay were not a rich man – but these wealthy insurance companies can be bled white without pity. Someone has had an accident due to some other person's act, and is not damaged; all sorts of people tell him that he will get nervous symptoms later on, and frighten him into an illness, which goes on until the damage is assessed and awarded. The damage to the recipient of the money, however, is great. Two quite undesirable emotional states have been stimulated, fear and greed, and the damage which they cause is by no means always repaired when the case is settled (Ross, 1941, p. 27).

Some countries, such as France, did not pay pensions for these neuroses, while the Germans did so until the finances prevented it in 1926. According to Shephard, following this administrative change, the German doctors reported that all the *Kriegszitterer* got better!

The role of compensation in encouraging continuing illness became an important discussion, but was supported by the fact that after the war the number of ex-soldiers receiving pensions for psychiatric illness increased over time rather than decreased.

Other wars followed. Classical patterns of hysterical breakdown were seen in the Second World War, and then in the wars in Korea, Vietnam and the Faulklands. By the time of the Second World War, shellshock, as a physical concept, had been officially abandoned, and the recognition of the psychological nature of the condition led to the widespread introduction of psychological interventions, but also, significantly, recommendations that those vulnerable to such breakdown should not be recruited.

At the outbreak of the Second World War, some 40 000 people in the UK were in receipt of pensions for psychiatric disorders from the Great War, and the Ministry of Pensions wished to avoid a repeat of such expense. It was pointed out that it was not the case that these neuroses were a direct result of front-line action, since nearly 60% of people in receipt of the pensions had not seen such action! The role of the claimant's constitution became the more relevant discussion, as did the possibility of simply refusing to give pensions for such problems. The line of argument was that such people would have developed psychiatric illness in any case, and to compensate them for an imaginary shellshock was illogical. As will be noted, the same arguments are now made in relation to those suffering from PTSD, in the eyes of some, another *malade imaginaire*.

In the Second World War, civilians were more directly involved, for example with the air raids. Air raids did not seem to provoke the huge increase in hysteria cases that may have been expected, but for the front-line, the clinical presentations with hysteria were the same. Abraham Kardiner was one psychiatrist who had experience of mental illness in both World Wars. He stressed that war evoked a syndrome, no different from that seen in peacetime, although he noted that in the Second World War, there were fewer cases of aphasia and paralyses, and more cases with 'a predominance of affect'.

T. A. Ross also agreed that the neuroses of peacetime and war were similar, and clinically he divided the problem into acute and chronic forms. In contrast to acute hysteria, chronic forms were different. 'But if a person gets into the chronic stage of neurosis, if he is given time to think over the situation, and to consider that he has done his bit, and that he has had enough of it; if there has been difficulty in coming to the diagnosis, and he has learned that there are considerable doubts about his case, or if immediate treatment has failed, then I do not think that it is possible to cure him, (Ross, 1941, p. 63).

Chronic symptoms included fatigue, insomnia, battle dreams, chronic pains, memory and concentration problems, myalgias, phobias, convulsions, visual disorders, deafness – the whole gamut of hysterical presentations of the First World War and bygones of the past.

Treatments may have been more effective over time, and in addition to psychological interventions, psychiatrists such as William Sargant (1907–88) and Eliot Slater (1904–83) introduced new physical therapies for hysteria for soldiers returning from the front, including prolonged sedation and barbiturate-induced abreaction.

New hysteria studies

The 'new hysteria studies' refer to the sociohistorical studies of hysteria that have mainly been published in the last 20 or so years, summarised and discussed by Mark Micale in his text *Approaching Hysteria* (1995). The inspiration for these studies has little to do with medicine, and has been driven by feminist interpretations of the literature. Essentially, hysteria is viewed as a diagnosis made by men (doctors) about women (patients), and is in essence a social construct of the historical timeframe of medical theories. Diagnosis is seen as a method of social control, and doctors as agents of the status quo.

Psychiatry has come in for particular critisism, with diagnoses based largely on subjectively based symptomology, and insistence on madness as a medical rather than a social construct. The substantial and influential contribution of

Elaine Showalter (1985) in her book gave pride of place to hysteria as the quintessential female disorder. Feminist reformers were seen as psychologically ill, while the hysterical personality, portrayed as Blanche Dubois (from Tennessee Williams' *A Streetcar Named Desire*) and Scarlett O'Hara (from Margaret Mitchell's *Gone with the Wind*), was seen as the epitome of feminine characterisation, the *femme fatale* with succubic exuberance which demands suppression.

Another interpretation, adopted for example by Edward Shorter (1992), is that hysteria is a recognisable psychiatric disorder, the symptoms of which vary over different social epochs. In a mistaken analysis of the clinical situation, he suggests that the Victorian faints, swoons and convulsions are now rare, and that various psychosomatic disorders have come to take their place. He documents several case histories of Victorian couch invalids, confined to their beds, often for years, including a well-known example such as Elizabeth Barrett Browning. He concluded that these pictures disappeared from the literature after 1900, based, in his view, on the culmination of several factors. These included patients' unconscious selection of symptoms, which was susceptible to various social and cultural pressures, assisted by a shifting medical paradigm, in which doctors influenced patients' behaviours.

In fact, although elegant and well argued, these texts are based on mistaken facts, and fail to acknowledge the continued existence of hysteria in the twentieth and twenty-first-century, not only in countless hundreds of thousands of men who came to medical attention in the various war settings, but also in the continued existence of classical hysterical presentations clinically over the decades. The nineteenth-century polysymptomatic Victorian invalid is simply a variant of today's Briquet's hysteria. In fact, far from going away after 1900, the numbers of cases of hysteria rose phenomenally in the twentieth century, and in the last 20 years, swoons and convulsions have once again become an important part of neurological practice, mainly referred to as pseudo- or psychogenic seizures.

Conclusions

This brief historical overview reveals a number of salient points of relevance for the later understanding of the syndromes considered in this book. First, patients with medically unexplained syndromes have been recognised in many different cultures for over 2000 years, and the term 'hysteria' has been used successfully to describe such patients. As early as the seventeenth century, the contribution of the emotions to the development of symptoms was discussed, and the pertinent role of trauma and accidents was an early observation.

The contributions of the personality were also commented on, and notably adjectives such as capricious, labile, emotionally unstable and suggestible were descriptors. Further, the tendency to deception as an integral part of the constitution is often commented on in this historical review, and links with malingering were recognised even by the time of Carter.

The role of unconscious forces and of physical abuse was also discussed, well before the contributions of Freud, but for a time the latter's more extensive consideration of sexual trauma came to dominate ideas. However, the fantasised nature of the trauma, and the role of epigenetic intrapsychic forces, had to give way to some extent to alternative theories from the extensive observations of shellshock and, later, war-related syndromes. Further, in a civilian setting, the role of extrinsic motivations, especially compensation, became central to all these discussions, especially medicolegal debates, as the cost of compensation began to rise.

The importance of railway spine in the development of the whole history of posttraumatic neuroses, including PTSD and the victim culture, cannot be underemphasised. The debates and arguments of Victorian physicians and surgeons over whether a patient's symptoms were organic echo down to us today, shielding and revealing a lack of knowledge about these fascinating medical syndromes. Chronic intractable forms of the disorder were well described in this historical literature, and patients today who are referred to as having somatisation disorder were central to these discussions. Hysteria, over two millennia, has never risen from the ashes: the fires have been burning brightly all along.

REFERENCES

American Psychiatric Association (1987). *Diagnostic and Statistical Manual of Mental Disorders* (DSM-III). Washington, DC: APA.

Breuer, J. and Freud, S. (1893/1956). *Studies in Hysteria*. New York: Nervous and Mental Diseases Publishing.

Briquet, P. (1859). *Traité Clinique et Thérapeutique de l'Hystérie*. Paris: J.-B. Baillière.

Brodie, B. C. (1837). *Lectures Illustrative of Certain Nervous Affections*. London: Longman.

Burton, R. (1621). *The Anatomy of Melancholy, What it is*. Oxford: Cripps.

Carter, R. B. (1853). *On The Pathology and Treatment of Hysteria*. London: Churchill.

Charcot, J.-M. (1889). *Clinical Lectures on Diseases of the Nervous System*, vol. 3. translated by T. Savill. London: New Sydenham Society.

Charcot, J.-M. and Marie, P. (1892). Hysteria. In: *Dictionary of Psychological Medicine*, ed. D. Hake Tuke, pp. 627–41. London: Churchill.

Cheyne, G. (1733). *The English Malady; or A treatise of nervous diseases of all kinds, as spleen, vapours, lowness of spirits, hypochondriacal and hysterical distempers, etc.* London: Strahan and Leake.

Dewhurst, K. (1980). *Thomas Willis' Oxford Lectures.* Oxford: Sanford Publications.

Erichsen, J. E. (1882). *On Concussion of the Spine: nervous shock, and other obscure injuries of the nervous system*. London: Longmans Green.

Fischer-Homberger, E. (1971). Der Begriff des freien Willens in der Geschichte der traumatischen Neurose. *Clio*, **6**, 121–37.

Griesinger, W. (1862). *Mental Pathology and Therapeutics*. Translated by C. Lockhart Robertson and J. Rutherford. London: New Sydenham Society.

Hecker, J. F. C. (1844). *The Epidemics of the Middle Ages*. Translated by B. G. Babbington. London: The Sydenham Society.

Hunter, R. and MacAlpine, I. (1963). *Three Hundred Years of Psychiatry*. Oxford: Oxford University Press.

Janet, P. (1901). *The Mental State of Hystericals*. Translated by C. R. Corson. New York: GP Putnam.

(1907). *The Major Symptoms of Hysteria*. London: Macmillan.

Jorden, E. (1603). *A Briefe Discourse of a Disease Called the Suffocation of the Mother*. London: Windet.

Kardiner, A. and Spiegel, H. (1941). *War Stress and Neurotic Illness*. London: Paul B. Hoeber.

Laycock, T. (1840). *An Essay on Hysteria*. Philadelphia: Haswell, Barrington and Haswell.

Merskey, H. (1995). *The Analysis of Hysteria*, 2nd edn. London: Gaskell.

Micale, M. S. (1995). *Approaching Hysteria*. New Jersey: Princeton University Press.

Micale, M. S. and Lerner, P. (2001). *Traumatic Pasts*. Cambridge: Cambridge University Press.

Mott, F. W. (1916). Special discussion of shell-shock without visible signs of injury. *Proceedings of the Royal Society of Medicine*, **3** (suppl. 9), 1–44.

Reynolds, J. R. (1869). Remarks on paralysis and other disorders of motion and sensation, dependent on an idea. *British Medical Journal*, **ii**, 483–5.

Ross, T. A. (1941). *Lectures on War Neuroses*. London: Edward Arnold.

Shephard, B. (2000). *A War of Nerves*. London: Johnathan Cape.

Shorter, E. (1992). *From Paralysis to Fatigue: A History of Psychosomatic Illness in the Modern Era*. New York: Free Press.

Showalter, E. (1985). *The Female Malady: Women, Madness, and the English Culture, 1830–1980*. New York: Pantheon.

Stone, M. (1985). Shellshock and the psychologists. In *The Anatomy of Madness*, vol. 2, Ed. W. F. Bynum, R. Porter and M. Shepherd, pp. 242–71. London: Tavistock.

Sydenham, T. (1850). *The Works of Thomas Sydenham*. London: Sydenham Society.

Trimble, M. R. (1981). *Post-Traumatic Neurosis*. Chichester: John Wiley.

Veith, I. (1965). *Hysteria, the History of a Disease*. Chicago: University of Chicago Press.

Whytt, R. (1751). *Observations on the Nature, Causes and Cure of those Disorders which have been Called Nervous, Hypochondriac, or Hysteric, to which are Prefixed some Remarks on the Sympathy of the Nerves*. Edinburgh: Becket and Du Hondt.

2

Classification and the somatoform disorders

Mr Purgon: I foretell that within four days you'll be in an incurable condition.
Argan: Oh Mercy!
Mr Purgon: You'll fall into a state of bradypepsia.
Argan: Mr Purgon!
Mr Purgon: From bradypepsia to dyspepsia.
Argan: Mr Purgon!
Mr Purgon: From dyspepsia to apepsia.
Argan: Mr Purgon!
Mr Purgon: From apepsia into diarrhoea and lientery.
Argan: Mr Purgon!
Mr Purgon: From lientery into dysentery.
Argan: Mr Purgon!
Mr Purgon: From dysentery into dropsy.
Argan: Mr Purgon!
Mr Purgon: And from dropsy to autopsy . . .   (Molière, *The Imaginary Invalid*, Act III)

Introduction

In Chapter 1, the gradual evolution of the hysteria concept was outlined, and the situation by the end of the last century was presented. The new hysteria studies, driven by sociological and often overt political considerations rather than medical realities, implied that the disorder had decreased in frequency, that cultural pressures and societal sophistication accounted for much of the variance in the presentation of hysteria over time, and that classical presentations were no longer seen. Nothing could be further from the truth. The acclaimed demise of hysteria, upon which many of the sociological theories were founded, received a further boost by the development, mainly in the USA of a succession of classificatory systems, which eventually saw the loss of the term 'hysteria' altogether, and the rise of the clumsy alternative, somatoform disorders, with the subcategory somatisation disorders.

The main classificatory manuals used by psychiatrists over recent years have been the ones developed by the World Health Organization, the *International Classification of Diseases* (ICD), and those of the American Psychiatric Association, the *Diagnostic and Statistical Manuals* (DSM). Currently the 10th edition of the ICD (World Health Organization, 1992) and the IVth edition of the DSM are in use (DSM-IV: American Psychiatric Association, 1994). A recent text revised version of DSM-IV (referred to as DSM-IV-TR (2000)) has been introduced, but the diagnostic criteria remain the same as for the original DSM-IV. These and related developments are now reviewed.

Classification – an introduction to modern concepts

Chapter 1 revealed how the concept of hysteria migrated over time, from the uterine to the cerebral to the psychodynamic, and how the later recognition of the traumatic hysterias led, back and forth, to and from the organic to the psychological, with different eras. This shift in concepts of aetiology and pathogenesis was not at all influenced by classification schemes, and even today, DSM-IV and ICD-10 avoid contamination of classification by theories of causation, with one exception – the diagnosis of posttraumatic stress disorder (PTSD), in which the cause is inherent in the name.

The first comprehensive classification of psychiatric disorders was that of Cullen, published in 1803. He divided diseases into four main categories, one of which was the neuroses. This was essentially a synonym for nervous disease. Thus, over time, the spleen and vapours of the seventeenth century became Whytt's disorders of the nerves, then the neuroses of Cullen, culminating in the rubrics hysteria and hypochondriasis of the nineteenth century. Charcot took up the hysteria challenge, George Beard (1839–1883) in the USA developed his ideas of neurasthenia, and Freud concerned himself with the psychoneuroses.

The challenge of classification in psychiatry in the twentieth century took two main directions. One was based on the ideal, the other on the statistical. The former has obvious Platonic overtones, the latter is Aristotelian. Neither approach is satisfactory, but the eventual preference of the psychiatric community for the former has had far-reaching consequences, especially in medicolegal practice.

Thus, attempts to define abnormality statistically, refining a core group of symptoms that on statistical grounds alone may identify a syndrome (like, for example, measuring blood pressure, noting population means and standard deviations, and defining those in an abnormal range), have been dominated by the alternative. Namely, the approach that conceives an ideal state (an essence), assumes it exists in nature, and then, by committee, lays down criteria for recognising it (essence precedes existence).

Symptoms, signs and diseases

The classification schemes used in psychiatry at the present time are based almost exclusively on symptoms. Thus, in medicine generally, we recognise two main types of data. Symptoms are those complaints of the patient that are spontaneously reported, or are elicited by taking the clinical history. They are subjective, and the enquiring physician is entirely dependent on what the patient tells him or her.

Signs are observed by the physician, the patient or a friend or relative of the patient which indicate the presence of some abnormal functioning of one or more bodily systems.

A syndrome is a constellation of signs and symptoms which seem to coalesce to provide a recognisable entity with its identifying characteristics. Attempts are made to classify syndromes, which are the clinical representatives of illness. However, a clear distinction needs to be drawn between illness and disease, and this is all the more important in psychiatric practice. Patients present with illnesses, that is, complaints, and they bring to the clinical picture their own idiosyncratic expressions. These idiosyncratic expressions are moulded by familial, environmental and cultural factors. Illness is then only a partial representative of any particular disease.

In psychiatry, the identification of underlying disease is very limited. In other words, the explanation for the psychopathology often does not lie with the identification of an underlying tissue pathology. This is more relevant for the neuroses, as opposed to the major mental disorders such as the psychoses. Indeed, the history of twentieth-century biological psychiatry has been one long, interesting and rewarding journey of discovery of the underlying pathologies associated with psychotic states. The triumph over general paralysis of the insane (GPI) was only one reflection of this. We now recognise substantial cerebral components to the psychoses associated with many conditions, including schizophrenia. However, the disorders under consideration here are rarely associated with any consistent biological markers, and the 'disease' identification is distinctly lacking. The illness that is observed and the symptoms reported are largely elicited by the physician from the patient as a witness to his or her own state. The physician then must mould what he or she has seen and heard to fit the relevant diagnostic pigeonhole.

The two main diagnostic systems in use at present are DSM-IV and ICD-10. In both, operational definitions are employed, and a checklist of symptoms is given. DSM-IV adopts a multiaxial approach: axis 1 refers to clinical syndromes, axis 2 covers developmental and personality disorders. Axis 3, 4 and 5 refer to physical disorders, psychosocial stressors and global assessment of functioning respectively.

Classification of the neuroses

The very term neurosis and its historical associations have caused psychiatrists many concerns, such that the later DSM series finally tried to abandon it altogether. Generally, the neuroses are what the general public refer to as 'nerves', and underlying many neuroses is the general affect of anxiety. The conditions embraced are generalised anxiety, more specific phobias, panic disorder, obsessive-compulsive disorder and the somatoform disorders. These have slightly different designations, depending on which classification system is preferred, and there is a variant of mood disorder defined, namely neurotic or reactive depression. In this condition the depression is reactive to environmental circumstances, and the symptoms tend to be less severe than in a major affective disorder, which is a synonym for old-fashioned endogenous depression. Reactive depression is confused with, but not the same as, dysthymia of the DSM, the latter being a variant form of minor, rather continuous mood disorder.

However, the neuroses shade off at the edges to other related diagnostic categories, including insomnias and parasomnias, sexual disorders and, notably, the personality disorders. The link with the latter is pertinent to an understanding of the somatoform disorders, since common threads between the latter and some personality disorders are both histrionic traits and dependence. While in DSM the terms neuroses and personality disorders belong to separate axes (1 and 2, respectively), this satisfying clarity begs the clinical reality of such associations, and is one source of confusion for an adequate understanding of these relationships.

The developers of the DSM, notably DSM-III (American Psychiatric Association, 1980), tried to abandon the term 'neurosis', on account of its historical association with Freudian psychoanalysis, and the failure of any single aetiological theory to explain the diverse manifestations of those conditions referred to under the neuroses category. The idea was to come up with a diagnostic manual that was free from aetiopathogenetical assumptions, but the compromise cop-out in DSM-III was to retain the term 'neurotic disorder', but for descriptive purposes only. As such, the word can be found in the later DSM-IIIR (American Psychiatric Association, 1987), and DSM-IV (American Psychiatric Association, 1994). The attempt to be free from aetiological implications failed entirely with one diagnosis – PTSD.

Somatoform disorders

Hysteria, along with neurosis, had to go. Conversion, on the other hand, the mechanism of symptom production, seems to have been retained in the manuals; conversion disorders are found in the diagnostic categories of both ICD-10 and DSM-IV.

Somatisation as a word can only have derived from the twentieth century, a clumsy compromise, a verb translated to a substantiative, a foreigner at home in the land of neologism. According to Berrios and Mumford (1995), it was originally introduced through the writings of the the psychoanalyst Wilhelm Stekel (1868–1940), who used *somatizieren* to refer to neurotic patients who expressed their mental states symbolically as somatic symptoms.

The era of psychosomatic medicine took this further, although did not take up the term. In these schemes, specific personalities were said to have predilections to develop various somatic diseases, for example defining a rheumatoid or an asthmatic personality, or certain fixed mental conflicts related to various bodily states. Two fundamental divisions of the nervous system, the autonomic and the somatomotor, reacted in different ways. Psychosomatic disorders classically affected the autonomic nervous system, chronic stress, for example, led to cardiac or dermatological abnormalities via the parasympathetic and sympathetic nervous system. The somatomotor and sensory abnormalities were seen in a Freudian sense, and thought to be related to 'conversion' of conflicts.

Somatisation made a limited appearance in the USA in the 1940s, but the concept seems to have been crystallised by three influential authors. Lipowski (1987), who published a paper entitled, 'Somatization: the experience and communication of psychological distress as somatic symptoms', considered somatisation to be, rather as conversion was becoming, a disorder as well as a process. Kleinman (1977), who defined somatisation as an expression of distress in the idiom of bodily complaints and medical help-seeking, placed the concept firmly in a cultural setting. In 1983, Ford wrote his book *The Somatizing Disorders*, subtitled 'Illness as a way of life'. This was a landmark contribution to the field, and he gave the definition of somatisation as follows: 'a process by which the body (the soma) is used for psychological purposes or for personal gain. Any one symptom or constellation of symptoms may concurrently serve more than one function, including issues related to intrapsychic conflicts, intrapersonal relationships and social or environmental problems' (p. 1).

Contemporary research into patients with somatisation disorder evolved from the work of Cohen and colleagues at Harvard, and Guze and colleagues at St Louis. Purtell *et al.*, in 1951, wrote up a small group of mainly female patients who had a wide variety of unexplained medical complaints. They referred to this condition as hysteria, but used the soubriquet Briquet to name the syndrome – hence Briquet's hysteria.

In DSM-II (1968), there are hysterical neuroses – conversion type (300.13) and hysterical neuroses – dissociative type (300.14). In conversion disorder, the special senses or the voluntary nervous system was affected, while in the dissociative type, alterations to the state of consciousness were seen. Further editions of the DSM retained a similar division. In DSM-III (1980), the term 'somatoform disorders' emerges, with various subtypes, including somatisation disorder (300.81), conversion disorder (300.11), psychogenic pain disorder (307.80) and hypochondriasis (300.70). Dissociative disorders are given as psychogenic amnesias, fugues and depersonalisation. Multiple personality disorder is also included here. The use of the subcategory somatisation relates to the studies of the St Louis group, and incorporated their concept of Briquet's hysteria. It was seen as separate from conversion disorder, and the eponym was seen as superfluous, and discarded.

Somatoform disorders in DSM-IV-TR and ICD-10

The concept of Briquet's hysteria has been taken up by the two diagnostic manuals now mainly in use, ICD-10 and DSM-IV-TR. Referred to as somatisation disorder in DSM-IV (300.81), and in ICD-10 (F 45.0), it represents a chronic condition, and the patients are by definition polysymptomatic. In contrast, there is conversion disorder, with a much more restricted symptomatology, which tends to run a shorter course.

The original criteria for Briquet's hysteria, as given by Perley and Guze (1962), required the patient to have 25 out of 59 possible medically unexplained symptoms, coming from nine out of a possible 10 symptom groups. However, over time, fewer complaints have been included, such that in DSM-III, the requirements were 14 symptoms for women, and 12 for men from a list of 37, and in DSM-IIIR, 13 symptoms from a list of 35 were needed.

The full criteria as given by DSM-IV are shown in Table 2.1. The requirements are a history of many physical complaints, over a period of several years, but with rather specific numbers of complaints from four main groups – pain symptoms, gastrointestinal and pseudoneurological symptoms and sexual complaints.

The diagnosis of somatisation disorder comes under the overall category of somatoform disorders, and the subdivisions of this and the ICD-10 counterpart are shown in Table 2.2. Somatisation disorder corresponds very well with the original concept of Briquet's hysteria, and the essential features are the development of medically unexplained symptoms, which usually emerge before the age of 30, for which the patient seeks advice and treatment, or which cause significant social and occupational impairment. Sometimes symptoms occur in association with some relevant somatic pathology, but in such settings, the complaint exceeds that which would normally be expected.

According to DSM-IV, patients often 'describe their complaints in colourful, exaggerated terms'; they are often inconsistent historians, and their lives can be as chaotic as their medical histories.

Table 2.1 Diagnostic criteria for somatisation disorder (300.81) as given in DSM-IV (American Psychiatric Association, 1994, pp. 449–50)

A. A history of many physical complaints beginning before age 30 years that occur over a period of several years and result in treatment being sought or significant impairment in social, occupational, or other important areas of functioning

B. Each of the following criteria must have been met, with individual symptoms occurring at any time during the course of the disturbance:

  1. *four pain symptoms:* a history of pain related to at least four different sites or functions (e.g. head, abdomen, back, joints, extremities, chest, rectum, during menstruation, during sexual intercourse or during urination)

  2. *two gastrointestinal symptoms:* a history of at least two gastrointestinal symptoms other than pain (e.g. nausea, bloating, vomiting other than during pregnancy, diarrhoea or intolerance of several different foods)

  3. *one sexual symptom:* a history of at least one sexual or reproductive symptom other than pain (e.g. sexual indifference, erectile or ejaculatory dysfunction, irregular menses, excessive menstrual bleeding, vomiting throughout pregnancy)

  4. *one pseudoneurological symptom:* a history of at least one symptom or deficit suggesting a neurological condition not limited to pain (conversion symptoms such as impaired coordination or balance, paralysis or localised weakness, difficulty swallowing or lump in throat, aphonia, urinary retention, hallucinations, loss of touch or pain sensation, double vision, blindness, deafness, seizures; dissociative symptoms such as amnesia; or loss of consciousness other than fainting)

C. Either 1 or 2:

  1. after appropriate investigation, each of the symptoms in criterion B cannot be fully explained by a known general medical condition or the direct effects of a substance (e.g. a drug of abuse, a medication)

  2. when there is a related general medical condition, the physical complaints or resulting social or occupational impairment are in excess of what would be expected from the history, physical examination or laboratory findings

D. The symptoms are not intentionally produced or feigned (as in factitious disorder or malingering)

As noted, lesser variants are accepted, referred to as undifferentiated somatoform disorder (300.81), and somatoform disorder not otherwise specified (300.81). The former designates patients with a 6-month or longer history of one or more unexplained physical complaints. The latter include patients who have unexplained symptoms which are not captured under any of the other groups, such as patients with pseudocyesis (false pregnancy), or an undifferentiated somatoform disorder lasting less than 6 months.

Table 2.2 The categorisation of somatoform
disorders in DSM-IV (American Psychiatric
Association, 1994) and ICD-10
(World Health Organization, 1992)

ICD-10: Somatoform disorders (F45)
Somatisation disorder (F45.0)[a]
Undifferentiated somatoform disorder (F45.1)[a]
Hypochondriacal disorder (F45.2)[a]
Somatoform autonomic dysfunction (F45.3)
Persistent somatoform pain disorder (F45.4)[a]
Other somatoform disorders (F45.8)
Somatoform disorder, unspecified (F45.9)[a]

DSM-IV: Somatoform disorders
Somatisation disorder (300.81)
Undifferentiated somatoform disorder (300.81)
Conversion disorder (300.11)
Pain disorder (300.7)
Hypochondriasis (300.7)
Body dysmorphic disorder (300.7)

---

[a] In common with DSM-IV.

The differences from ICD are quite substantial. Thus, in ICD, dissociative (conversion) disorders (F44) are distinct from somatoform disorders (F45). The former relate to Janet's concept of dissociation, reflecting a partial or complete loss of conscious integration:

There is normally a considerable degree of conscious control over the memories and sensations that can be selected for immediate attention, and the movements that can be carried out. In the dissociative disorders it is presumed that this ability to exercise a conscious and selective control is impaired, to a degree that can vary from day to day or even from hour to hour. It is usually very difficult to assess the extent to which some of the loss of functions might be under voluntary control (World Health Organization, 1992, p. 152).

These dissociative disorders are of presumed 'psychogenic' origin. The term 'conversion' is retained to imply that 'the unpleasant affect, engendered by the problems and conflicts that the individual cannot solve, is somehow transformed into the symptoms' (World Health Organization, 1992, p. 152).

The subdivisions are into dissociative amnesia, dissociative fugue, dissociative disorders of movement and sensation, and other dissociative disorders. The latter includes the Ganser syndrome (a well-known form of pseudodementia characterised by *Vorbeireden*, or approximate answers), and the multiple personality disorder.

The dissociative disorders of movement and sensation cover many of the typical symptoms of hysteria, and convulsions are included here.

With regards to conscious awareness, the ICD again comments:

> The degree of disability resulting from all these types of symptoms may vary from occasion to occasion, depending on the number and type of other people present, and upon the emotional state of the patient. In other words, a variable amount of attention seeking behaviour may be present in addition to a central and unvarying core of loss of movement or sensation which is not under voluntary control (World Health Organization, 1992, p. 157).

The somatoform disorders (F45) are characterised by the repeated presentation of physical symptoms, with repeated requests for medical examinations, in spite of reassurance that the symptoms have no physical basis. Somatisation disorder (F45.0) finds its place here, along with hypochondriacal disorder, somatoform autonomic dysfunction, persistent somatoform pain disorder and other somatoform disorders. As with DSM-IV, somatisation disorder is the presentation of 'multiple recurrent, and frequently changing physical symptoms, which have usually been present for several years before the patient is referred to a psychiatrist. Most patients have a long and complicated history of contact with primary and specialist medical services, during which many negative investigations or fruitless operations may have been carried out' (World Health Organization, 1992, p. 162).

The diagnostic guidelines require:

1. at least 2 years of multiple and variable physical symptoms for which no adequate physical explanation has been found
2. persistent refusal to accept the advice or reassurance of several doctors that there is no physical explanation for the symptoms
3. some degree of impairment of social and family functioning attributable to the nature of the symptoms and resulting behaviour.

If the full picture is not seen, but the diagnosis seems secure, then the term 'undifferentiated somatoform disorder' can be used. Somatoform autonomic dysfunction refers to presentations with supposed alterations of the autonomic nervous system, such as cardiac, respiratory or gastrointestinal symptoms. Somatoform pain disorder is used when the predominant symptom is pain, persistent, severe and distressing, which cannot be fully explained by underlying physiological dysfunction.

Medicolegal aspects of the use of diagnostic manuals

For reasons that are not too clear, the courts in the UK have preferred to rely on DSM-IV diagnostic criteria, as opposed to ICD-10. Certainly the former tend to be more precise, with better-defined inclusion and exclusion criteria. However, part of the push came from the inclusion of PTSD in DSM-III, a diagnosis which then found its way into the ICD. PTSD, however, was only a refinement of the old-fashioned concept of posttraumatic neurosis, with a new transatlantic gloss. The latter, coloured by an enthusiasm which so often accompanies the finding of old wine in new bottles, seems to have been intoxicating for both lawyers and court experts.

As can be seen from the above descriptive diagnostic categories of both the DSM and ICD, they are rather arbitrary, cooked up by committees, and can hardly be seen to have been set in stone by a Moses. Over successive generations, the ICD and DSM categories have more and more come together, but they still reveal major differences, as presented above. Is it that patients in the USA are different from those in the rest of the world? The more likely explanation is that the categories outlined pretend to deal with discrete Platonic entities, which it is hoped with more refinement will reach their ideal state, whereas the real world begs for Aristotelian interpretations, and patients often simply refuse to conform to ideal clinical pictures.

The ICD model is less precise than the DSM; the latter insists on quite rigid inclusion and exclusion criteria. Yet both have get-out clauses, with categories such as undifferentiated somatoform disorder. To be fair, the authors of DSM-IV acknowledged this difficulty. However, the main points are that these manuals reflect – but should not dictate – clinical practice, and that in a medicolegal setting their use can be not only misleading, but also mischievous.

Many people fail to read the introductions to these manuals. ICD-10 is 'intended for general clinical, educational and service use' (World Health Organization, 1992, p. 1). More specifically, DSM-IV was 'developed for use in clinical, educational and research settings . . . to be employed by individuals with appropriate clinical training and experience in diagnosis. It is important that DSM-IV not be applied mechanically by untrained individuals. The specific diagnostic criteria included in the DSM-IV are meant to serve as guidelines to be informed by clinical judgement and are not meant to be used in a cookbook fashion' (American Psychiatric Association, 1994, p. xxiii).

The text of DSM-IV then goes on specifically to discuss the use of the manual in forensic settings. When used for forensic purposes there are 'significant risks that diagnostic information will be misused or misunderstood . . . These dangers arise because of the imperfect fit between the questions of ultimate concern to the law and the information contained in a clinical diagnosis'. The authors note that fulfilling criteria does not equate with any specific level of impairment or disability, and

non-clinical decision makers should also be cautioned that a diagnosis does not carry any necessary implications regarding the causes of the individual's mental disorder or its associated impairments . . . Moreover, the fact that an individual's presentation meets the criteria for a

DSM-IV diagnosis does not carry any necessary implication regarding the individual's degree of control over the behaviours that may be associated with the disorder . . . The proper use of the criteria requires specialised clinical training (American Psychiatric Association, 1994, p. xxvii).

In other words, the manuals are to be used only by the clinically informed, as a guide to clinical or research practice, and they are not secure, and have not been developed for use in a legal setting.

Personality disorders (axis 2) and psychiatric illness (axis 1)

The hysterical personality

The move against the unitary of the concept of hysteria was partially accelerated by the writings of Slater (Slater and Glithero, 1965). In a follow-up study, reviewed in greater detail in Chapter 6, he noted that, after 9 years, the majority of patients diagnosed as having hysteria still displayed symptoms, and nearly 30% were totally or partially disabled. He further noted that the frequency of misdiagnosis was high, with a number of patients going on to develop other recognised psychiatric or neurological diagnoses. He commented on the fragility of the whole hysteria concept, and the false clinical security which the name gave. He referred to hysteria as a guise for ignorance and a fertile source of clinical error (Slater and Glithero, 1965).

However, in Slater's sample, he felt that 25% sustained the 'hysteria' diagnosis. These fell into two groups. The first consisted of young patients with acute psychological reactions presenting as a conversion disorder. The second were patients with long-lasting personality disorders. Since he was unable to uncover any genetic associations in family and twin studies, and since the disorder fractionated into mainly anxiety states and personality disorders, he concluded that the adjectival use of the term was acceptable, but not the substantive. Symptoms could be hysterical, but hysteria had no uniformity, no essence.

Others writing about the same time pointed out that no satisfactory meaning of the term had ever been found, and that there were in any case several meanings, depending on lay or medical usage. In lay parlance, hysterical meant immature, overreacting and childish behaviour. Patients who got angry easily, who tended to act out and in whom the doctor–patient relationship became fragile were referred to as hysterical by frustrated medical staff. Hysterical became a pejorative term, even within medical settings.

An interesting partial resolution to this dilemma had already been achieved though the writings of two American psychiatrists, Chodoff and Lyons. Their 1958 paper was entitled 'Hysteria, the hysterical personality and hysterical conversion'. They distinguished between hysteria, a particular kind of psychosomatic symptomatology often referred to as conversion hysteria or conversion reaction, and the hysterical personality, a pattern of behaviour habitually exhibited by certain individuals. Conversion was a postulated mechanism for the development of the symptoms.

The hysterical personality was not necessarily linked to hysterical conversion, and indeed, several studies, including that of Chodoff and Lyons, noted this personality style in a minority of patients presenting with conversion symptoms.

The main features of the hysterical personality (renamed histrionic personality disorder by DSM-III) include egocentric attitudes, exhibitionism and dramatism, labile affects and excitability, emotional shallowness, flirtatiousness associated with sexual frigidity, dependence and suggestibility. In its florid form this style is easily recognised (the essence of femininity – hence the feminists' revolt!), but some authors have revealed these trait patterns as identifiable factors using personality questionnaires in population studies.

Most studies suggest that about 20% of patients with conversion disorders have this style, but other personality styles are also noted, including passive-immature-dependent types, and borderline personalities. The point is that it is a spectrum of personality attributes that lends towards conversion, and that not all patients with hysteria conform in personality attributions to one type. This has important implications for those who subscribe to psychoanalytic interpretations, in the sense that in these theories, personality development and illness go hand in glove, but this does not appear to be the case with this paradigmatical psychoanalytic disorder.

There are however overlaps, and hysterical personalities are commonly found in patients with conversion disorders. In one of the best descriptions of the hysterical style given, Shapiro (1965) re-emphasised the close links of the latter to the processes of cognition. Memory is likely to be inexact, and impressionistic. This flavour is revealed during the clinical interview. Ask the patient where the pain is; the response will be: 'all over'. Ask when the symptoms began; the answer will be: 'way back when'. This, for example, is in stark contrast to the descriptions of the obsessional, who not only catalogues exactly the development of the symptoms, but will also give precise descriptions, sometimes so tedious and circumstantial that they also become misleading to the medical enquirer.

The impressions of the hysteric are vivid but opaque, global not specific, diffuse and not sharpened. Shapiro makes the point that such a cognitive style itself has nothing to do with repression; it represents a form of cognition. As such, it is not surprising that memory complaints are frequently encountered in such personalities, that chronologies of their illnesses are unclear, and that performance on neuropsychological tasks sometimes seem odd.

The impressionability of hysterics means that their attention is easily captured and swayed. Shapiro refers to their 'relatively non-factual subjective world'; their cognitions relate not so much to facts but to impressions. He felt that such a cognitive style favoured repression as a defence: 'clear, detailed, factual recollection of contents that are highly charged emotionally is hardly imaginable' (Shapiro, 1965, p. 116). This leads on to a failure of self-monitoring, and to self-deception. 'The capacity of hysterical people to become so ungenuine without being aware that they are so, is quite striking' (p. 120). This feeds into *la belle indifférence* of patients towards their clinical symptoms, and, as noted later, into the shaded world of conscious deception.

Impulsive personalities also have overlaps with the hysterical style, in addition being what Shapiro refers to as concrete. The impulsive cognition perceives only what strikes: there is no meditation or mediation, things are viewed only in their most personally relevant ways. Planning, concentration, ability to shift attention and logical objectivity are all impaired, leading again to poor performance on neurocognitive tests, but also to seeing the world as 'a series of opportunities, temptations, frustrations, sensuous experiences, and fragmented impressions' (p. 154). The point is that there are obvious overlaps between cognition, performance on neuropsychological tests and personality styles or types.

Another eminent psychopathologist who has written about the hysterical personality is Karl Jaspers (1883–1969). Jaspers distinguished the hysterical attack from hysterical stigmata, and both from the hysterical personality. The hysterical personality can be distinguished by one enduring trait, namely: 'far from accepting their given dispositions and life opportunities, hysterical personalities crave to appear, both to themselves and others, as more than they are, and to experience more than they are ever capable of. The place of genuine experience and natural expression is usurped by a contrived stage act, a forced kind of experience' (Jaspers, 1972, p. 443). For Jaspers this was not conscious, but a reflection of the hysteric living within his or her own drama. In the end they lose the centrality of their existence, and with exaggerated expressions, end up deceiving themselves and others.

Jaspers further opined that:

hysterical personalities have to ensure their own importance and so play a role and try to make themselves interesting everywhere even at the expense of their calling or integrity. If unnoticed for even a brief period, or if they feel they somehow do not belong, they grow unhappy ... If they cannot otherwise succeed, they will get attention by falling ill and playing the part of a martyr, a sufferer. Under some circumstances they will be reckless with themselves and inflict self-injury; they have a wish to be ill, provided they reap the reward of some corresponding effect on others. In order to heighten life and find new ways of making an effect, they will resort to lying, at first quite consciously but this soon becomes unconscious and they come to believe themselves (p. 444).

The profound insights delivered by Jaspers in this descriptive typology hits at the heart of the medicolegal dilemma to be discussed later, namely the inherent wish to be ill that some people crave, and the fluctuating boundary between what is conscious and unconscious. Anderson and Trethowan (1967) put it thus:

One of the most effective ways in our society of achieving and attracting individual attention and commiseration is through sickness. The *malade imaginaire* who takes to her bed from which she dominates her whole family, playing one member off against another, inducing with consumate skill in each member a sense of guilt and unworthiness to serve such a 'devoted mother' . . . is a commonplace in medical practice (p. 178).

Throw in a complacent and compliant physician, instruct a lawyer, and the full catastrophe blossoms like a flower watered by the spring rains.

The borderline personality and sociopathy

The overlaps between impulsivity and psychopathy noted above lead on to discussion of another personality profile often associated with the presentation of somatised symptoms – the borderline personality. Some brief history is needed. There are various people, in all times and in all societies, who offend against the societal rules to the extent that they either make society or themselves suffer in some tangible way. Such people are rarely creative, but when they are, they are more lightly forgiven. Various terms have been used to delineate this group, including psychopaths, sociopaths and antisocial personalities. They display recurrent recidivist behaviour, starting early in life, with poor interpersonal relationships, negligible school achievements, a poor work record and criminal convictions, varying in severity. They lack the power of empathy, and have a disregard for the rights of others. Drug abuse, alcoholism, pathological lying and episodes of impulsive aggression are features. This disorder has been recognised in the psychiatric literature for centuries, and in the past was referred to as moral insanity. It has now found a place in DSM-IV as the antisocial personality disorder, in ICD-10 as the dissocial personality. It appears to have genetic contributions, and biological associations include evidence of aberrant frontal lobe functioning (Trimble, 1996). These personality types are a constant feature of one part of the law, the criminal division. They also have a tendency to somatise.

A long-recognised personality anlage, the passive-dependent personality is marked by an ever-ready tendency to seek help and attention, easily becoming dependent on others. By responding to these needs, they increase their latent yearning for prolonged infantilisation.

The borderline personality by contrast has appeared late in the diagnostic manuals, emerging for the first time in DSM-III. It derives its name from certain psychoanalytic concepts, but its main representative features are impulsivity, unpredictability, intense but unstable interpersonal relationships, rapid mood swings, a tendency to self-harm with overdoses and wrist cutting, feelings of emptiness and boredom, and a poor concept of self-identity. Such personalities tolerate anxiety badly, and seek relief through acts of self-mutilation or drug taking. The overlaps with the antisocial personality are obvious, and both have roots in disruptive early family relationships.

The presentation of somatic, unexplained medical symptoms and dissociative states in borderline patients is common, and seems a feature of the underlying personality organisation. Further, a common psychodynamic mechanism is that of splitting, in which ambivalence is poorly tolerated, and things are seen as either black or white. Objects or people are seen as good or bad – there is no in-between. People are either with them, or against them. As such, idealisation of one group of people becomes contrasted with another, who are seen as hostile and as aggressors. In a medicolegal context it is obvious how such a thinking style easily leads to compartmentalisation of a claimant's view in his or her own mind, and to a fostering of, and crystallisation of, the adversarial positions inherent in the English legal system.

Abnormal illness behaviour

One elegant attempt to bring uniformity to and to unite the above disparate categorisations was the introduction of the term 'abnormal illness behaviour (AIB)' by Pilowsky (1997). This concept evolved from the term 'illness behaviour' used initially by David Mechanic (1982). 'Illness behaviour describes the manner in which persons monitor their bodies, define and interpret their symptoms, take remedial actions and utilise the health care system' (p. 1). It suggests a considerable social variability of behaviours related to illness, and derives from a social rather than a medical perspective. Mechanic pointed out how ethnic variations and cultural and developmental experiences determine a person's reaction to threat. What may not seem rational behaviour to a doctor, to patients with symptoms may seem a logical approach to their problems.

Presentations to doctors and the manner of the presentation are essentially culturally and socially determined, and not primarily directed by underlying disease. Thus, distinctions need to be made between symptoms and signs, syndromes and diseases, and, as already discussed, between these concepts and illness. The latter is the patient's representation of any underlying signs and symptoms to doctors. Illness is a recognised social currency, and one that can be exchanged for alternatives. It can, for example, be exchanged for health, or for dependence, or for compensation. Medical understandings of illness (your cough is caused by a bacterium that causes tuberculosis) differ from patients' (my cough is caused by my damp house), and the latter rely much more on what might be referred to as folk understanding. This forms the basis for acting in relation to symptoms, and is influenced not only by lay understandings of disease, but by prevailing cultural beliefs and pressures, and beliefs about causation. There is then a chain, which may be written as follows:

Cause → Disease → Signs and
Symptoms → Syndrome → Illness

This chain applies well from a medical perspective to a number of recognised diseases, from diabetes to tuberculosis. However, with many psychiatric syndromes, especially the ones discussed in this book, the chain would have to be rewritten omitting or bracketting both cause and disease; signs go in lower carriage and syndrome and illness remain prominent:

(Cause) → (Disease) → Signs and Symptoms → Syndrome → Illness

This is because the causes are usually not clear, and underlying disease (brain pathology, for example), even if present, is often hard to demonstrate. What is outstanding is the syndromic presentation and the patient's illness. In hysteria, and many of the somatising conditions, the gapi Disease → Illness is simply not transcribable.

To describe this chasm, physicians adopting the first model above use epithets such as supratentorial or functional overlay. However, these merely shield ignorance, and lead to a false security of understanding.

Thus, within any social group, normal illness behaviour can be recognised. A patient develops a rash, seeks help (by going to a doctor), is prescribed a cream (treatment) and returns to his normal lifestyle. In a given context, normal illness behaviour could be measured (given those kind of rashes, how often the average person goes to a doctor, how many times on average he applies the treatment, and the mean stay away from work, as a sick person, before being well again). The 'sick role' which the person with illness adopts, usually temporarily, defines certain privileges, but also carries with it obligations. Amongst these are an obligation to comply with treatment and to get better.

Thus, if normal illness behaviour has given parameters, it should be possible to define AIB. Pilowsky (1997) defined AIB as: 'the persistence of an inappropriate or maladaptive mode of experiencing, evaluating or acting in relation to one's own state of health' (p. 25). It is noted by the patients' ways of behaving and responding with respect to their symptoms, and by their interactions with physicians and other helpers.

The concept allows for a further understanding of a number of overlapping clinical phenomena which cover a spectrum from illness-denying to malingering. Thus, Pilowsky classified AIB into illness-affirming and illness-denying subcategories, as shown in Table 2.3. He further subcategorises into those which are predominantly with conscious and those with predominantly unconscious motivation. In this

Table 2.3 Abnormal illness behaviour syndromes

	Somatically focused	Psychologically focused
Illness-affirming	*Motivation predominantly conscious* 1. Malingering 2. Chronic factitious syndrome with physical symptoms (Münchausen syndrome) 3. Factitious disorder with physical symptoms	*Motivation predominantly conscious* 1. Malingering 2. Factitious disorder with psychological symptoms (Ganser syndrome)

	Motivation predominantly unconscious
	1. Neurotic (somatoform disorders)
	  • Somatisation disorder
	  • Conversion disorder
	  • Psychogenic pain disorder
	  • Hypochondriasis
	2. Psychotic hypochondriacal delusions associated with:
	  • Major depressive disorder with mood-congruent psychotic features
	  • Schizophrenic disorder
	  • Monosymptomatic hypochondriacal psychoses
		Motivation predominantly unconscious
		1. Neurotic
		  • 'Psychic hypochondriasis'
		  • Dissociative reactions
		  • Psychogenic amnesia
		2. Psychotic
		  • Delusions of memory loss or loss of brain function

Illness-denying	*Motivation predominantly conscious* 1. Denial to obtain employment 2. Denial to avoid feared therapies 3. Denial of illness (e.g. sexually transmitted disease) due to shame and guilt	*Motivation predominantly conscious* 1. Denial of psychotic symptomatology to avoid stigma or hospital admission, or to gain discharge from care 2. Denial of psychotic illness to avoid perceived discrimination by health care professionals or employers

	Motivation predominantly unconscious
	1. Neurotic
	  • Non-compliance following myocardial infarction
	  • Counterphobic behaviour in haemophilia
	  • Non-compliance with antihypertensive therapy
	2. Psychotic
	  • Denial of somatic pathology, e.g. as part of hypomania or schizophrenic disorder
		Motivation predominantly unconscious
		1. Neurotic: refusal to accept 'psychological' diagnosis or treatment in the presence of neurotic illness, personality disorder or dependence syndromes (alcohol, opiates, etc.)
		2. Psychotic: denial of illness ('lack of insight') in psychotic depression, manic states and schizophrenia

	Neuropsychiatric 1. Anosognosia	*Neuropsychiatric* Confabulatory reaction in Korsakoff's psychosis and other organic brain syndromes

context, hysteria is thus a form of predominantly unconscious, somatically focused AIB, while malingering is somatically or psychologically focused, predominantly conscious AIB. Within this classification we also find some other states that are considered in this book, such as fictitious disorders and the Münchausen syndrome.

Although subject to some criticisms, the most obvious being that perhaps it is the doctor and not the patient who is mistaken about the diagnosis, the concepts of illness behaviour, the sick role and AIB reveal the need to consider sociological and cultural components to a patient's or a claimant's symptoms, and their likely influence by external factors, of which compensation must be relevant.

Conclusions

This chapter has reviewed contemporary classifications, and suggested an important role of personality variables in relation to clinical presentations of patients with somatic and dissociative symptoms. In general the modern classifications uphold emerging divisions noted in the historical overview, namely of distinctions between acute and chronic disorders, and of the presence of a particularly intractable form of somatoform disorder, referred to as somatisation disorder or Briquet's hysteria. Although slow in acknowledgement, somatisation disorder has an established place in current diagnostic manuals, with well-defined criteria for diagnosis.

Some personality styles lend themselves to the clinical phenomena of somatoform and dissociative disorders, and this must in part be considered a constitutional given. In other words, the cognitive style of these individuals reflects on their symptoms as patients and their behaviour both within and without the clinical setting. While the diagnostic manuals make distinctions between psychiatric disorders (DSM-IV, axis 1) and personality disorders (DSM-IV, axis 2), the two are actually carefully entwined in some psychiatric settings, especially through cognitive styles. Memory, recall, performance on psychological tasks, impulsivity, suggestibility – all relate to individual underlying personalities. For some personalities, impressions can dominate over detail; deception of the self and others is a given, as is the desire to achieve the unachievable. The yearning to be ill in some people is stronger than the will for wellness; some take flight into illness, while others are nurtured and encouraged into dependence. Several differing but related personality styles are relevant here, especially the hysterical, the passive-dependent, the psychopathic and the borderline.

The relative exertion of consciousness over the control of somatic symptoms is hedged, by both DSM and ICD classifications, but the fluctuating nature of such control over time is perhaps a feature of these personalities. This is discussed in more detail later.

It is imperative to be very wary of the use of diagnostic manuals in settings they were not devised for, and respect their very limited view of many clinical phenomena. They should be used with utmost caution in the medicolegal setting, and only by the experienced.

AIB provides a particularly useful concept to take our understanding of the somatoform disorders further, and emphasises the important cultural and sociological nature of patients' emerging symptoms. However, by and of itself it says little of relevance for aetiology (the ultimate cause), but more for pathogenesis (the development of the disorder from causes), and gives some insight into pathoplastic (moulding) variables in the development of symptomatology.

REFERENCES

American Psychiatric Association (1968). *Diagnostic and Statistical Manual of Mental Disorders* (DSM-II), 2nd edn. Washington: American Psychiatric Association.

(1980). *Diagnostic and Statistical Manual of Mental Disorders* (DSM-III), 3rd edn. Washington, DC: American Psychiatric Association.

(1987). *Diagnostic and Statistical Manual of Mental Disorders* (DSM-IIIR), 3rd edn. Washington, DC: American Psychiatric Association.

(1994). *Diagnostic and Statistical Manual of Mental Disorders*, 4th edn. Washington, DC: APA Press.

(2000). *Diagnostic and Statistical Manual of Mental Disorders* (DSM-IV) – Text Revision. Washington: American Psychiatric Association.

Anderson, E. W. and Trethowan, W. H. (1967). *Psychiatry*, 2nd edn. London: Baillière Tindall and Cassell.

Berrios, G. E. and Mumford, D. (1995). Somatoform disorders: clinical section. In *A History of Clinical Psychiatry*, ed. G. E. Berrios and R. Porter, pp. 384–409. London: Athlone Press.

Chodoff, P. and Lyons, H. (1958). Hysteria, the hysterical personality and hysterical conversion. *American Journal of Psychiatry*, **114**, 734–40.

Cullen, W. (1803). *Nosology or the Classification of Diseases*. Edinburgh: self-published.

Ford, C. V. (1983). *The Somatizing Disorders – illness as a way of life*. New York: Elsevier Biomedical.

Jaspers, K. (1972). *General Psychopathology*. Translated by J. Hoenig and M. W. Hamilton. Manchester: Manchester University Press.

Kleinman, A. (1977). Depression, somatization and the new cross-cultural psychiatry. *Social Science and Medicine*, **11**, 3–10.

Lipowski, Z. J. (1987). Somatization: the experience and communication of psychological distress as somatic symptoms. *Psychotherapy and Psychosomatics*, **47**, 160–7.

Mechanic, D. (ed.) (1982). *Symptoms, Illness Behaviour, and Help Seeking*. New York: Prodist.

Perley, M. G. and Guze, S. B. (1962). Hysteria: the stability and usefulness of clinical criteria. *New England Journal of Medicine*, **266**, 421–6.

Pilowsky, I. (1997). *Abnormal Illness Behaviour*. Chichester: John Wiley.

Purtell, J. J., Robins, E. and Cohen, M. E. (1951). Observations on clinical aspects of hysteria. *Journal of the American Medical Association*, **146**, 902–9.

Shapiro, D. (1965). *Neurotic Styles*. New York: Basic Books.

Slater, E. and Glithero, E. (1965). A follow-up of patients suffering from hysteria. *Journal of Psychosomatic Research*, **9**, 9–13.

Trimble, M. R. (1996). *Biological Psychiatry*, 2nd edn. Chichester: John Wiley.

World Health Organization (1992). *The ICD 10 Classification of Mental and Behavioural Disorders*. Geneva: World Health Organization.

3

Clinical presentations

What we know is that, in an unclichéd way, nobody knows anything. You *can't* know anything. The things you *know* you don't know. Intention? Motive? Consequence? Meaning? All that we don't know is astonishing. Even more astonishing is what passes for knowing.

(Philip Roth, *The Human Stain*, Vintage, 2000, p. 209)

Introduction

The preceding two chapters have outlined the history of hysteria and posttraumatic hysteria, and hints at their clinical presentations have been given. Several important issues have arisen. These include the extent to which the concept of the somatoform disorders is contaminated with malingering, the role of unconscious as opposed to conscious mechanisms in symptom production and maintenance, and the special role of the medicolegal process in some cases. In this chapter, the main clinical varieties of somatoform disorder are presented, while malingering is discussed in the next chapter.

Incidence and prevalence

In reality, no one knows the true extent to which patients somatise. In one study, in which patients kept a health care diary, a new symptom was reported on average every 5–7 days (Demers *et al.*, 1980). It is estimated that perhaps a quarter to a half of patients in medical clinics attend with symptoms that are medically unexplained. Thus, in the UK, many thousands of patients go daily to their general practitioners (GPs) with physical complaints, which, with the passage of some brief period of time, gentle persuasion and perhaps a prescription, soon resolve. In many cases, some minor muscular ailment is translated into a syndrome or disease, given the imprimatur of medical approval, and patient, doctor and employers are all satisfied. Minor anxiety, occasioned by a boss, bereavement or a broken promise, transmogrifies to the somatic realm, but with the balm of calming exercises or gentle tranquillisation soon dissipates. The notation in the GP notes may read: '? Anxiety'. However, in some patients, symptoms such as palpitations, giddiness, episodes of light-headedness, breathlessness and feeling tired pepper the GP notes like barely disguised road signs in the night, ambiguous yet directional.

The system of general practice in the UK has been very important in documenting the pattern and distribution of various illnesses from an epidemiological point of view. Such a system does not exist in the USA, where the population is much more mobile, and most symptoms are first evaluated by specialists. In general, in the UK, patients stick with one or two GPs throughout their lives, and, in any case, when they transfer from one GP to another, their notes (sometimes referred to as Lloyd George notes), which are the GP's handwritten comments, and any associated specialist letters are sent on to the new GP. Thus, for most of the population, the medical biographical record of a patient, or a claimant, is readily available for scrutiny. These are vital in the assessment of patients in a medicolegal context, and are even more important when assessing a person's tendency to somatise. On average, female patients visit the GP five times a year, males slightly less, with four attendances.

Medically unexplained symptoms abound. It is estimated that up to half of primary care consultations are for pains in the head, chest, back or abdomen, fatigue, dizziness, shortness of breath, swelling joints, insomnia and numbness, of which only a minority have an obvious organic basis (Katon and Walker, 1998). However, as noted, most such symptoms resolve, barely become endorsed under a syndrome rubric, and are not usefully referred to as variants, however minor, of hysteria. Their presence however may reflect on mechanisms, to be discussed in Chapter 8, since they suggest that the tendency to somatise is universal, and that the inclination to use medical facilities for reassurance, reification or ratification of such symptoms is very common.

When it comes to estimating the frequency of syndromes, especially in psychiatric practice, the problem of 'caseness' becomes important. It seems clear that the diagnostic criteria for psychiatric disorders differ, say between DSM-IV (American Psychiatric Association, 1994) and ICD-10 (World Health Organization, 1992), and that, in any case, most practitioners do not apply such criteria when sitting in a surgery making a diagnostic judgement. Indeed, DSM-IV makes it clear that informed clinical judgement is the basis for diagnosis. However, in research settings, criteria are more specifically applied, in particular so that work at one centre can be replicated at another, with some certainty that the cases included in and excluded from a particular study have coherence.

It is obvious that the prevalence of a particular disorder, defined as the proportion of individuals within a population affected with the disorder at a particular time, will vary not only with the definition of the syndrome, but also with the setting of the study, namely the population under investigation. The incidence, which refers to the frequency with which new cases occur in a population, also relates to these factors. Further, estimates of both the prevalence and the incidence of medically unexplained symptoms are very dependent on the symptoms remaining unexplained! In theory this can only be obtained through complex follow-up studies, few of which have been carried out, and most that have been done have examined patients attending specialist centres. A further interesting issue that relates to the history of these disorders and the nature of the symptoms is that they often derive from neurological centres. These follow-up studies are discussed in more detail in Chapter 6.

The epidemiology of conversion disorders, excluding somatisation disorder (Briquet's hysteria), has recently been reviewed by Akagi and House (2001). They surveyed all the literature on prevalence or incidence between 1966 and 1999 where cases 'broadly in line with DSM or ICD criteria' could be identified. However, certain groups were not included, such as studies of pseudoseizures (seizures not due to epilepsy but which resemble epileptic seizures clinically; these are alternatively called non-epileptic seizures) or those that were concerned with symptoms related to the special senses, and studies of prisoners and war veterans.

The annual incidence of conversion disorders in general practice is given at 8.9 per 100 000; higher figures of 11 and 22 are given for data obtained from case registers from Iceland and New York respectively. Incidence estimates obtained from neurological referrals were 5–12 per 100 000. The rates for prevalence were more varied, from 53 per 100 000 point prevalence to 408 per 100 000 lifetime prevalence.

In a recent study (Lieb et al., 2000), in which over 3000 adolescents and young adults (age 14–24) were surveyed, the overall prevalence rate was given as 12.6%. These figures for conversion disorder attest to the frequency of the syndrome in the community, and their presence in young adults.

The data from more specialist centres support the vivid presence of these syndromes in practice. Rates vary from 1.2% of general medical and surgical patients to higher rates of up to 10% in neurological settings. Carson et al. (2000) give a rate of 11% for unexplained and 19% for somewhat explained symptoms in neurological outpatients, and, in the survey of Perkin (1989), 26.5% of neurological outpatients finished their consultations with no diagnosis. For inpatients, Creed et al. (1990) give a figure of 24% 'non-organic' cases out of 133 female neurology inpatients. Table 3.1 shows the rates in psychiatric liaison practice. Not surprisingly, rates are highest here, although again, considerable variability is seen.

Although there is good evidence that conversion disorder or its variants are common in medical practice, it will be noted that most of the studies quoted are over a decade old, and may not reflect on clinical practice at the present time. Indeed, the introduction of more sophisticated medical investigations has shifted the

Table 3.1 Numbers of referrals with conversion disorders in psychiatric liaison practice

Patient population	Area	No. of cases	Rate among referrals (%)	Case definition	References
Inpatients	London, UK	45	15	Hysteria Criteria not stated	Fleminger and Mallett (1962)
Accident and emergency	London, UK	6	18.8	Hysteria Criteria not stated	Bridges et al. (1966)
Outpatients		10	4.9		
Inpatients		10	7.0		
General hospital	Yale, New Haven, USA	144	14	Conversion reaction Own diagnostic criteria	McKegney (1971)
General hospital	New Haven, West Haven, USA	20–289	6–12	Conversion reaction Criteria not stated	Kligerman and McKegney (1971)
Liaison referrals	London, UK	36	14	Hysteria Criteria not stated	Anstee (1972b)
Neurology and neurosurgery	Montreal, Canada	34	8	Conversion reaction: Engel's definition (Engel, 1970)	Lipowski and Kiriakos (1972)
General hospital	New York, USA	74	4.5	DSM-II Hysterical neurosis, conversion type	Stefansson et al. (1976)
General hospital	New Hampshire, USA	52	5	Hysterical neurosis, conversion type Criteria not stated	Shevitz et al. (1976)
General hospital	New York, USA	3	2	Conversion reaction Criteria not stated	Karasu et al. (1977)
General hospital	Alabama, USA	50	5[a]	DSM-III Somatoform conversion disorder	Folks et al. (1984)
General hospital	New York, USA	11	0.61	DSM-III Conversion disorder	Snyder and Strain (1989)

[a] Includes 1.7% with coexisting somatisation and conversion sympotms.

For references, see original article.

From Akagi and House (2001), p. 81.

trend for these diagnoses in two directions. Some patients previously diagnosed with conversion can now be shown to have some undiagnosed medical diagnosis, but others, with apparently known neurological diagnoses, such as epilepsy, can be rediagnosed as patients with conversion or dissociation (non-epileptic or pseudoseizures). The estimated frequency of non-epileptic seizures in patients with a diagnosis of chronic epilepsy ranges up to 25%, and about half of the patients receive a diagnosis of conversion or dissociation after re-evaluation (Trimble, 2001).

The above studies confirm that the somatoform disorders are predominantly diagnosed in women, and interestingly, in an assessment of the few studies where two investigations were carried out in the same city separated by a number of years, that the condition is not decreasing in incidence (Akagi and House, 2001).

Somatisation disorder, one would suspect, was rarer. In population surveys, Robins and Regier (1991) reported a prevalence of 0.01%, Deighton and Nicol (1985) of 0.2%, and Escobar et al. (1987) of 0.3–0.7%. However, Kroenke et al. (1997), in a study of 1000 primary-care patients reported multisomatoform disorder in 8%.

Somewhere in between the studies quoted above by Akagi and House for conversion disorders, and the patients with somatisation disorder, are those with abridged forms of somatisation, with prevalence rates of up to 19% (Gureje et al., 1997).

The rates for hypochondriasis have been determined less often, but the survey of Escobar et al. (1998) used a structured interview to estimate levels of disability. The prevalence of hypochondriasis using DSM-IV criteria was approximately 3%.

There are no specific studies of the prevalence or incidence of these syndromes in a medicolegal setting, but it has been observed from the historical studies that it is males rather than females who tend to develop hysteria in posttraumatic settings, and Akagi and House concluded that sex differences are least in neurological surveys. Goodwin and Guze (1984) note that nearly all men with symptoms of hysteria have been involved with compensation. In practice, many patients with conversion disorders are not so diagnosed in the legal setting; the reasons for this are discussed later.

Somatoform disorder

To list the symptoms of conversion and dissociation disorders is merely to give a list of all the symptoms that patients complain of – they are legion. As noted, DSM-IV provides lists of symptoms for patients diagnosed as having somatisation disorder, broken down into categories. The original list given by Feighner et al. (1972) for diagnosing Briquet's syndrome is shown in Table 3.2. Essentially, nearly all of these can present acutely, and be monosymptomatic, or be noted in polysymptomatic combinations, and chronically as Briquet's syndrome.

Table 3.2 Symptoms for Briquet's syndrome according to Feighner *et al.* (1972)

Group 1
Headaches, sickly majority of life

Group 2
Blindness, paralysis, anaesthesia, aphonia, convulsions, unconsciousness, amnesia, deafness, hallucinations, urinary retention, trouble walking, other unexplained neurological symptoms

Group 3
Fatigue, lump in the throat, fainting spells, visual blurring, weakness, dysuria

Group 4
Breathing difficulty, palpitation, anxiety attacks, chest pain, dizziness

Group 5
Anorexia, weight loss, marked fluctuation in weight, nausea, abdominal bloating, food intolerances, diarrhoea and constipation

Group 6
Abdominal pain, vomiting

Group 7
Dysmenorrhoea, menstrual irregularity, amenorrhoea, excessive bleeding

Group 8
Sexual indifference, frigidity, dyspareunia, other sexual difficulties, vomiting all 9 months of pregnancy at least once, or hospitalised for hyperemesis gravidarum

Group 9
Back pain, joint pain, extremity pain, burning pains of the sexual organs, mouth or rectum, other bodily pains

Group 10
Nervousness, fears, depressed feelings, need to stop working, or inability to undertake regular duties because of feeling ill, crying easily, feeling life was hopeless, thinking a good deal about dying, wanting to die, thinking of suicide, suicide attempts

The list reveals that there are many variants, neurological, gynaecological, gastroenterological, orthopaedic, respiratory, intermixed with psychiatric symptoms. It needs to be reinforced that the symptoms must remain medically unexplained, and the clinical presentation often initially gives no such clues. Further, it is a considerable diagnostic error to make a diagnosis of conversion or dissociation on negative grounds alone, i.e. with no positive physical, psychiatric and behavioural features to back up the diagnosis.

Suspicion may first arise with failure of investigations to confirm initial clinical impressions, and the persistence of the symptoms beyond their expected time.

History-taking usually reveals more than one symptom. It is not the rule that conversion disorders are single-symptom presentations, but a single symptom may attract the lion's share of attention. This is often the beginning of the slippery slope to misdiagnosis. In other words, a dramatic neurological symptom will lead to specialist neurological referral, to specialist neurological investigations and to specialist blinkers. The adjacent gynaecological history, the associated history of asthma or the non-anatomical sensory symptoms attending a motor paralysis are either not noted, or, if noted, ignored.

In clinical enquiry, the history must come first. While it is fashionable in evaluating patients to direct attention to the history of the presenting complaint, where there is a suspicion of medically unexplained symptoms, three other features are important in the assessment. These are the patient's personality, the past illness history and the presence of abnormal illness behaviour (AIB).

Much has already been said in Chapter 2 of the personality of patients with conversion disorder. The main point in the history-taking is that many of these patients are notoriously poor at describing their symptoms. Their verbal imprecision, poor memories and often dramatic behavioural styles tend to mislead even the most attentive medical archivist. The history taken by one doctor differs from that of another; the severity of the symptoms is often descriptively florid, with interspersed superlatives serving to reinforce the severity of the problem. An immaturity of behaviour is reflected in emotional lability, evanescent enthusiasms and evident egocentricity. There is a shallowness to their emotional expression, a lack of insight into their own dilemmas, sometimes a seemingly pleased attachment to a symptom. A classical *belle indifférence* is rarer than the textbooks suggest, but the bland smile of the patient whose pain is 'excruciating', or whose paralysis has rendered the arm useless is readily detectable.

The onset of the disorder is often an emotional crisis. Bereavement is a common precipitant, but Chapter 1 reviewed the literature on the war neuroses, emphasising the varieties of emotional trauma that may be involved. It is not unusual for there to be a phase of emotional tension that precedes the symptom onset, that may mount to the early phases of a depressive illness. In some settings, notably those involving accidents, an initial physical symptom, such as a pain following trauma, becomes embedded as a chronic symptom, extending in time far beyond that expected. Some initial alteration of consciousness, a minor concussion, may become self-sustaining, with continuing complaints of episodes of daydreaming, lapses of attention, memory impairments or full-blown fugue states. In these fugue states, patients wander, 'coming to' in a strange place not knowing how they have got there. Typically they do not draw attention to themselves by acting strangely during the fugue, which lasts hours, days and, rarely, weeks, and on coming to they may have lost their personal identity. Such complaints readily get misinterpreted as epileptic seizures.

A link between emotional events and physical symptoms will usually be denied by the patient, as will that between any motivating and maintaining factors. This may in part be a reflection of the very processes of dissociation and conversion (the conversion in psychodynamic terms being protective of the emotional distress), or of denial for other reasons. The onset of symptoms and the occurrence of life events need to be carefully explored, at first not making such direct links that the patient becomes defensive, thus blocking off further lines of psychological enquiry. Subtle gestures, a momentary eye avoidance, a word introduced by the patient, all may hint that the topic under consideration has more significance for the patient than overtly given. It is an interesting paradox that in the general run of medical practice, organic illness is often attributed by patients to psychological factors ('Oh, I've been under a lot of stress lately'), while in these disorders such links are usually specifically denied.

The illness history is one aspect of the patient's anamnesis that is often so poorly documented, and yet is the clue to the diagnosis, especially with the more chronic, polysymptomatic forms of conversion disorder. A past history of conversion is reported in about 20% of cases. Patients should always be asked if they have had any other illnesses which have not been well diagnosed, or which have led to an unclear diagnosis. Childhood and adolescence are important, especially illness that has led to prolonged time away from school, or any other evidence of school refusal. A propensity to seek surgery, or at least to persuade surgeons to operate, seems a feature of many patients. Appendectomy, hysterectomy, cholecystectomy, operations on adhesions, laporoscopies, tonsillectomy and the like are noted in the history. An appendix operation should always be held with suspicion. When examined pathologically, about 50% of removed appendices are normal; in effect the surgeon has operated on a case of abdominal pain, which still remains unexplained after the operation! Such people usually give a history of grumbling abdominal pain, rather than acute appendicitis.

The hysterectomy reflects most often on the gynaecological history, with menorrhagia or dysmenorrhoea, while operations on 'adhesions' suggest ongoing abdominal pains after index operations.

An essential part of the work-up, in the collection of information about the past history, is to obtain the GP records. Therein is often a wealth of biographical information that allows the current illness symptoms to be evaluated in the context of past symptoms, and past episodes of possible medically unexplained symptoms to be noted. In a medicolegal context this is mandatory.

The response of patients to medical enquiry may give away the obvious AIB. There is an immediate hostility to psychological enquiry, a rejection to explore even superficial personal details. Answers are not so much evasive, but in the mould of 'what is the relevance of . . .' or 'I don't see the point of . . .'. It should be noted that such attitudes are not necessarily unfounded, or unexpected. It is not an unfamiliar scenario that patients, having been examined and referred for specialist opinion by their GPs, have a battery of investigations carried out in hospital. The results turn up nothing positive, at which point the patient is either discharged back to the GP, or referred on to other specialists. Further referrals and examinations follow, and, at the end of a long trail through negative findings, the patient is triumphantly given the news that there is nothing abnormal found. The immediate assumption, often encouraged by the medical messenger, is that if it is not in the body, it must be in the mind, and if it is in the mind, then the patient must be putting it on. As noted in the next chapter, this may be a valid conclusion in some cases, but in terms of the illness descriptions given in this chapter, such an exchange is damaging. The suggestion that 'since there is nothing wrong with you, you need to see a psychiatrist' is demeaning to both the patient and the psychiatrist!

The medical exchange however has embedded within it certain rules – those of normal illness behaviour. The patient's insistence that the doctor, along with a dozen other doctors, has got it wrong reveals a failure of the normal mechanisms of reassurance. Their insistence on yet more tests, or on yet another scan, or, even worse, another operation reflects the tendency to procure medical attention. There may be obvious signs of a breakdown in the relationships between the patient and staff responsible for their management. Patients become referred to as 'difficult' or 'non-compliant'; later in the negative diagnostic process they become 'crocks' or 'lead swingers'. Sometimes patients put unreasonable limits on what a doctor can and cannot do. An obvious one is: 'I'll do anything to get well, doctor, except see a psychiatrist'.

As noted, it is up to the physician to explore links between life events and physical symptoms, but in AIB, the relevant life events may be buried in decades of biography. Resistance to any form of psychological exploration is nearly always a reflection of AIB, but elicitation of important details such as early physical or sexual abuse requires considerable tact, and if handled badly can only increase the patient's negative feelings towards psychiatric intervention. However, often such events are slyly hinted at, provocatively slipped into conversation, as if the patient is fly-fishing for the doctor's response. Any flirtation between the doctor and the patient can lead to an erroneous trail, and false attributions. This, in another context, discussed later, can flourish into false memories, and the so-called false-memory syndrome, in which fantasised or elaborated events, usually of sexual seduction, are reified and held responsible for the person's tragic life trajectory, which may include presentations with medically unexplained symptoms.

The worrisome, importunate insistence of the hypochondriac on the physical basis for symptoms is usually obvious, but in lesser forms, the anancastic valetudinarian can be very persuasive that his or her symptoms have not been properly evaluated. What for most people is good news, namely that the tests are negative, is greeted by the hypochondriac as bad news, and a further reflection of the obvious need for more investigation. Interestingly, hypochondriasis is the only somatoform condition described in DSM-IV in which non-response to medical reassurance is given as a key criterion, and the disorder was used by Pilowsky (1970) as a paradigm for the concept of AIB.

The physical examination

It is important to let the patients know that the reported symptoms are being taken seriously, and a physical examination should be conducted when the patient is first assessed, or when obvious new symptoms arise. However, repeated requests for examinations, a reflection of AIB, should be declined. Invasive investigations should be avoided, since one of the complications of medically unexplained symptoms is iatrogenic damage from physically invasive tests.

It is important to ascertain that the symptoms complained of, and the signs revealed, do not obey anatomical and physiological laws, and do not fit the pattern of an alternative medical diagnosis. It is generally said that the symptoms of conversion fit those of folk law – in other words, what lay people think the symptoms of, say, a stroke might be. In fact, while this is undoubtedly so in many cases, the situation is much more complicated in reality. It is simply often very difficult to mimic some conversion symptoms, and others, such as the anaesthesias, are often revealed by the physical examination, not having previously been reported or acknowledged by patients.

The commonest groups of medically unexplained symptoms in medicolegal practice relate to neurology and orthopaedics, and certain signs herald the diagnosis. In neurological practice, common ones are the elicitation of obvious muscle contraction in supposedly paralysed muscles. There are several ways of eliciting this; one of the more reliable is referred to as Hoover's sign. In a hemiparesis, while lying down, the patient is asked to flex the unaffected leg at the hip against resistance. The affected leg will physiologically extend, and the increasing muscle tone can be felt or measured by a hand placed under the foot. Thus, the hand under the affected heel will detect the downward pressure of the apparently paralysed leg. There are several tests of this type which effectively reveal the non-anatomical nature of the motor symptoms (Stone *et al.*, 2002).

Non-physiological anaesthetic patches (Figures 3.1 and 3.2), anomalous visual fields, with tubular fields of vision or spiral fields, and simply either a bizarre

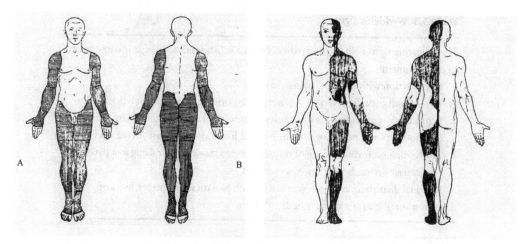

Figure 3.1   Anaesthetic patches in hysteria. From Charcot (1889).

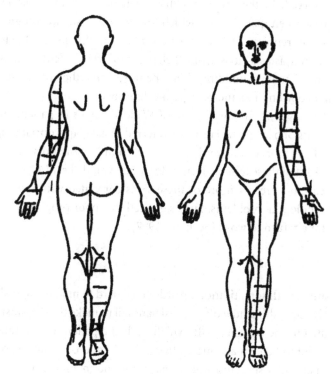

Figure 3.2   Anaesthetic patches from a contemporary patient.

Table 3.3 Waddell's signs

The following signs help identify patients with a substantial non-organic component
to their problem:

1. Overreaction with obvious 'pain behaviour'
2. Widespread superficial tenderness not corresponding to anatomical distribution
3. Reproduction of symptoms by simulated stress on the spine. Elicited by rotation of
    the shoulders and pelvis together or by axial loading by pressure on the skull
4. The finding on formal testing of severely limited straight-leg raising in a patient
    who can sit forwards with the legs extended
5. Regional disturbances with severe lower-limb weakness or sensory loss not
    corresponding to any nerve root distribution

Reproduced from Jason (1992), with permission.

clinical presentation or an obvious hysterical sign such as a typical hysterical gait
may all be observed. In the same way that a left-hemisphere stroke leads to a
right-sided spastic hemiparetic gait, which any neurologist can recognise, some
hysterical gaits can represent, to the experienced eye, nothing else. One feature of
such gaits, including astasia–abasia, in which patients struggle deftly to maintain an
upright posture, virtually stumbling along the way, is that they reveal quite intact
neuromuscular coordination and balance mechanisms.

Orthopaedic surgeons employ the use of Waddell's signs in patients with persistent complaints of back pain. These are referred to as 'inappropriate' signs, and
are categorised as tenderness, simulation, distraction, regional disturbances and
overreaction. A list of these tests is given in Table 3.3. Waddell *et al.* (1984) reported
that the presence of three or more of these signs correlated with scores on tests
indicating psychological problems. Such signs reflect a poor prognosis for lumbar
surgery, and for a return to work (Scalzitti, 1997).

Somatisation disorder

The classic patient with somatisation disorder is so hard to miss in clinical practice
that it is simply astonishing how often physicians fail to make the diagnosis. In part
this is attributed to the patient's AIB, which leads the patient to several different
specialists. All fail to take an adequate illness history, and concentrate exclusively
on their own particular specialist signs, symptoms and investigations, and return
the patient to the referring doctor with various conditions ruled out. Further, it
reflects on an ignorance of psychiatry generally among non-psychiatrists, and a
failure to come to terms with the fact that, for some patients, illness simply is 'a
way of life' (Ford, 1983). After all, in medical school the conventional teaching is
that most people are well, that when they fall sick they do so with disorders that

have been empirically charted, over several centuries and that they come to doctors to be diagnosed, treated and made well again. The idea that patients may develop non-illnesses, present with anomalous symptoms and signs, and seek illness rather than wellness, not only makes little sense – to many it is simply repugnant.

The reluctance of non-psychiatrists to accept the frequency with which they meet psychiatric illness in their practice is hard to understand, especially after so many years of improved medical education, but it remains a fact. It also remains a fact that much psychopathology goes undetected and hence untreated, and that many patients with somatoform disorders are undetected and overtreated, but with the wrong interventions!

The typical patient is female, and usually between 20 and 30 years old by the time she presents to neurological specialists. She will have come from a turbulent background, perhaps with a family history of sociopathy or alcoholism, often from a broken home; there may be a hint or acknowledgement of some form of early abuse. School refusal for some minor childhood complaints may be noted. Often this is recurrent abdominal pain, but headaches and 'growing pains' may be documented in the GP notes (which are so important in unearthing such early histories, since these symptoms are often simply not related or perhaps even recalled by the patient). The patient may just have been 'a sickly child'.

The abdominal pains lead on to the first operation (although the tonsils may have already been extracted), a normal appendix being removed. Further abdominal pains may follow, although there may be a medically quiescent phase. There may be conduct problems at school, some truancy, perhaps an early pregnancy or marriage. Then other medical problems arise, but exactly when is often difficult to tie down. The symptom history is imprecise, often dramatically described, and invariably complicated.

Table 3.4 lists the relative frequency of symptoms reported; all organ systems are included. Visits to gynaecologists, neurologists and other specialists are common, and a glance at the GP notes will reveal that the use of medical facilities is above average. Other operations ensue. While 70% will have had an appendectomy, nearly 50% have a gynaecological procedure, and other interventions follow. Table 3.5 is taken from the controlled study of Cohen *et al.* (1953), showing the various operative procedures in 50 patients with somatisation disorder, compared with healthy controls and a comparison group of patients from the same hospital who had other non-psychiatric illness. Figure 3.3 shows the dramatic difference in the number of operations in this group, and the distribution of the procedures. Dilation and curettage (D&C) occurred nearly five times more frequently in the hysteria group, hysterectomy four times, and by the age of 35, 20% of the hysteria patients were rendered sterile, compared with none in the controls. It was estimated that three times the weight of body organs is removed from patients diagnosed as having hysteria compared with controls!

Table 3.4 The frequency of symptoms in hysteria

Symptom	%	Symptom	%	Symptom	%
Dyspnoea	72	Weight loss	28	Back pain	88
Palpitation	60	Sudden fluctuations in weight	16	Joint pain	84
Chest pain	72	Anorexia	60	Extremity pain	84
Dizziness	84	Nausea	80	Burning pains in rectum, vagina, mouth	28
Headache	80	Vomiting	32	Other bodily pain	36
Anxiety attacks	64	Abdominal pain	80	Depressed feelings	64
Fatigue	84	Abdominal bloating	68	Phobia	48
Blindness	20	Food intolerances	48	Vomiting all 9 months of pregnancy	20
Paralysis	12	Diarrhoea	20	Nervous	92
Anaesthesia	32	Constipation	64	Had to quit working because felt bad	44
Aphonia	44	Dysuria	44	Trouble doing anything because felt bad	72
Lump in throat	28	Urinary retention	8	Cried a lot	60
Fits or convulsions	20	Dysmenorrhoea (premarital only)	4	Felt life was hopeless	28
Faints	56	Dysmenorrhoea (prepregnancy only)	8	Always sickly (most of life)	40
Unconsciousness	16	Dysmenorrhoea (other)	48	Thought of dying	48
Amnesia	8	Menstrual irregularity	48	Wanted to die	36
Visual blurring	64	Excessive menstrual bleeding	48	Thought of suicide	28
Visual hallucination	12	Sexual indifference	44	Attempted suicide	12
Deafness	4	Frigidity (absence of orgasm)	24		
Olfactory hallucination	16	Dyspareunia	52		
Weakness	84				

From M. Perley and S. B. Guze, N.E.J.M. 266; 421–426, 1962.
Reproduced from Goodwin and Guze (1984, p. 96), with permission.

It is of interest that, when males are examined, this excess of surgery is not seen (Robins *et al.*, 1952).

The illness history progresses, but who knows in what direction. Classic chronic hysteria tends, as noted, to end up in gynaecological or neurological practice, and certainly the contractures, seizures and inevitable loss of muscle power lead to

Table 3.5 Comparison of the frequency of major surgical procedures in hysteria patients and control subjects

	Hysteria patients	Control patients	
		Healthy	Medically ill
No. of patients	50	50	30
Operation	Rate per 200 patients[a]		
Gynaecological operations[b]	166	24	57
Mixed operations[c]	84	14	20
Dilation and curettage	70	6	30
Appendectomy	68	28	47
Tonsillectomy	58	50	57
Oophorectomy	48	8	10
Salpingectomy	32	10	7
Hysterectomy	24	6	7
Sterilising surgical procedures prior to age 35	20	0	7
Adhesiotomy	18	0	0
Uterine suspension	16	0	7
Caesarean section	14	0	0
Cholecystectomy	14	0	17
Haemorrhoidectomy	12	0	7
Nephropexy	8	2	0
Ovariotomy	4	2	3
Spinal fusion	4	0	0
Scaleanotomy	4	0	0
Nephrectomy	2	0	0
Coccygectomy	2	0	0
Laminectomy	2	0	0

[a] The rate includes: (1) any operation on that organ; (2) a reoperation on that organ; and (3) an operation on that organ done as part of an operation involving several organs. Bilateral organs, e.g. ovaries, are considered as one organ in these calculations.
[b] Gynaecological operation = operation involving ovaries, tubes, uterus or vagina.
[c] Mixed operation = operations involving more than one organ.
Reproduced from Cohen *et al.* (1953, p. 978), with permission.

neurological referral at some stage. The state of dependence often increases, encouraged by physicians, who make a pseudodiagnosis such as rheumatism which leads to the prescription of steroids, or myalgic encephalomyelitis (ME), which encourages patients to languish in bed. It is further encouraged by well-meaning paramedical staff who make suggestions such as 'perhaps you have a touch of multiple

50 Healthy controls   50 Hysteria patients

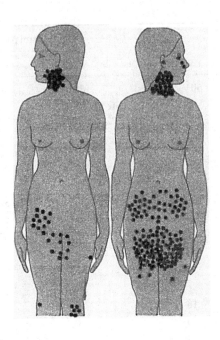

● = 1 operation

Figure 3.3   Comparison of number and location of major surgical procedures in 50 hysteria patients and 50 healthy controls. Reproduced from Cohen *et al.* (1953), with permission.

sclerosis'. It is encouraged by local authorities, which adapt patients' houses to become cocoons of illness, with all kinds of special aids, often provided at considerable expense. It is encouraged by spouses who give up their job to become full-time carers.

By this time the patient is often bed-bound, if not wheelchair-bound, and requiring full-time care. Patients wear splints for orthopaedic complaints, dark glasses for visual problems and carry other insignias of the sick role. In the more severe but rarer cases, urinary symptoms have led to self-catheterisation, or even worse, to operations to provide false bladders. Eating difficulties can lead to abdominal percutaneous endoscopic gastrotomies (PEGs); painful dystonias and recurrent infections to amputations. Patients take a compendium of medications, usually with opiates somewhere in their regimen, on which they have become dependent. It is estimated that some 10% of patients become wheelchair-bound, and average patients spend about a quarter of their time in bed (Bass and Murphy, 1991).

The course of somatisation disorder is to some extent predictable, in the sense that it is by definition chronic and it seems to be a lifelong disorder, embedded within a patient's personality. Since it is lifelong, at some point the patient will be involved in an accident.

Hypochondriasis

There are arguments about the precise validity of this diagnosis, as there are about hysteria. For Pilowsky (1997), there are three cardinal elements: bodily preoccupation, disease phobia and disease conviction. Hypochondriasis differs from hysteria in that in this disorder patients are preoccupied by ill health and disease. They fear they have some dreadful ailment, sometimes having insight into their predicament but, at another end of the spectrum, becoming delusional. 'Hypochondriasis is defined as a concern with health or disease in oneself which is present the major part of the time. The preoccupation must be unjustified by the amount of organic pathology and must not respond more than temporarily to clear reassurance given after a thorough examination of the patient' (Pilowsky, 1970).

It is not an infrequent condition, occurring in up to 10% of medical outpatient consultations and, unlike hysteria, the sex incidence is reported to be equal for males and females (Kenyon, 1964, 1976).

Patients are at the same time clinging, demanding, importuning and ungrateful and inevitably are eventually dissatisfied. Their complaints go back over a number of years, have been investigated elsewhere and have dominated the patient's life. They become isolated from their tired lay helpers, and their appointments with doctors and their association with clinics become their most meaningful contacts.

Symptoms are referable to the musculoskeletal system of the head and neck, but gastroenterological and neurological symptoms are common. Unlike the often vague descriptions of the patient with hysteria, hypochondriacs often keep well-documented details of their illness career, and have a good lexicon of medical terms. Most patients have multiple complaints, but monosymptomatic presentations are common (monosymptomatic hypochondriasis), with persistent headaches, abdominal pains, skin lesions, and the like. Often patients are convinced they have some specific disease, such as an ulcer, cancer or multiple sclerosis, and may be demanding some very recently developed test. Some patients are convinced they have an infestation, and collect evidence for this, like skin shavings, which they take to dermatologists. The more obsessional develop compulsions about checking their body parts. Others believe they give off some offensive smell, washing, changing their clothes and persistently deodorising themselves. Patients may come to the clinic armed with the latest literature about their preoccupation, and nowadays the internet feeds the information (cyberchondria).

Anancastic, worrying personalities hide in the background of these states, but some underlying psychiatric disorder (usually depression) may be present. However, psychological interpretations and psychiatric interventions are strongly resisted, patients often lacking appropriate vocabularies for emotional expression – so-called alexithymia.

Another variant of hypochondriasis, listed in the diagnostic manuals under somatoform disorder, and by Pilowsky as a form of AIB, is dysmorphophobia or body dysmorphic disorder. In this condition, patients are convinced that some body part is abnormal, deformed or defective, and are preoccupied by this in the same way as hypochondriacs. It usually starts in the teenage years, and can be lifelong and unremitting. In most cases, the imagined anomaly represents an overvalued idea, but in some patients it becomes delusional. Such patients present with frequency to plastic surgeons (in some series up to 15% of consultations) for nose, chin, breast or other body part realignment, even when an observer, be it friend, relative or doctor, can see nothing abnormal for correction. Patients have little insight, and develop repetitive behaviours surrounding their preoccupation. These include camouflaging or covering up the offending part, mirror-seeking, checking the body part of concern with others, excessive grooming and seeking excessive medical attention. The concerns preoccupy patients' waking lives, and dissatisfaction is an inevitable outcome of medical consultation. However, it is not uncommon for people to persuade some surgeon to operate on them, with an obviously (for the patient) unsatisfactory outcome, which may lead on to a civil action.

Body dysmorphic disorder is often comorbid with other psychiatric disorders, especially obsessive-compulsive disorder and depression. It can become delusional, and has links with eating disorders such as anorexia nervosa, in which the body image is clearly distorted. About 25% of patients will have attempted suicide, and most have quite severe problems with social and interpersonal relationships.

Pain

Although pain is considered the cardinal symptom of tissue damage, it is also a very common psychiatric complaint. It is a subjectively reported experience, very difficult to measure, and one whose significance is universally appreciated. It is a cardinal symptom bringing patients and doctors into contact, and one that is often so elusive to tie down. Doctors recognise typical patterns of pain, such as the hemicrania of migraine, the left brachial pain of angina or the facial agony of a *tic douloureux*. But, in so many presentations, the patients' descriptions do not fit those of the textbooks, and fail to meet requirements of committee-derived manuals.

Pain is a common problem in AIB, although there have been arguments over time as to what extent pain should be accepted at all as a hysterical symptom. However, the inclusion of somatoform pain disorder in DSM-IIIR is an acceptance that pain should be included within this spectrum, and in fact Pilowsky developed his AIB questionnaire using chronic pain patients.

Merskey and Bogduk (1994) suggest the following criteria for the diagnosis of hysterical pain:

1. the absence of an adequate organic explanation
2. the absence of schizophrenia or a depressive illness or a psychophysiological mechanism which could account for the symptom
3. the presence of a very well-marked syndrome, such as somatisation disorder, identified by detailed criteria
4. or, ideally, the presence of an emotional conflict, which has caused repression (p. 161).

As Merskey pointed out, fulfilling these criteria is hard in practice, but it seems accepted wisdom that pain can arise either as an idea, in other words from thoughts, or from hysterical mechanisms, whatever they may be (conversion). As an example of the former he gives the *couvade* syndrome, in which abdominal pains arise in the spouses of pregnant females.

Perhaps the most cogent writer on the psychodynamic aspects of pain was George Engel, himself a twin, who suffered recurrent illnesses on the anniversary of the death of his twin brother.

His classic paper '"Psychogenic pain" and the pain prone patient' (Engel, 1968), stemmed from his view that pain was the most common conversion symptom seen in clinical practice. Conversion pain was viewed mostly in relation to struggling with feelings of aggression and guilt, when pain brought a degree of atonement. 'Pain-prone' people offered the enquiring physician a certain profile. Patients inevitably had a long history of various pain disorders, and described their pains with vivid imagery. Some presented as martyrs, others as victims, and in the background was a history of abuse and brutality. Relationships with peers and parents were distant and cold, although sometimes the reported early family relationships of love and harmony sounded too good to be true. Engel noted that pain-prone women emphasise hardships, bad marriages and difficulties and defeats, although do little to avoid the offending situations. 'Their bitter lives are reported with a certain relish, suggesting masochism, and curiously an inverse relationship often exists between the occurrence of pain and the difficulties of the life situation. When life is treating them badly, they are pain free; when they have a success or prospect of relief, pain develops and denies them of its enjoyment' (Engel, 1970, p. 662).

In contrast, men tended towards sadism, struggling with hostility, which is sometimes diverted into intense but solitary activities, for example they become of the super-fit type. They often develop a pain syndrome when they suffer 'defeat or loss' or are thrust into a position of too great a responsibility. Engel further noted that 'an accident on the job may be the final step precipitating the chronic pain, permitting the patient to rationalise his defeat and subsequent activity'.

Another subgroup identified are patients with narcissistic personalities (Blazer, 1980). They tend to be mistrustful of others, but strive for prestige and seek the admiration of others. They are often body-proud, and 'work out' regularly. They excel at sports, and remain (even in a state of debility) proud of their achievements. Insults, often trivial, and not always physical, puncture their narcissistic skein, and anger with fairly prompt physical decompensation ensues.

Although such profiles have not been empirically tested, and are open to the critisisms of much psychodynamic theorising, such patients are commonly seen in medicolegal practice. However, while their pain-proneness may not be understood, closer evaluation of their history may reveal overlaps with somatisation disorder, including excessive surgery.

In clinical practice, there are links between depression and chronic pain, and it is not infrequent to find pain of somatic origin intensified and maintained by a depressive illness, which makes the pain more vivid and intense. The initial clinical examination may not identify depression, which the patient may deny, but careful enquiry will reveal the associated affective symptoms.

The location of the pain in hysteria is remarkably variable, and the mechanisms of localisation speculative and barely verified. The concepts vary from pain as an idea (*couvade*); an identification (in a similar location to that of a loved one who has suffered); to a conformation to a common belief (anterior chest pain and heart disease); to pain based on a physiological basis (muscular tension); to the psychoanalytic ideas of symbolism. Following an accident, the site of the physical injury may become the locus from which pain originates and spreads, the pain itself persisting far longer than can be predicted by the nature and intensity of the original insult.

Chronic fatigue syndrome

There is no better example of old somatised wine in new bottles than this revived version of the nineteenth-century neurasthenia. Neurasthenia (nerve weakness) and its cerebral counterpart psychasthenia, were reported in epidemic proportions in France, Germany and the USA at that time. Neurasthenia referred to undue exhaustion with minimal effort. It was accompanied by waning powers of attention and concentration, and was associated with a variety of somatic symptoms.

The history and current state of research in this disorder are well described by Wessely *et al.* (1998). Fatigue is, by all accounts, a very common symptom, difficult to measure and entirely subjective. It is reported to be 10 times commoner than weakness or being run down, and, when questioned, about a third of the population report periods of fatigue lasting 6 months or more. It is one of the commonest reported symptoms (headache is commoner), it affects women more than men, and, while it can obviously be associated with physical illness, it is associated with depression. However there are considerable arguments over the existence of a primary fatigue syndrome (chronic fatigue syndrome: CFS) and, if such a syndrome exists, about its aetiology.

The background to neurasthenia was rather like that of shellshock, in that initially physical causes were sought, only to be supplanted later by social and psychological explanations. Although as a diagnosis, neurasthenia temporarily left the stage in the middle of the twentieth century, it was retained in ICD-9 and 10, and remained a popular diagnosis in many countries. However, the more recent story begins with ME, a condition which was first reported in 1956, and became popularly referred to as Royal Free disease, named after the hospital where it was first described.

A glut of patients presented with myalgia and a variety of other motor and sensory symptoms, which were considered to be due to some infective illness. The latter was supported by an apparent mild pyrexia and the finding of scattered enlarged lymph nodes. In spite of the arguments, which still go on, about the organic basis for this and related outbreaks, no infective agent was or ever has been isolated, and the reality of what caused this syndrome will never be known.

The fact that emotional factors were interlinked with these presentations was recognised early on (McEvedy and Beard, 1970), and associations were made to the well-known social phenomenon of mass hysteria. This refers to outbreaks of hysteria among groups of susceptible people, which have been well documented over the centuries (Merskey, 1995). A variety of somatic symptoms are reported, but excessive motor activity, hyperventilation, convulsions, fainting and the like are the most dramatic. The outbreak of illness is attributed to various factors, depending on the time in history and the geographical location of the outburst. Possession, poisoning by food or gas, and contagion by some epidemic infection are common themes.

These community outbreaks tend to occur in groups which possess certain central characteristics. These include an atmosphere of tense restraint, with some internal paranoia, and often within the group some who share a dissatisfaction or grudge against the possible perpetrators or alleged poisoners. In the work setting, antagonism to the conditions of work is significant. Symptoms tend to spread down from high-status to lower-status individuals within the group. Sometimes shared delusions of such damage occur in small groups or families, so-called *folie à deux* or *trois* or *communiquée*. In a medicolegal context, such a sequence of events may be encountered, for example, in families who may believe that they have been poisoned by carbon monoxide from a faulty gas boiler, or communities who believe they have been collectively contaminated by a polluted communal water supply.

The supposition that psychological as opposed to organic factors were most relevant for understanding ME, and then subsequently its variant CFS, had, as Wessely *et al.* observed, 'the paradoxical effect of reinforcing the organic allegiances of the supporters of the new illness. The mass hysteria hypothesis led to a retrenchment of the organic school of thought, and a polarised, bitter, and acrimonious debate which continues to this day' (Wessely *et al.*, 1999, p. 130).

Wessely *et al.* concluded that, while there is an independent fatigue syndrome, it is nearly always comorbid with psychiatric illness, and it can properly be referred to as either a fatigue syndrome or neurasthenia. There are obvious associations between chronic fatigue, as an unexplained medical symptom, and somatisation. In general, fatigue is a common complaint of patients with somatoform disorders, and as a symptom it is often noted in a patient's biography along with other unexplained medical symptoms.

The typical patient presents with gradually progressive fatigue, associated with a variety of other loosely bound somatic symptoms; dizziness is common, as are muscle pains. What is striking is the complaint of easy fatigability with minimal effort, and the obvious retraction of the patient's daily vitality. Sometimes the condition comes on after an operation or an episode of acute vertigo; in the latter setting an initial diagnosis of an acute inner-ear infection (vestibular neuronitis) may be made. Patients will have reported feeling unwell, with flu-like symptoms, and premonitory fever is commented on. Swollen glands, infected tonsils, and tender livers and spleens are reported. However, it is often difficult to confirm the infective background with any clarity.

Cognitive complaints are common, especially difficulties with attention and concentration, and a multitude of lesser symptoms ranging from swollen joints and tingling to tachycardia may be reported. In more severe forms, and as the disorder progresses, the entrapments of AIB become apparent, perhaps with the adoption of a wheelchair lifestyle and a destiny of dependence. Some disuse atrophy of muscles appears, bringing alarm to patients and physicians alike, and the resulting minor abnormalities on electromyogram testing reinforce the neurological credo. Much time is spent in bed, and, on account of the lack of muscle use, the fatigue becomes more profound, as a vicious cycle is portrayed of reported fatigue leading to lack of activity, which increases the fatigue of activity. The condition continues, often without intervention, and while less severe cases may resolve over time, the more entrenched the AIB, the gloomier is the prognosis.

The literature is replete with attempts to show that CFS is related to this or that viral or immunological factor. Epstein–Barr virus is important here, the virus related to infectious mononucleosis or glandular fever. It had been recognised for some years that a syndrome of persistent fatigue could follow on from several infections, and the postviral fatigue of glandular fever has been well documented, although this rarely lasted more than a few months. However, since a specific test is available to look for the viral antibodies (the Paul–Bunnell test), it is commonly looked for in patients with CFS. It is usually negative, but the finding of a negative test result in the GP notes of a patient with possible somatisation is relevant in the sense that it suggests an episode of unexplained fatigue, and supports the psychiatric diagnosis.

Following a very thorough review of the literature on the possible underlying organicity of CFS, Wessely *et al.* (1998) conclude that it is not a neuromuscular disorder, and that the evidence for any consistent viral metabolic or immunological abnormality is lacking. The medical jury may still be out, but the idea that CFS has some as yet unidentified somatic cause becomes more untenable as the research data accumulate.

The personality profile of patients with CFS is different from those with somatisation disorder. Instead of histrionic and borderline personalities, it is rather more likely in the obsessional, driving, egotistical person, often with an earlier preoccupation with physical prowess and excellence at one or many sports. Their strict training regimes come to an end with infection, operation or accident, and they simply wither from their former fitness. They seem dedicated to return to their former lifestyles and responsibilities but, like Gulliver, are bound down to immobility by the threads of their demons.

Although most agree that psychiatric illness is commonly comorbid with CFS, the link is often denied, especially by patients. When present it is more a dysthymia than a major depressive illness, although anxiety-related disorders are also prominent. The arguments about causality are unresolved. The depression may be secondary to having chronic fatigue, rather than the fatigue and depression both being attributes of the same disorder. As Wessely *et al.* conclude, the CFS represents a final common pathway in which psychological and sociological factors play a defining role. The risk factors to the development of chronicity are those more generally related to the encouragement of AIB, whether or not following acute insults, including accidents.

Fibromyalgia

Related to chronic fatigue is the complaint of myalgia (muscle pain) and the condition fibromyalgia. Fibromyalgia, like CFS, is commoner in females, and also has quite indiscrete boundaries. It is characterised by pain and tenderness of muscles, but also specific points of tenderness. It too has a long history, from the fibrositis of old, through idiopathic myalgia to the official fibromyalgia criteria given by the American College of Rheumatology (Wolfe *et al.*, 1990). Their criteria are shown in Table 3.6, and emphasise pain in various tender points of the body on palpation.

Table 3.6 The criteria given for fibromyalgia

1. **History of widespread pain**
Definition: Pain is considered when all of the following are present:
Pain in the left side of the body, pain in the right side of the body, pain above the waist and pain below the waist. In addition, axial skeletal pain (cervical pain or anterior chest or thoracic spine or lower back) must be present. In this definition shoulder and buttock pain is considered as pain for each involved side. Low back pain is considered to be lower segmental pain

2. **Pain in 11 of 18 tender point sites on digital palpation**
Definition: Pain, on digital palpation, must be present in at least 11 of the following 18 tender point sites:
- Occiput: bilateral; at the suboccipital muscle insertions
- Low cervical: bilateral; at the anterior aspects of the intertransverse spaces at C5–C7
- Trapezius: bilateral, at the midpoint of the upper border
- Supraspinatus: bilateral, at origins, above the scapular spine near the medial border
- Second rib: bilateral, at the second costochondral junctions, just lateral to the junctions on upper surfaces
- Lateral epicondyle: bilateral, 2 cm distal to the epicondyles
- Gluteal: bilateral, in upper outer quadrants of buttocks in anterior fold of muscle
- Greater trochanter: bilateral, posterior to the trochanteric prominence
- Knees: bilateral, at the medial fat pad proximal to the joint line

Digital palpation should be performed with an approximate force of 4 kg. For a tender point to be considered positive the subject must state that the palpation was painful. 'Tender' is not considered painful.

For classification purposes patients will be said to have fibromyalgia if both criteria are satisfied. Widespread pain must have been present for at least 3 months. The presence of a second clinical disorder does not exclude the diagnosis of fibromyalgia

Reproduced from Wolfe *et al.* (1990), with permission.

Fibromyalgia has become a popular diagnosis, second only to osteoarthritis in rheumatological clinics. In community surveys, the full syndrome affects up to 3% of women. Tender points are crucial, and manuals have been written on how and where they can be elicited; local muscle spasm is the cardinal perpetrator of pain. Most of these are on the neck and back, and are often said to be distant from the site of referred pain. Aside from this, the general medical examination yields nothing abnormal.

However, as with the other conditions discussed in this chapter, such patients are not usually monosymptomatic, but present with associated somatic symptoms, overlapping with fatigue. Minor depression and sleep disturbance are frequent accompaniments, although any psychological disturbance is usually denied by the patient. It remains unclear whether any depression is secondary to chronic pain, or if the lowered threshold for reporting pain is a consequence of the altered mood.

The elicitation of tender points is open to much discussion and criticism, not the least being the subjective nature of the whole exercise. It is reminiscent of the detection of hysterogenic points in the abdomen to diagnose hysteria in the clinics of Charcot. In reality, it depends on the patient's pain perception and on the examining physician's expectations. In research studies, their detection has poor reliability and specificity, and no abnormalities have been detected in the offending muscles (Bohr, 1995). In reality, no one has explained why the 18 bodily points should be so specific. It is also bizarre that they are referred to as tender points, and yet if the patient describes them as 'tender' it is not counted as a symptom! It seems likely that patients complaining of such tender points have a decreased pain threshold generally, and that tender points can also be elicited from other sites, such as over bone. Thus many examined patients report pains wherever they are touched (Mikkelson *et al.*, 1992).

In the official criteria, 11 or more of 18 tender points need to be demonstrated. Fatigue, sleep disturbances and morning stiffness are noted as accompanying symptoms, but are not central to the diagnosis. The fatigue is as in CFS, often severe following minimal exertion. Patients wake feeling unrefreshed, with muscle stiffness. They sometimes complain of additional symptoms such as swelling or paraesthesias of the extremities, urinary frequency, dysmenorrhoea and abdominal pains with altered bowel habits. The overlap with CFS is obvious.

A related disorder is the myofascial pain syndrome. It is less disseminated than fibromyalgia, and has also been referred to as regional fibromyalgia. It seems to be characterised by trigger points of pain, rather than tender points, the former often developing after muscle trauma. Taut bands of muscle can be palpated which with pressure trigger pain, often at referred sites. However, the distinction between trigger and tender points seems quite a fine one, and it is not clear if there are any anatomical or pathological distinctions between them. The exact relationship between fibromyalgia and the myofascial pain syndrome remains blurred.

In reviewing the literature on fibromyalgia, Malleson (2002) quoted a Dutch study in which three different rheumatological conditions were examined, namely rheumatoid arthritis, ankylosing spondylitis and fibromyalgia. The level of functional disability and clinical observations were compared. There was good agreement between these two for ankylosing spondylitis, less so for rheumatoid arthritis and very little for fibromyalgia (Hidding, 1994). Malleson quotes with approval the study from the Arthritis and Rheumatism Council Epidemiological Research Unit, which concluded that tender points were a measure of general distress and that fibromyalgia did not exist as a distinct entity (Croft *et al.*, 1994).

Reflex sympathetic dystrophy (RSD)

If fibromyalgia seems difficult to tie down as a clinical entity, the confusion over the role of the sympathetic nervous system in the mediation of pain, and the characteristics and history of RSD are even more complicated. There are no reliable diagnostic criteria (van de Beek *et al.*, 2002).

The typical patient has a minor injury to an extremity, often with only minimal tissue damage. This is followed by pain, swelling and hyperalgesia, but over time skin atrophic changes are noted with changes of temperature, and then sometimes muscular involvement with the development of tremors and then dystonias. Many of these changes were observed to be relieved by blocking activity of the sympathetic nervous system, and thus emerged the concept of sympathetically maintained pain and the related name of RSD. The terminology has recently evolved to the complex regional pain syndrome, a broad diagnosis covering a number of pain disorders associated with vasomotor and sudomotor disturbances. However, in the past, other terms used have been Sudeck's atrophy, neuralgodystrophy and the shoulder–hand syndrome.

One definition is given by Blumberg and Jaenig, as follows:

RSD is a descriptive term meaning a complex disorder or group of disorders that may develop as a consequence of trauma affecting the limbs, with or without obvious nerve lesion. RSD may also develop after visceral disease, and central nervous lesions or rarely without any obvious antecedent event. It consists of pain and related sensory abnormalities, abnormal blood flow and sweating, abnormalities in the motor system and changes in structure of both superficial and deep tissues ('trophic changes'). It is not necessary that all components are present. It is agreed that the name 'reflex sympathetic dystrophy' is used in a descriptive sense and does not imply specific underlying mechanisms (Blumberg and Jaenig, 1999, p. 685).

Essentially the disorder consists of a triad of autonomic, sensory and motor symptoms. One of the puzzles is its onset, often after trivial trauma, and, as with fibromyalgia, the lack of specific pathological findings.

Over time, the response to sympathetic blockade has been well investigated, and the role of the sympathetic nervous system in initiating or maintaining the symptomatology been brought into doubt.

The most common symptom is spontaneous pain, which may be anything from shooting to throbbing to burning, which is felt deep to the surface of the affected limb. Swelling is usually reported, hyperalgesia is common and the affected limb will be reported to be hotter or colder that the unaffected side. It may be redder in colour, and either hypo- or hyperhydrotic, with later cyanosis and mottling. Pain may be evoked by movements, and muscular movements become reduced. Tremor, abnormal postures and then dystonias can develop, the latter picture being referred to as the causalgia–dystonia syndrome. Eventually disuse atrophy, osteoporosis and total limb disuse ensue.

Although most patients have only one limb affected, cases are reported of all four limbs being involved. The effect occurs distally, but there is no obvious anatomical distribution directly related to the distribution of the peripheral nerves. Like many of the conditions described in this chapter, it is commoner in women. It usually emerges fairly acutely following trauma, and in many people it is a self-limiting condition, but in the minority a chronic form develops.

Psychiatric illness is conspicuous by its absence, although continuous pain and disability can lead to secondary depression, or substance abuse with analgesics. Whether or not some form of excessive autonomic activity is engendered in these patients by some emotional trauma, leading to a susceptibility to develop the syndrome, is purely speculation, but secondary physical problems can emerge from the ensuing immobility and overprotection of the limb to which patients resort, to avoid it being knocked or further damaged. Some physicians have even suggested that the whole syndrome could be a result of disuse, and that active exercise is the best treatment.

In clinical practice, based on the supposed involvement of the sympathetic nervous system, several tests were introduced for the diagnosis of this syndrome, essentially observing the intensity of the pain following blockade of the sympathetic nerves supplying the affected limb. This can be done with analgesics or drugs such as guanethidine. More recently, scintigraphic bone scanning has been used in chronic cases, but it is unclear how specific any bone changes noted are in making the diagnosis.

Sympathectomy and various of the sympathetic nerve blockade techniques were used as a treatment, although the value of these is held in doubt, and in any individual patient the response is unpredictable (Schott, 1998). This, of course, raises further doubts about the underlying specificity of the sympathetic nerve involvement.

The term 'complex regional pain syndrome' avoids the specific anatomical identity. Type 1 refers to those cases in which all the features of RSD are present, but there is no definable nerve injury, while in type 2 syndrome, formerly called causalgia, evidence for a nerve injury is present. The International Association for the Study of Pain (IASP) gives criteria for complex regional pain syndrome as shown in Table 3.7. Unfortunately there is a lack of empirical validation for these definitions, stressful life events frequently precede the onset of the disorder, and the aetiology is totally unknown.

Ochoa (1999) has persistently argued that these syndromes are heterogeneous, that the clinical signs may often be due to disuse, and that there is little evidence that they are either induced by the sympathetic nervous system or relieved by sympathetic blockade – hence the abandonment of 'sympathetic' from the new term 'complex regional pain syndrome'. He points out that the great majority of patients with RSD show no evidence of nerve fibre injury, and that the limbs of normal

Table 3.7 International Association for the Study of Pain (IASP): diagnostic criteria for complex regional pain syndrome (CRPS)

1. The presence of an initiating noxious event, or a cause of immobilisation
2. Continuing pain, allodynia or hyperalgesia with which the pain is disproportionate to any inciting event
3. Evidence at some time of oedema, changes in skin blood flow or abnormal sudomotor activity in the region of the pain
4. This diagnosis is excluded by the existence of conditions that would otherwise account for the degree of dysfunction

Associated signs and symptoms of CRPS listed in the IASP taxonomy but not used in the diagnosis:
1. Atrophy of the hair, nails and other soft tissues
2. Alteration in hair growth
3. Loss of joint mobility
4. Impairment of motor function, including weakness, tremor and dystonia
5. Sympathetically maintained pain may be present

Reproduced from Merskey and Bogduk (1994), with permission.

volunteers placed in plaster casts and immobilised, or limbs with tourniquets tied around them, as can occur in flagrant malingerers, can show all the objective signs of RSD.

Dystonia

As noted, RSD is often associated with movement disorders, and prominent are tremor and dystonia. Dystonia is a painful sustained spasm of a muscle group or groups, which may become chronic (fixed dystonia). It frequently presents as a focal dystonia, for example as persistent head jerkings in spasmodic torticollis, but it may be more generalised, affecting the trunk and leading to bizarre posturings, in flexion or extension. More extreme forms of the latter used to be referred to as dystonia musculorum deformans.

The contractures of hysteria have been discussed, and it must be clear that a considerable overlap exists between them and various dystonias, especially of the limb extremities. In the past, no neurological explanation was known for any of the dystonias, and, partly on the grounds that the developed postures were so odd, it was assumed that they must be somehow psychosomatic in origin. However, the discovery of dopamine, one of the brain's main neurotransmitters, now known to regulate motor and emotional behaviours, changed this view. Dopamine was given to relieve Parkinson's disease, and it was noted that, as a side-effect, many patients developed dystonias, often similar to those seen in idiopathic dystonia.

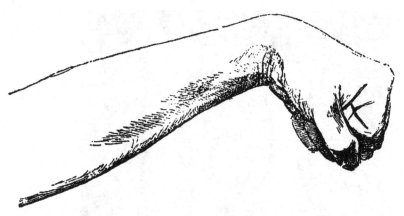

Figure 3.4   Example of contracture. Reproduced from Charcot (1889).

In some variants, genetic associations have now been identified, and genetic tests are used in clinical practice to diagnose such patients. The latter clinical pictures soon became understood as 'neurological', and the concept of psychogenic dystonia became discredited.

However, in recent years this view has again shifted. Psychogenic dystonias are again recognised, and they are seen in medicolegal practice because the onset is, as with RSD, often following some injury to a limb. The abnormal movements may appear quite suddenly. In the upper extremity, the dystonia starts with contraction and flexion of the fingers of the hand, eventually affecting the wrist and then the arm. In the legs, the foot becomes inverted; eventually the patient walks (if still able) on the lateral border, or even the surface of the foot. Examples of dystonias taken from the works of Charcot and from the present time are shown in Figures 3.4 and 3.5.

The most relevant clinical paper on this syndrome is that of Bhatia *et al.* (1993). They refer to the causalgia–dystonia syndrome, but the term 'psychogenic dystonia' is now more widely used for some of these patients (Fahn and Williams, 1988; Lang, 1995). In the causalgia–dystonia syndrome, most patients are female, and it usually comes on following trauma, often minor. In the study of Bhatia *et al.*, initially all patients had sudomotor and vasomotor changes, and went on to develop causalgia and dystonia. In some cases the clinical picture emerged within days of an injury, and in over half of them, the causalgia and dystonia developed almost simultaneously.

In contrast to neurological dystonias, the dystonia is characteristically 'fixed' and patients find it difficult to move the affected part. The causalgia may wane, and the patients may be left with the dystonia alone, which may progress or migrate to another limb, either spontaneously or with additional trauma. If the limb becomes very painful or disfigured, amputation may become necesssary.

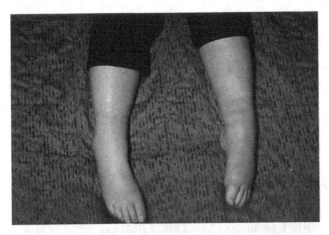

Figure 3.5   Examples of dystonias taken from the author's collection.

Again, the cause of this syndrome is unknown, but Bhatia *et al.* point out that, while peripheral sensory nerve input may be relevant, the causalgia is not abolished by deafferentating or anaesthetising the offending limb, and in any case, explanations relying on afferent inputs from the offending limb would not explain the migration and spread of the syndrome. Bhatia *et al.* could not discount a psychogenic aetiology.

Fahn and Williams (1988) list several clues to the diagnosis of psychogenic dystonia (Table 3.8). They recognise an overlap with multiple somatisations, chronic pain at sites distant from the dystonia, factitious disorder and malingering. A contrast can be made between neurogenic dystonias, which are commoner in the upper parts of the body in adults (they commonly start in the lower limbs in children), and the psychogenic dystonias which commonly begin in the leg or foot. In their series, most of the patients had a spread of the dystonia. Lang (1995) noted how

Table 3.8 Clues suggesting psychogenic dystonia

False weakness

False sensory complaints

Multiple somatisations

Self-inflicted injuries

Obvious psychiatric disturbances

Inconsistent dystonic movements over time

Incongruous dystonic movements and postures

Dystonia usually presents as a fixed dystonia or as a
paroxysmal dystonia

Other movement disorders, usually presenting as incongruent
or bizarre movements, including bizarre gait and often as a
paroxysmal disorder

Reproduced from Fahn and Williams (1988), with permission.

the progression to maximum disability is commoner with psychogenic dystonia (idiopathic torsion dystonias progress slowly) and he suggested some other clues in the differentiation. Psychogenic dystonia is not improved after sleep, but this is commonly found in idiopathic torsion dystonias. Patients with the psychogenic movement disorder commonly show a slowness of voluntary movement, which may be observed on neurological examination, for example during the finger–nose test of coordination, and show a resistance to passive movement. Further, the curious phenomenon of the *geste antagoniste* is absent in psychogenic dystonia. This refers to the fact that even severe idiopathic dystonias can be momentarily relieved by a light sensory input, for example touching the chin of a patient with a torticollis and gently moving the head back to its central anatomical position.

While the incidence of trauma before the onset of psychogenic dystonia is high, this is rare in idiopathic forms.

Whiplash injury

It is not uncommon for patients to be involved in a rear-end collision while in a car, and for them to develop neck pains, often of considerable intensity. They may not come on for an hour or two after the accident, but they may lead the sufferer to the Accident and Emergency department of the local hospital. There the patient will be examined, and the attending staff may do a cervical X-ray and discharge the patient with a soft collar and some analgesics. A diagnosis of whiplash will be given. The median time to recovery is about 4 weeks (Spitzer and the Task Force, 1995).

While that all sounds straightforward, things sometimes do not progress as expected. The patient deteriorates, the clinical picture diversifies and the debates begin. This is entirely reminiscent of the arguments over concussion of the spine, one major difference being that this occurred following railway accidents, whereas whiplash injuries, although first reported in pilots of catapult-assisted take-off aircraft on aircraft carriers, are mainly, but by no means exclusively, diagnosed after road traffic accidents (RTAs). The incidence of this diagnosis has risen, and continues to rise, except in certain settings (see below) and whiplash has become a worldwide epidemic and a multibillion-dollar industry (Malleson, 2002). However, diagnostic criteria are confusing and not standardised (Spitzer and the Task Force, 1995).

Of all RTAs, 35% are the result of one vehicle running into the back of another, leading to sudden head movements. There is extension followed by flexion, often beyond the normal range of movement; the former however may be limited by appropriate seat head-restraints. If the head is turned at impact the effect is likely to be greater. Soft-tissue injury may result, and in more severe acceleration–deceleration injuries, considerable force can be applied to the intracranial structures, and central nervous system symptoms may develop. These may include headache, dizziness, tinnitus, paraesthesiae and the like, and although momentary loss of consciousness is often reported, concussion is rare. In very severe whiplash injuries, there is a hint from experimental models that diffuse axonal injury to the cerebral white matter can result.

In most cases the neck symptoms clear in weeks (Radanov *et al.*, 1995), but in about 30% of cases, symptoms persist; this delayed recovery is sometimes referred to as the late whiplash syndrome or chronic whiplash. Factors predicting a poorer prognosis include radicular damage and pre-existing damage or degeneration of the cervical spine. The symptoms include pain, but also headache, concentration and memory problems, fatigue and minor affective complaints. Back pain is also frequently reported.

It is this late whiplash variant which causes controversy, and is a frequent presentation of patients in a medicolegal setting. As with the other syndromes discussed in this chapter, arguments abound as to the natural history of this disorder, the causes of delayed recovery and its overlap with other syndromes.

Crash severity is one obvious factor that relates to prognosis. Physical outcome has been shown to be related to various variables. Factors associated with a poor outcome include symptom duration, increasing age, being female, upper-limb radiation of symptoms, thoracic and lumbar pain, occipital headache and neurological signs (Mayou and Radanov, 1996).

Oddly, there are few scientific studies specifically dealing with the chronic syndrome, and the existing data are unclear. The search for any underlying cerebral damage for the majority of cases with minimal or no loss of consciousness has proven elusive, and psychological factors are thought to be predominant; the longer-lasting the syndromes, the more likely it becomes that they are relevant. Pearce (1999) summarised data on magnetic resonance imaging of the brain and neck and studies of brainstem evoked potentials, of 350 published examples of whiplash complaints, affirming that none had shown unequivocal attributable pathology.

The final outcome of a small group of these patients is a full state of dependence, with multiple symptoms, which include pain well beyond the original site of injury, eventually adopting the use of braces, splints, catheters and wheelchairs.

The role of compensation in promulgating the chronic cases has been discussed endlessly. Reports of a rising incidence and rising insurance claims for whiplash injury over the past two decades need some explanation. The very term implies cause and effect, like posttraumatic stress disorder (PTSD). As with conversion, it is used to describe symptoms, but also a mechanism. The term 'whiplash' was introduced by Crowe in 1928, and was referred to by MacNab (1974) as having 'evil connotations'. The latter's own study reported a follow-up of 266 patients, 2 years or more after settlement of a legal claim. Of 145 examined, 121 continued to have symptoms. MacNab concluded that compensation made little difference to outcome, and supported this with data from animal studies of whiplash injuries, which revealed muscular tears, haemorrhages and haematomas which could form the basis of the symptoms in patients.

In contrast, Gotten (1956) reported that 88 of 100 patients were 'largely recovered' following settlement, and, although only 54 were totally symptom-free, he suggested his data cast doubt on the validity of the diagnosis. Gay and Abbott (1953) reported that the incidence of psychoneurotic disturbance in people presenting with chronic symptoms of whiplash was about 50%, a figure that was vigorously disputed in subsequent journal correspondence.

This older controversy has recently been revived and well reviewed by Malleson (2002). Livingston (2000) noted an observation by Melville from 1963. The latter had observed several thousand vehicle accidents, some at speed, in contests in Canada, and had seen heads flailing all over the place. However, the pit stewards and the insurance companies knew of no reported whiplash injuries.

Two recent controversial studies have been carried out in Lithuania, professing to study the natural history of whiplash disorders in consecutive patients involved in rear-end collisions outside a medicolegal setting. Essentially, in that country there is no compensation for whiplash injuries, and no involvement of therapists, insurance companies or lawyers. In a controlled cohort study, none of 202 people involved in a car collision with rear-end impact had persistent symptoms that could be linked to the accident at a 1–3-year follow-up. The authors reported initial symptoms in nearly 50% of patients, but no excess of chronic neck pain and headache compared with controls, who had not been involved in accidents, at follow-up (Schrader et al., 1996; Obelieniene et al., 1999).

Cassidy et al. (2000) reported some supportive data to the view that compensation is a relevant factor in promoting symptoms. They noted that elimination of compensation for such injuries was associated with an improved prognosis. Similar findings have been reported in several places where the compensation laws have been changed, namely Singapore and Victoria, Australia (Balla, 1982). Since New Zealand adopted a no-fault accident compensation scheme, the prognosis and time off work for disability from whiplash has improved (Carron et al., 1985; Mills and Horne, 1986). In Saskatchewan, Canada, the introduction of the no-fault system has also led to a significant reduction in claims for chronic pain, despite a coincidental increase in the number of road traffic accidents (Malleson, 2002).

Livingston (2000) summed up the present state of knowledge of nearly 50 years of research, comment and observation of whiplash injuries by noting that the relationship between the accident and injury remains unclear. He quoted Barnsley et al. (1994) thus: 'The usual expectation would be that sprains or tears of muscle would heal in a matter of weeks, forming a scar within the muscle but leaving the patient with no residual pain' (p. 526). In this context the observation of Farbman (1973), that uncomplicated whiplash patients employing a lawyer maintained their symptoms for a longer time than others, may be relevant.

Mayou and colleagues (1996; Mayou and Bryant, 2002), have conducted studies and reviewed the literature on the psychiatric aspects of whiplash injury. Most patients do not develop any psychopathology. Some patients, because of the nature of their accidents, develop PTSD, others anxiety and depression. Phobias about driving or travel as a passenger are also common. The depression may be secondary to chronic physical symptoms, or loss of amenities. They reported that predictors of a poor psychological outcome include previous psychological problems, initial severe distress and chronic social difficulties.

They also noted a high proportion of patients with preaccident treatment for headaches compared with the general population, hinting that the reporting of previous pain syndromes facilitates the reporting of whiplash symptoms, either because patients are used to using medical facilities, or that they have a lower threshold for reporting pain.

They rather discounted the role of litigation in outcome, making several points. In all reported series, the rate of litigation is high, and they cannot conclude that the outcome is different in those who seek compensation when compared to those who do not. Patients may gain improvement during the litigation process, and, in any case, settlement of compensation is usually not followed by marked improvements in the clinical state. However, in one of their follow-up studies, pain outcome for whiplash and other soft-tissue injuries at 1 year was predicted by claiming compensation at 3 months. They concluded: 'compensation is just one of the many social variables that may affect the rate of symptomatic recovery and of return to full activities, but that in individual instances compensation may be especially significant' (Mayou and Radanov, 1996, p. 470).

The role of compensation and the litigation process in maintaining the symptoms of so-called whiplash injuries has recently been thoroughly reviewed by Malleson (2002). He refers to whiplash as the 'prince of all faked injuries' (p. 270). He points out that the **g**-forces created by low-velocity rear-end collisions are no more than plopping backwards in a chair, and are simply not compatible with the forces required to induce brain damage and to explain associated cognitive symptoms. Further, symptoms of concussion, such as headache, irritability, fatigue, concentration problems and the like, are higher in non-head-injured litigants (i.e. including those with whiplash) than the head-injured (Lees-Hayley and Brown, 1993). The animal experiments he points out are useless (as monkeys cannot complain of symptoms), noting that 'much confusion [about whiplash] has arisen from observations of orthopaedic surgeons who know too little psychiatry and psychiatrists who know too much' (Norris, 1991).

Occupational disorders of the upper limb

A number of occupational related disorders, particularly of the upper limb, have been known to medicine for generations. These include, for example, writer's cramp, tennis elbow and various abnormal hand and finger postures that afflict musicians and prevent them from playing their chosen instrument to high capacity. However, a variety of other disorders are noted, some of which have been collectively entitled 'repetitive strain injury' (RSI). A review of RSI is given by Barton *et al.* (1992).

These authors considered that RSI was a misleading term since it implied the existence of a physical condition with an identifiable cause. However, the physical signs are imprecise, no pathological lesions have been clearly identified and the word 'strain' is not used in its 'true mechanical sense'.

They commented on a related term, tenosynovitis. Although a more 'clear-cut entity', since the synovium around the tendon becomes inflamed, they further stated that, strangely, the term is often applied to conditions where there is, in fact, no synovium involved. The term 'tenosynovitis' is often given by a factory doctor or a GP on a sick note, and they say: 'this initial misdiagnosis of tenosynovitis is the most frequent source of misunderstanding and may start the patient on a course towards litigation'. They specifically referred to two large studies (one from Edinburgh and one from Birmingham) that have examined relationships between occupational tasks and symptoms and they opine as follows:

'we concluded that it was disappointing that after so great an expenditure of time and money so few conclusions could be drawn from these two studies' (*ibid.*, p. 309). It seems that disorders such as tennis elbow (lateral epicondylitis), carpal tunnel syndrome and, their preferred term for RSI, non-specific arm pain, cannot be reliably shown to be linked to any occupational group or particular activity.

It seems to have become particularly popular in Australia where it was referred to as kangaroo paw. It afflicted keyboard operators, and soon became so popular that 30% of public service workers were affected (Malleson, 2002). However, following evidence that social rather than physiological factors were responsible for the condition, and subsequent reduced compensation, the epidemic declined. In the UK, where there was a similar outbreak of the diagnosis in the 1970s and 1980s, the tide of claims was reduced by a court ruling that the diagnosis was meaningless.

The spectrum of somatoform and related disorders

The syndromes discussed in this chapter have several features that unite them. Individually they have all been presented either as a discrete disorder with characteristic signs and symptoms, often ratified by some committee, or as a vague collation of similarly sounding symptoms without clear boundaries. They are all characterised by a failure, often after many years of research, to define a clear pathological cause. Further, there is more than a hint that sociological and psychological factors play a predominant role, not only in their presentation, but also in their perpetuation. The ignorance about their aetiology is revealed by partisans who are either strong advocates that the syndrome exists and has such-and-such an identifiable cause, in this or that patient or others who question not only the boundaries of the syndrome, but its very essence. Causes for these physical symptoms are often couched in the unknowable; euphemisms such as 'stress' apparently explain the unexplainable. These arguments are met in respectable academic circles, but abound in the medicolegal setting.

The reasons for this are discussed further in a later chapter, but one obvious problem is that many of the above syndromes are seen by specialists, say rheumatologists with a special interest in fibromyalgia, who do not know much about irritable bowel syndrome, fixed dystonias or somatoform disorders. Ignorance of psychiatry blinkers their view to obtaining a broader clinical picture, embracing the patient's personality and any AIB. However, what has been clear for many years, but has now been discussed more widely, is the overlap of these syndromes. Wessely and his group (1999) have convincingly argued this, providing empirical support. They refer to 'functional somatic syndromes', and argue for an underlying unifying theme. They point out that each medical speciality seems to have its own syndrome (Table 3.9).

Table 3.9 Functional somatic syndromes by speciality

Speciality	Functional somatic syndrome
Gastroenterology	IBS; non-ulcer dyspepsia
Gynaecology	Premenstrual syndrome; chronic pelvic pain
Rheumatology	Fibromyalgia
Cardiology	Atypical or non-cardiac chest pain
Respiratory medicine	Hyperventilation syndrome
Infectious diseases	Postviral fatigue syndrome
Neurology	Tension headache
Dentistry	Temporomandibular joint syndrome; atypical facial pain
Ear, nose and throat	Globus syndrome
Allergy medicine	Multiple chemical sensitivity

IBS, irritable bowel syndrome.
Reproduced from Wessely *et al.* (1999, p. 936), with permission.

Thus, the rates of somatisation in patients with chronic fatigue vary from 0 to over 30%, with most studies giving rates of 10–20% (Wesseley *et al.*, 1998). Seventy per cent of those with chronic fatigue have significant muscle pain, and so-called tender points are common. In chronic fatigue patients, complaints of food intolerance are common, and sometimes this leads to diagnoses such as coeliac or Crohn's disease (Manu *et al.*, 1993). The syndrome of recurrent abdominal pain and distension with intermittent diarrhoea or constipation, referred to as irritable bowel syndrome (IBS), affects between 10 and 20% of the population (Jones and Lydeard, 1992). This is also associated with the reporting of other somatic symptoms, including fatigue, atypical facial pain, allergies, myalgia and hyperventilation. Hyperventilation, a pattern of dysfunctional breathing, can be misinterpreted as asthma (Keeley and Osman, 2001). There is an overlap between causalgia, dystonia, somatisation and factitious disorder.

Wessely *et al.* (1999) point out that the core diagnostic features of these syndromes overlap. For example, bloating appears in eight, and both fatigue and abdominal pain in six of 12 published definitions for the individual disorders. The authors ran a Medline search of the different somatic syndromes. They

found 13 references for chronic fatigue syndrome that described symptoms that overlapped with fibromyalgia, tension headache, multiple chemical sensitivity, food allergy, premenstrual syndrome and irritable bowel syndrome. Conversely, irritable bowel syndrome was linked with hyperventilation syndromes, fibromyalgia, chronic fatigue syndrome, tension headaches, atypical facial pain, non-cardiac chest pain, chronic pelvic pain, non-ulcer dyspepsia and the premenstrual syndrome (Wessely *et al.*, 1999, p. 937).

These syndromes share several features in common. They pursue a chronic course, often responding only for a while to interventions. One diagnosis, such as IBS, gets repeated or replaced by another. They are nearly all more frequent in females, they are associated with minor psychiatric disorders in the anxiety–depression spectrum, and there is persistent reference to a history of a disrupted early family life and childhood abuse. Difficult doctor–patient relationships are apparent, patients express dissatisfaction with their care, they are viewed as difficult by the medical staff. This last point reflects on the underlying AIB, a common behavioural pattern.

The implication is that these apparently diverse syndromes may share aetiologies, or even be reflections of a single syndrome, pathoplastically moulded by the speciality under whose care the patient falls. The reporting of one medically unexplained symptom is associated with the tendency to report others. Using the statistical technique of principal-components analysis it is possible to identify a general factor contributing nearly 40% to individual symptom variance (Deary, 1999). Basically, some people tend to be serial somatisers!

These syndromes are not simple expressions of a psychiatric disorder, although they are often comorbid with the reporting of psychiatric symptoms in the depression–anxiety spectrum. However, they are a reflection on the process of somatisation, and the way in which illness is perceived and reflected through AIB.

The longer the symptoms go on, the more obvious it is that non-organic factors are involved, and the more the gap between symptoms and pathology is apparent and requires some form of explanation, common sense, dynamic or otherwise. However, arguments about these syndromes and their aetiology reign outside the legal setting, with one camp strongly advocating the physical, the other the psychological. No wonder that in the medicolegal context they represent a minefield of confusion, and ideal grounds for acolytes of fashion to parade their Emperor's clothes.

Conclusions

The clinical syndromes discussed in this chapter all have as a feature the problem of definition. They are difficult to diagnose, because their presentations overlap with other syndromes, and the patients presenting these disorders themselves often have complicated medical histories, difficult social lives and comorbid psychiatric diagnoses.

There may well be core syndromes, with well-defined features, that one day will be subject to biological markers, which will help with diagnosis. As Oscar Wilde said: 'I am now a neurasthenic. My doctor says I have all the symptoms. It is comforting to have them *all*, it makes one a perfect type'. However, in a medicolegal setting, so often the clinical picture is atypical, and often evokes alternative diagnoses, depending on the special interest of the examining doctor.

Important points in evaluation include the total illness history of the claimant, his or her personality style, the assessment of any AIB, and features on examinations, with orthopaedic, neurological or other relevant specialist investigations. Attempts to explain symptoms by resorting to a pseudodiagnosis, and ignorance of the psychological and sociological factors that both mould and maintain symptoms, remain powerful forces in the retention of patients as patients and claimants as claimants.

Wessely *et al.* (1998) sum up these pressures by quoting the experience with ME, and the change of focus to the CFS:

> The remarkable acceptance of CFS/ME in the late 1980s left the research community with a dilemma. Although little convincing evidence had been provided for the existence of a discrete syndrome, researchers were faced with a *fait accompli*. Chronic mononucleosis had captured the public imagination. The professional disillusionment with the role of the Epstein–Barr virus in the syndrome did nothing to diminish or de-legitimise this – a new syndrome appeared to be here to stay. The medical reaction was therefore to change the label (*ibid.*, p. 134).

The latest chapter in this story is from the Working Group on CFS/ME (2002). This begins by using the term 'a genuine illness' ('a real entity') for CFS/ME. Thus, although it is referred to as CFS in the text, ME is still retained as a rider. The report goes on to note that 'the aetiology and pathogenesis are unclear . . . [CFS/ME] assumes many different clinical forms and is highly variable in severity and duration, but lacks specific disease markers'. However, we are confidently informed we are dealing with just 'one condition'!

REFERENCES

Akagi, H. and House, A. (2001). The epidemiology of hysterical conversion. In *Contemporary Approaches to the Study of Hysteria*, ed. P. W. Halligan, C. Bass and J. C. Marshall, pp. 73–87. Oxford: Oxford University Press.

American Psychiatric Association (1994). *Diagnostic and Statistical Manual of Mental Disorders*, 4th edn. Washington, DC: APA Press.

Balla, J. I. (1982). The late whiplash syndrome: a study of an illness in Australia and Singapore. *Culture, Medicine and Psychiatry*, **6**, 191–210.

Barnsley, L., Lord, S. M. and Bogduk, N. (1994). Whiplash injury. *Pain*, **58**, 283–307.

Barton, N. J., Hooper, G., Noble, J. and Steel, W. M. (1992). Occupational causes of disorders of the upper limb. *British Medical Journal*, **304**, 309–11.

Bass, C. and Murphy, M. (1991). Somatisation disorder in a British teaching hospital. *British Journal of Clinical Practice*, **45**, 237–44.

Bhatia, K. P., Bhatt, M. H. and Marsden, C. D. (1993). The causalgia–dystonia syndrome. *Brain*, **116**, 843–51.

Blazer, D. G. (1980). Narcissism and the development of chronic pain. *International Journal of Psychiatric Medicine*, **10**, 69–79.

Blumberg, H. and Jaenig, W. (1999). Clinical manifestations of reflex sympathetic dystrophy and sympathetically maintained pain. In *Textbook of Pain*, ed. P. Wall and R. Melzack. Edinburgh: Churchill Livingstone.

Bohr, T. W. (1995). Fibromyalgia syndrome and Myofascial pain syndrome. Do they exist? *Neurological Clinics*, **13**, 365–84.

Carron, H., DeGood, D. E. and Tait, R. (1985). A comparison of low back pain patients in the United States and New Zealand: psychosocial and economic factors affecting severity of disability. *Pain*, **21**, 77–89.

Carson, A. J., Ringbauer, B., Stone, J. *et al.* (2000). Do medically unexplained symptoms matter? A prospective cohort study of 300 new referrals to neurology outpatient clinics. *Journal of Neurology, Neurosurgery and Psychiatry*, **68**, 207–10.

Cassidy, J. D., Carrol, L. J., Cote, P. *et al.* (2000). Effect of eliminating compensation for pain and suffering on the outcome of insurance claims for whiplash injury. *New England Journal of Medicine*, **342**, 1179–86.

Charcot, J. M. (1889). *Clinical Lectures on Diseases of the Nervous System*. Translated by Sarll, T. London: New Sydenham Society.

Cohen, M. E., Robins, E., Purtell, J. J., Altmann, M. W. and Reid, D. E. (1953). Excessive surgery in hysteria. *Journal of the American Medical Association*, **151**, 977–86.

Creed, F., Firth, D., Timol, M., Metcalf, R. and Pollock, S. (1990). Somatization and illness behaviour in a neurology ward. *Journal of Psychosomatic Research*, **34**, 427–37.

Croft, A. C., Schollum, J. and Silman, A. (1994). Population study of tender point counts and pain as evidence of fibromyalgia. *British Medical Journal*, **309**, 696–699.

Deary, I. (1999). A taxonomy of medically unexplained symptoms. *Journal of Psychosomatic Research*, **47**, 51–9.

Deighton, C. M. and Nicol, A. R. (1985). Abnormal illness behaviour in young women in a primary care setting: is Briquet's syndrome a useful category? *Psychological Medicine*, **15**, 515–20.

Demers, R., Altamore, R., Mustin, H. *et al.* (1980). An explanation of the dimensions of illness behaviour. *Journal of Family Practice*, **11**, 1085–94.

Engel, G. L. (1968). "Psychogenic pain" and the pain prone patient. *American Journal of Medicine*, **26**, 899–918.

    (1970). Conversion symptoms. In *Signs and Symptoms*, 5th edn, C. M. MacBryde and R. S. Blacklow, pp. 650–68. New York: Lippincott/Williams & Wilkins.

Escobar, J. I., Burnam, M. A., Karno, M. *et al.* (1987). Somatisation in the community. *Archives of General Psychiatry*, **44**, 713–18.

Escobar, J. I., Gara, M. and Waitzkin, H. (1998). DSM IV hypochondriasis in primary care. *General Hospital Psychiatry*, **20**, 155–9.

Fahn, S. and Williams, D. T. (1988). Psychogenic dystonia. In *Dystonia*, ed. S. Fahn, C. D. Marsden and D. B. Calne. *Advances in Neurology*, vol. 50, pp. 431–55. New York: Raven Press.

Farbman, A. A. (1973). Neck sprain. Associated factors. *Journal of the American Medical Association,* **223**, 1010–15.

Feighner, J., Robbins, E., Guze, S. *et al.* (1972). Diagnostic criteria for use in psychiatric research. *Archives of General Psychiatry,* **26**, 57–63.

Ford, C. V. (1983). *The Somatizing Disorders: Illness as a Way of Life.* New York: Elsevier Biomedical.

Gay, J. R. and Abbott, K. H. (1953). Common whiplash injuries of the neck. *Journal of the American Medical Association,* **152**, 1698–1704.

Goodwin, D. W. and Guze, S. B. (1984). *Psychiatric Diagnosis,* 3rd edn. Oxford: Oxford University Press.

Gotten, N. (1956). Survey of 100 cases of whiplash injury after settlement of litigation. *Journal of the American Medical Association,* **162**, 865.

Gureje, O., Simon, G. E., Ustun, T. B. *et al.* (1997). Somatisation in cross-cultural perspective: a World Health Organization study in primary care. *American Journal of Psychiatry,* **154**, 989–95.

Hidding, A. (1994). Comparison between self-report measures and clinical observations of functional disability in ankylosing spondylitis, rheumatoid arthritis and fibromyalgia. *Journal of Rheumotology,* **21**, 813–18.

Jason, M. I. V. (1992). Trauma, back pain, malingering, and compensation. *British Medical Journal,* **305**, 7–8.

Jones, R. and Lydeard, S. (1992). Irritable bowel syndrome in the general population. *British Medical Journal,* **304**, 87–90.

Katon, W. J. and Walker, E. A. (1998). Medically unexplained symptoms in primary care. *Journal of Clinical Psychiatry,* **59** (suppl. 20), 15–21.

Keeley, D. and Osman, L. (2001). Dysfunctional breathing and asthma. *British Medical Journal,* **322**, 1075–6.

Kenyon, F. E. (1964). Hypochondriasis: a clinical study. *British Journal of Psychiatry,* **110**, 478–88. (1976). Hypondriacal states. *British Journal of Psychiatry,* **129**, 1–14.

Kroenke, K., Spitzer, R. L., deGruy, F. V. *et al.* (1997). Multisomatoform disorder. An alternative to undifferentiated somatoform disorder for the somatising patient in primary care. *Archives of General Psychiatry,* **54**, 352–8.

Lang, A. E. (1995). Psychogenic dystonia: a review of 18 cases. *Canadian Journal of Neurological Science,* **22**, 136–43.

Lees-Playley, P. R. and Brown, R. S. (1993). Neurological complaint case rates of 170 personal injury claimants. Archives of Clinical Neuropsychology, **8**, 202–9.

Lieb, R., Pfister, H., Mastaler, M. and Wittchen H.-U. (2000). Somatoform syndromes and disorders in a representative population sample of adolescents and young adults: prevalence, co-morbidity and impairments. *Acta Psychiatrica Scandanavica,* **101**, 194–208.

Livingston, M. (2000). Whiplash injury: why are we achieving so little? *Journal of the Royal Society of Medicine,* **93**, 526–9.

MacNab, I. (1974). The whiplash syndrome. *Clinical Neurosurgery,* **20**, 232.

Malleson, A. (2002). *Whiplash and other useful illnesses.* Montreal: McGill-Queens University Press.

Manu, P., Matthews, W. D. and Lane, T. (1993). Food intolerance in patients with chronic fatigue. *International Journal of Eating Disorders*, **13**, 203–9.

Mayou, R. and Bryant, B. (2002). Psychiatry of whiplash injury. *British Journal of Psychiatry*, **180**, 441–8.

Mayou, R. and Radanov, B. P. (1996). Whiplash neck injury. *Journal of Psychosomatic Research*, **40**, 461–74.

McEvedy, C. P. and Beard, A. W. (1970). Royal Free epidemic of 1955, a reconsideration. *British Medical Journal*, **I**, 7–11.

Merskey, H. (1995). *The Analysis of Hysteria*, 2nd edn. London: Gaskell Press.

Merskey, H. and Bogduk, N. (1994). *Classification of Chronic Pain: Descriptions of Chronic Pain Syndromes and Definitions of Pain Terms*. Seattle: IASP Press.

Mikkelson, M., Latikka, P. *et al.* (1992). Muscle and bone pressure pain threshold and pain tolerance in fibromyalgia. *Pain*, **73**, 814–18.

Mills, H. and Horne, G. (1986). Whiplash – man made disease? *New Zealand Journal of Medicine*, **99**, 373–4.

Norris, J. W. (1991). Whiplash. *Lancet*, **338**, 1207–8.

Obelieniene, D., Schrader, H., Bovim, G., Miseviciene, I. and Sand, T. (1999). Pain after whiplash: a prospective controlled inception cohort study. *Journal of Neurology, Neurosurgery and Psychiatry*, **66**, 279–83.

Ochoa, J. L. (1999). Truths, errors, and lies around "reflex sympathetic dystrophy" and "complex regional pain syndrome". *Journal of Neurology*, **246**, 875–9.

Pearce, J. M. S. (1999). The myth of chronic whiplash syndrome. *Spinal Cord*, **37**, 741–8.

Perkin, G. D. (1989). An analysis of 7836 successive new outpatient referrals. *Journal of Neurology, Neurosurgery and Psychiatry*, **52**, 447–8.

Pilowsky, I. (1970). Primary and secondary hypochondriasis. *Acta Psychiatrica Scandinavica*, **46**, 273–85.

(1997). *Abnormal Illness Behaviour*. Chichester: John Wiley.

Radanov, B. P., Sturzenegger, M. and Distefano, G. (1995). Long term outcome after whiplash injury. *Medicine*, **74**, 281–97.

Robins, L. N. and Regier, D. (1991). *Psychiatric Disorders in America. The Epidemiologic Catchment Area Study*. New York: Free Press.

Robins, E., Purtell, J. J. and Cohen, M. E. (1952). Hysteria in men: a study of 38 male patients so diagnosed and 194 control subjects. *New England Journal of Medicine*, **246**, 677–85.

Scalzitti, D. A. (1997). Screening for psychological factors in patients with low back pains. Waddell's non-organic signs. *Physical Therapy*, **77**, 306–12.

Schott, G. D. (1998). Interrupting the sympathetic outflow in causalgia and reflex sympathetic dystrophy. *British Medical Journal*, **316**, 792–3.

Schrader, H., Obelieniene, D., Bovim, G. *et al.* (1996). Natural evolution of late whiplash syndrome outside the medicolegal context. *Lancet*, **ii**, 1207–11.

Spitzer, W. O. and the Task Force (1995). Scientific monograph of the Quebec Task Force on Whiplash-Associated Disorders. *Spine*, **20** (suppl. 8S), 1S–72S.

Stone, J., Zeman, A. and Sharpe, M. (2002). Functional weakness and sensory disturbance. *Journal of Neurology, Neurosurgery and Psychiatry*, **73**, 241–5.

Trimble, M. R. (2001). Non-epileptic seizures. In *Contemporary Approaches to the Study of Hysteria*, ed. P. W. Halligan, C. Bass and J. C. Marshall, pp. 143–54. Oxford: Oxford University Press.

Van de Beek, W. J. T., Schwartzman, R. J., van Nes, S. I. *et al.* (2002). Diagnostic criteria used in studies of reflex sympathetic dystrophy. *Neurology*, **58**, 522–6.

Waddell, G., Main, C. J., Morris, E. W. *et al.* (1984). Chronic low back pain, psychological distress and illness behaviour. *Spine*, **9**, 209–13.

Wessely, S., Hotopf, M. and Sharpe, M. (1998). *Chronic Fatigue and its Syndromes*. Oxford: Oxford University Press.

Wessely, S., Nimnuan, C. and Sharpe, M. (1999). Functional somatic syndromes: one or many. *Lancet*, **354**, 936–9.

Wolfe, F., Smythe, H., Yunis, M. *et al.* (1990). The American College of Rheumatology 1990 criteria for the classification of fibromyalgia. *Arthritis and Rheumatism*, **33**, 160–73.

Working Group on CFS/ME (2002). *Report to the Chief Medical Officer*. London: Department of Health.

World Health Organization (1992). *The ICD 10 Classification of Mental and Behavioural Disorders*. Geneva: World Health Organization.

4

Malingering

Mendacity is the system we live in.   (Tennessee Williams, *Cat on a Hot Tin Roof*, Act II)

To the ingénue it often comes as a shock to realise that virtually the whole of the civil litigation process is about money. Claimants feel they have been injured, and have been told to expect, as a right, compensation. The advocates will ensure that the claimant is adequately represented, but will command a proportion of the eventual settlement. The insurance company who has underwritten any claim wants to minimise cost to its shareholders. No medical claim can proceed without medical reports, hence the need for experts, who themselves require fees. As the neurologist Purves-Stewart observed in 1928, 'The litigation neurosis may be likened to an originally innocuous drink to which exciting ingredients are added at the bar – the legal bar. Such a cocktail is expensive, mainly because of its legal ingredients' (Trimble, 1981, p. 139).

Since those words were written, the relative cost of litigation, and the amounts of money paid out in compensation, have risen enormously. This is discussed further in Chapter 7, but suffice it to say here that there are two opposing trends, one from those who wish to push up the costs of settlements, and the other from those who want to bring them down. Experts are not directly involved in this process, at least initially, but are called upon to provide medical reports, nowadays solely for the court, and supposedly not be biased towards one side of this process or another. Although the issue of malingering features widely in medicolegal practice, strangely it is rarely discussed openly, it does not attract any informed research, and is not much written about. Indeed, it did not evoke significant medical comment until the early part of the twentieth century, when, as we have seen, industrial and railway accidents provided ideal circumstances for opportunist plaintiffs, and those paying out became suspicious.

Some early examples

Genesis 32.35 recalls that Rachel, the wife of David, hid some stolen goods in the camel's furniture, and sat on them. When David came to look for them she pleaded: 'Let it not displease my lord that I cannot rise up before thee, for the custom of woman is upon me', and the goods were not detected.

Examples of malingering were well known in prisons and the armed forces. In 1403 the First Earl of Northumberland 'lay craftily sick' to avoid taking part in the Battle of Shrewsbury, and in the 1785 version of *Grove's Dictionary*, malingering was defined as a 'military term for one who under pretence of sickness evades his duty'.

An example of compensation for illness attribution is given by Falstaff in *2 Henry IV*, when he says (I, ii) ''Tis no matter if I do halt; I have the wars for my colour. And my pension shall seem the more reasonable. A good wit will make use of anything; I will turn diseases to commodity.'

In the seventeenth century, a well-known beggar at the Temple, Gennings, lay in filthy clothes with body abrasions and blood on his face, complaining of pains, a 'sight monstrous and painful'. One suspicious Thomas Harman hired two boys to watch him, and follow him. After his day of begging he went home to a more fashionable part of London, where he 'renewed his stains from a bladder of sheep's blood and daubed fresh mud over his legs and arms'. He was apprehended by the parish watch, and was found, after being washed, to be a healthy young man, in possession of an admirable sum of money. This is possibly the first recorded incidence of the hiring of others to rumble malingering (Ackroyd, 2001, p. 609).

In the late eighteenth century it was reported that a Thomas Cooke, who preferred not to pay for his own food and drink, would fall down in 'a pretended fit opposite a house of one whose bounty he sought'. Dressed in powdered wig and ruffs, he seemed respectable, and was taken into the house and refreshed. A few days later he would return to thank his benefactors for saving his life, only to receive further sustenance.

The earliest treatise on the subject was probably Gavin's *On Feigned and Factitious Diseases, Chiefly of Soldiers and Seamen* (1843), resulting from the wars in France in which 'a thousand reasons induced the young men to feign disease to avoid conscription'.

The whole area was given a considerable boost around the turn of the twentieth century with the introduction of various Acts of Parliament relating to employers' liability and workman's compensation, and the term 'compensation neurosis' was introduced by Rigler in 1879. He was reflecting on the increase in invalidism reported following railway accidents with the introduction of the compensation laws in Prussia in 1871. As noted in Chapter 1, those involved in such accidents had a champion in England, Dr Erichsen, and soon concussion of the spine became a medical reality, with all its medicolegal consequences. In his book, Erichsen dismissed the whole topic of compensation in a few pages.

However, the railway companies had their own protagonist, Dr Herbert Page, surgeon to the London and North-West Railway. His book, *Injuries of the Spine and Spinal Cord without Apparent Mechanical Lesions* (1885), essentially served as a rebuttal to the ideas of Erichsen. Page opined that concussion of the spine was an indefinite expression, scientifically inaccurate, and illogical. Erichsen had quoted the celebrated case of the Count de Lordat, who in 1761 was involved in a carriage accident on his way to join his regiment. Essentially, following an apparently minor injury, over the next 3 years he sank into a state of physical decrepitude, eventually dying, and at a postmortem was shown to have spinal cord damage. Page revealed the cause of many a claimants' symptoms:

A terrible case, forsooth, to be pointed out as 'typical'; and typical of what? Of the whole class of injuries of the spine grouped together under the one common term 'concussion' . . . Small wonder when a man gets a slight sprain of his vertebral column in the most trifling collision on a railway that, labouring under the belief he has received a 'concussion of the spine', his anxiety should be needlessly great and prolonged if he learns that the result of the injury in this often-quoted case of the Count de Lordat is the typical result of such a 'concussion of the spine' as he himself received . . . The dust of the unhappy Count must have undergone a 'molecular disturbance' in its tomb when, in the very opening pages of the book, this painful history was transcribed as 'typical of the whole class of injuries' grouped under the term 'concussion of the spine'.

Page referred to the concept of nervous shock, which he felt played an important part in all medicolegal cases of so-called concussion of the spine. In his own reported 234 cases, he found no obvious cases of organic damage that could be attributed to the accident *per se*, and referred to the importance of 'some functional disturbance of the whole nervous balance or tone'. Thus, Page and other contemporaries recognised a subgroup of cases that were best diagnosed as hysteria, which one author commented: 'thanks to the labours of Charcot and his pupils, has vastly outgrown its old and vague meaning, and is constantly acquiring a more precise and practical significance' (Putnam, 1881).

Page (1885) thought that 32 of his reported cases were fraudulent or were wilfully exaggerated, but commented that 'exaggeration is the very essence of many of those emotional or hysterical disorders which are so common in both sexes after the shock of collisions'.

The other relevant contribution to the malingering debate at that time was the introduction of workman's compensation. It became required by law that employers regulated their business so that injury would not result to others. The Employers'

Liability Act, passed in 1880, provided compensation to 'workmen' who received injury in the course of their employment, provided that the injury was not the direct result of the workman's own negligence. However, under the 1906 Act, anyone who entered into a contract of service or apprenticeship with an employer was covered, and the defence of serious or wilful misconduct on the claimants' part was no longer allowed if the injury resulted in permanent disablement.

In the first 6 years after the passing of the 1906 Act, the number of reported industrial accidents rose by 44%, in spite of the number of people in work remaining the same. Compensation payouts in the same period rose by 63.5%. One observer, Dr Collie (1917), medical examiner to the Sun Insurance Company, commented:

Workmen have now a greater tendency to make what they think is the best of an injury which befalls them – that is, get the most money out of it! . . . there is ample scope for exaggeration and I fear the opportunity is frequently seized.

Collie's scepticism was supported by the fact that the Act specifically laid down that an injured workman would only receive compensation for a full 2 weeks if he was on the sick list for 2 weeks. No compensation was paid if he returned to work in the first week; he received compensation for each day he was off work in the second week, but only if he was on the sick list for 14 days was the compensation dated back to day one. Not surprisingly (for Collie), the number of cases of injury putting people off work remained the same, but those injuries lasting over 2 weeks rose dramatically!

This link between compensation and presentation of physical symptoms has been demonstrated more recently in the papers reporting on compensation from countries where compensation for certain civilian injuries is not allowable. In 1995, the tort-compensation system in Saskatchewan, Canada changed to a no-fault scheme, which excluded payments for pain and suffering. Cassidy *et al.* (2000) examined the insurance claims from traffic injuries for whiplash injury before and after this date, and reported that the incidence declined by 43% for men and 15% for women following the change. Similar reductions for whiplash claims occurred in Victoria, Australia after limitations were introduced for compensation for whiplash injuries. The involvement of a lawyer in any case was associated with delay in the time to any settlement! As already noted in Chapter 3, posttraumatic whiplash injuries are hardly seen in Lithuania.

Malingering in the diagnostic manuals

Malingering finds no place in DSM-II, but does appear in DSM-III and in subsequent versions. In DSM-IV, the following are the specified criteria for malingering (V65.2):

The essential feature of Malingering is the intentional production of false or grossly exaggerated physical or psychological symptoms, motivated by external incentives such as avoiding military duty, avoiding work, obtaining financial compensation, evading criminal prosecution, or obtaining drugs. Under some circumstances, malingering may represent adaptive behaviour – for example feigning illness while a captive of the enemy during wartime (American Psychiatric Association, 1994).

Malingering should be strongly suspected if any combination of the following is noted:

1. Medicolegal context of presentation (e.g. the person is referred by an attorney to the clinician for examination)
2. Marked discrepancy between the person's claimed stress or disability and the objective findings
3. Lack of cooperation during the diagnostic evaluation and in complying with the treatment regimen
4. The presence of antisocial personality disorder

Distinctions are made between both conversion disorders and factitious disorders, on account of the external incentives involved and intentional production of symptoms in malingering.

In this manual, malingering falls under the rubric of 'additional conditions that may be a focus of clinical attention', rather than being listed as an axis 1 or 2 disorder *per se*. A similar exclusion is found in ICD-10 (World Health Organization, 1993), where malingering is not listed in the index, and is only briefly mentioned under Z76, relating to 'factors influencing health status and contact with health services'.

In fact, it can be argued, reinforced by the positioning of malingering in these manuals, that malingering is not a psychiatric diagnosis at all, and should not be treated as such. It is a social concept, and reflects on the way society encourages certain behaviours, and it is not pathological, in the way that for example a major depressive illness is. To categorise a patient as a malingerer, which implies fraud, is rightly the province of a judge, and for a medical expert to offer such an opinion could be seen as usurping judicial authority.

Some have argued otherwise, popularising the idea that malingering should be viewed as a mental illness. The concept 'attitude pathosis' was introduced by Thorne in 1949, and expanded on by Kamman (1951). In compensation neurosis, the neurosis was, in part, created by a conviction on the patient's behalf that he or she had been in an accident for which compensation would be payable. Resentment can easily follow, especially if the claimant meets with scepticism on behalf of doctors or others, and with this goes a wish for 'atonement from the privileged'. In attitude pathosis, the resentment was taken one step further, with the development of a nuclear core attitude. From this other related attitudes developed: 'If he

Table 4.1 On the distinction between hysteria
and malingering

Condition	Symptom for gain	Conscious
Malingering	Yes	Yes
Hysteria	Yes	No

Reproduced from Trimble (1981, p. 64), with
permission.

(an injured workman) adopts as his nuclear attitude that because he has been hurt he is unable to work, he is going to interpret reality according only to attitudes which are consistent with his basic or core attitude'. However, for Kamman this was not conscious malingering, but a composite of the original pathological attitude, and personality and environmental influences, somehow intermediate between conversion and the usual concept of malingering.

Others have attempted medical/psychiatric interpretations of malingering. Malingering has been seen as a psychological defence of a constitutionally weak ego against anxiety, or as an abnormal nervous reaction serving a conscious purpose; one author used the term 'teleophrenia' for such a condition. In general, such attempts to wrap malingering in psychiatric camouflage have stemmed from neo-Freudian psychoanalytic theories, and may not have held much sway in a legal setting.

One well-rehearsed distinction between conversion and malingering resides in the distinction between whether or not the symptoms are conscious or unconscious. This problem is discussed in detail in Chapter 9, but some observations are pertinent here. Table 4.1 is reproduced from an earlier review, and summarises the position (Trimble, 1981). Huddleston (1932) defined malingering as the deliberate feigning, induction or protraction of illness with the object of personal gain, which could be contrasted with a neurosis, which could protract illness but was not deliberate. Schilder (1940) was more precise in his definition that malingering was 'the conscious attempt to imitate symptoms to bring either economic or social gains to the individual'. Henry Miller (1961) expanded the net: 'the term malingering is used to encompass all forms of fraud relating to matters of health. This includes the simulation of diseases or disability which is not present; the much commoner gross exaggeration of minor disability; and the conscious and deliberate attribution of a disability to an injury or accident that did not in fact cause it, for personal advantage'. Turner (1999) pithily noted that 'the cardinal feature of malingering is the attempt to abdicate social responsibilities without cost' (p. 196) – cost, that is, to the claimant!

Whatever the definition, they all note that symptoms are deliberately contrived, and the purpose is gain, usually but not exclusively financial. These discussions have not considered in much detail malingering in the armed forces, where motivation is usually very different, but attitudes nevertheless remain the same. There are arguments over whether or not malingering is a psychiatric diagnosis needing understanding and treatment, or whether it is a social judgement, in the armed forces related to cowardice and avoidance of duty (Eissler, 1986). The obvious life-preserving value of the development of symptoms at the front may be reflected in conversion, as discussed in Chapter 1, but may also lead to malingering, or any of the subtle variants in the spectrum in between.

In fact, it seems that many patients in a military setting may exaggerate their traumas. Ross (1941) noted that many soldiers recounted being blown up or buried, when eyewitness accounts revealed that such things had not happened. He suggested that in the shock and confusion of warfare these men may have had false memories, but suppose they had lied: 'who shall blame him? A man who really feels at his last gasp, who feels his whole world has had the bottom knocked out of it, who has ceased to care about anything may I think be excused such a terminological inexactitude, especially as the responsibility for having got into this mess is partly at least someone else's' (Ross, 1941, p. 39). This issue merges into the problem of malingered posttraumatic stress disorder (PTSD), discussed in Chapter 8.

Several authors have tried to subdivide malingering. Richard Asher (1972) noted three varieties, depending on the motive: fear, desire and escape. Compensation claims fell in the second group. Mock (1930) defined neurotics proper, liars and mixed types; Travin and Protter (1984) separated self-deceivers, other deceivers and mixed deceivers. Resnick (1984) distinguished pure malingering, which was the feigning of disease or disability when it does not exist at all, from partial malingering, which is the conscious exaggeration of symptoms that do exist.

More recently, Rogers and Neumann (2003) proposed three models for explaining malingering. The motivations are: (1) an underlying psychopathology with a deteriorating course; (2) a manifestation of antisocial behaviour and attitudes; and (3) an attempt to respond to adversarial circumstances that takes into account other alternatives. In the first model, overtly intentional acts of malingering are gradually transformed into involuntary behaviour, while the second represents rather that suggested by DSM-III and DSM-IV criteria. The third model assumes that malingerers attempt to resolve difficult circumstances with a kind of cost-benefit analysis.

The DSM-IV definition has obvious relevance for medicolegal practice, and notably, high on the list of suspicion for the examining doctor is that the patient is referred from a solicitor! While there are no figures that compare the incidence of malingering in medicolegal practice to ordinary doctor–patient encounters, as a generalisation in the latter setting, malingering is said to be rare. Quite how such comments square up with the thousands of patients who go every day to their general practitioner (GP) for sick notes for short-term absence from work is unclear, and how many patients on long-term disability who have had their compensation assessed by tribunals, based upon favourable medical reports from their physicians, actually have defined medical as opposed to social causes for their disabilities has not been assessed. In general, compensation is coming from the public purse, not from private companies, and to investigate individual cases with the vigour sometimes necessary in medicolegal cases is financially (in the short term) not viable, and politically unacceptable. However, surveys suggest that a third of all 'sick days' have nothing to do with disease (*Times*, 2002)! More than a third of the 1.92 million sick days taken off in 2000 were not related to ill health at all, at an estimated cost to the UK taxpayer of £4 billion (Halligan *et al.*, 2003). In the USA, the workers' compensation payouts in the 1980s and 1990s grew at an annual rate of 14%, considerably higher than the general rise in consumer spending (Dembe, 1998).

Only the naive write in medicolegal reports that, in their experience, malingering is rare, and they therefore would not expect it in a particular case! They will have had little experience of the tougher end of medicolegal practice, assessing the more difficult cases, and will have not had their fingers burnt by supporting deceptive claimants down to the wire. Another naive gamble is to assert, in a report, that the information contained within, and the opinions derived, stem from what the patient has said to them, which they (the physician) have no reason to believe to be untrue. Again, this stems from years of ordinary medical practice, where it is expected that the rules of normal illness behaviour apply, that abnormal illness behaviour (AIB) is the exception, not the rule, and that patients come to doctors for medical and not for social reasons. In fact, civil medicolegal practice is a quite different speciality, with its own clientele, and very different patterns of doctor–patient interactions. The patient is not coming to the doctor for medical help, but for financial reward, and any expert who does not recognise this is also practising some (self)-deception!

The second criterion used by DSM-IV is usually the first clinical indication of suspicion: patients with relatively trivial injuries, normal X-ray examinations, discrepant signs and severe disability, forming a clinical picture which simply does not hang together. This gap, between somatic pathology and signs, or between signs and symptoms, is often, curiously, initially at least, ignored in many medicolegal assessments. It is not uncommonly first noted when patients come under the scrutiny of experts retained by the defence, at which point in time the patient, not unexpectedly (whether a case of hysteria or malingering), is aggrieved at the suggestion that the symptoms may not be bona fide.

The third criterion, lack of compliance, is sometimes easy to note, especially in patients' hospital or GP records. Failure to attend, missed appointments, lapsed prescriptions, refused referrals and the like may be noted. Patients may or may not be cooperative during the medicolegal assessment; a range of responses from utter civility and politeness to downright anger and indignation is found. The argument is often put by claimants that they are fed up with the whole medicolegal process, and that they resent seeing yet another specialist, especially one 'from the other side'. However, this understandable lament is not related to the malingering issue, while a more hostile, aggressive truculence may be.

The final criterion, the presence of antisocial personality disorder, is rarely brought forward in civilian practice to support a formulation of malingering, but should be. It has already been noted how there are close associations between such personality styles and deception, interlinked with labile emotions, frail, readily perforated memory processes, and the obvious requirement to be antisocial. To malinger in this context must be considered an antisocial act. While malingerers come from all social classes and backgrounds, and in some settings, such as escape from imprisonment, or the front line, malingering may be adaptive to the individual, many authors have noted the association with antisocial personality disorder.

Turner (1999) put it thus:

As one moves from malingering in essentially normal individuals along a continuum of behaviour towards malingering in the context of antisocial tendencies it becomes apparent that there is an increasing willingness and indeed a propensity to use malingering behaviour to pursue personal gain without regard for other individuals' or society's respective goals . . . there is always a risk of being caught out and this itself is a type of cost which serves to limit malingering in less antisocial persons (pp. 195–6).

There have been several studies seeking links between antisocial personality and malingering, but they mostly derive from forensic psychiatric settings, and have evaluated the frequency of malingering in antisocial people, rather then the other way round (Clark, 1997). In one study of this question, Sierles (1984) reported a significant association between self-reported measures of sociopathy and malingering.

Before discussing the issue of malingering further, a number of conditions in the malingering–hysteria penumbra will be described.

Factitious illness

Factitious disorders refer to patients who deliberately produce symptoms in order to assume the sick role but, in contrast to malingering, the symptoms are psychologically motivated, and external motives are not apparent. DSM-IV-TR recognises three main varieties, factitious disorder with predominantly psychological symptoms (300.16), factitious disorder with predominantly physical symptoms (300.19) and factitious disorder with combined symptoms. ICD-10 refers to factitious disorder (F68.1) as the intentional production or feigning of symptoms or disabilities, either physical or psychological.

Hawkins *et al.* (1956) drew attention to a group of patients who manifest 'deliberate disability', most of whom were female. They showed skilful simulation of illness, sometimes involving severe disfigurement, pain and even a threat to life. Many were paramedical personnel, and their medical knowledge was obviously relevant to the symptom presentation. They did not show any severe personality disorders, but were emotionally immature, and had disturbed relationships with their sibs and parents. Direct external material gain or advantage was not apparent.

The symptoms vary, as do the mechanisms of production, but dermatologists are well aware of the resulting dermatitis artefacta, chronic ulcerative lesions that continually reinfect. Injection of insulin to produce hypoglycaemia and coma, subcutaneous injections of faeces to provoke pyrexia, the use of drugs to alter the mental state, anaemia from self-bleeding, putting blood in the urine or vomit to create the impression of haematuria and bleeding ulcers, and, more recently, simulation of AIDS are all reported.

Psychological variants include factitious bereavement, PTSD and multiple personalities, all of which depend on the reporting of subjective symptoms, which can be difficult to discount.

Little is known of its prevalence, but in terms of the frequency of somatoform disorders, factitious disorder is uncommon. The presentations are often sporadic rather than chronic, and the evasiveness and convictions of the patients can render suspicion and then detection very difficult. Patients will often continue to deny their deceit, even when the evidence is laid out in front of them (e.g. needles, syringes and ampoules of insulin hidden in their clothes). Direct confrontation rarely resolves the situation.

Münchausen's syndrome

Neither the DSM-IV nor ICD-10 distinguishes Münchausen's syndrome from factitious disorder, but there are reasons to do so. The cardinal feature of Münchausen's syndrome is that patients present themselves to hospital, as opposed to being sent there by doctors. They present often for the procurement of drugs, in particular opiates, and they are more likely to be males. Crucial to the behaviour is the attempt to gain admission to hospital, one pseudonym being the hospital-hopper syndrome. Typically, any suggestion of a psychiatric referral is met with abuse, and on being confronted, these patients instantly discharge themselves. They verge and merge with patients who have a pseudologia fantastica, hence the diagnostic triad given by Bursten (1965) of: (1) a severe and chronic course of factitious disorder; (2) peregrination; and (3) pseudologia fantastica.

Münchausen-by-proxy is now well recognised, having been first described by Meadow (1977). Parents, usually the mother, but sometimes the father, present their children to doctors reporting symptoms in the child that initially seem valid but which, with time, do not conform to expectations. The parent may have good medical knowledge, perhaps being a paramedic and, after a time, it dawns on those attending the child that there is a direct correspondence between the presence of the parent and the signs of illness. Often the cardinal features of the problem are never witnessed, only reported (such as seizures), or there is obvious failure to respond to treatments that are usually effective. In more sinister settings, illness is deliberately created, by giving the child drugs, or by direct trauma, including, for example, smothering. The health of the child may be endangered by unnecessary medical interventions.

There is a relationship between Münchausen's syndrome and the syndrome by proxy in that a percentage of those involved in the latter will themselves have a history of factitious illness or hospital peregrination. However, the epidemiology of these disorders is really unknown. A mild form of Münchausen's-by-proxy is probably quite common. These are over concerned mothers, with unhappy marriages, overusing medical facilities, who present their children rather than themselves to doctors for attention. It is not uncommon in the histories of patients with medically unexplained symptoms to see such a catalogue of surgery visits as a child in the GP records.

Pseudologia fantastica

Lying, self-deceit and deception of others are universal human attributes. This interesting fact has much bearing on medicolegal practice, and intersects well with any consideration of somatoform disorders. Pathological lying, referred to as pseudologia fantastica, is a well-recognised psychopathology, which is encountered clinically, but also in media expositions of the rich and the famous.

Pseudologues spin a weave of tales about themselves and their lives that are not credible, although at first are believed by the fascinated listener. They may talk of their military exploits, of their work with the secret service, of political connections or of their academic achievements. They may use alias names, conceal to reveal (everything they do is top-secret), boast of linguistic prowess or claim to have invented some wonderful device.

Such pathological lying can be seen in patients with cerebral damage and with schizophrenia, in which settings some evidence of learning disability, neurological impairment or psychosis will be found. The pseudologia fantastica of the psychotic takes on totally unrealistic proportions, is less coherent than in non-psychotics and the lies will be maintained against all evidence of their falsity.

Habitual liars are a lesser variant, often coming to the fore in childhood or adolescence, when the tissue of fabrication may bolster a lagging self-esteem, or may be interwoven with a fantasy mythology that satisfies an impoverished imagination. Ford (1996) lists the following factors associated with habitual lying:

- a dysfunctional family of origin
- childhood physical or sexual trauma
- neuropsychological abnormalities, including learning disabilities and borderline mental retardation
- suggestible or accommodating personality features
- disorders particularly of the sociopathic, borderline, histrionic and narcissistic types
- frequent association with substance abuse, either personal or in the family of origin

What is interesting about these associations is the underlying bridge with dysfunctional families, disordered upbringing and the spectrum of personality profiles noted in many patients with somatoform disorders. However, not everyone fits such profiles, and in everyday life successful psychopaths with a lifestyle of habitual lying are encountered. Famous impostors include those who adopt the role of doctors, such as the famous Ferdinand Walter Demara. He became famous for his heroic surgical exploits in the Korean war, in spite of having no medical qualifications. His background revealed that he had also posed as a schoolteacher, a doctor of psychology and a warden of a prison. So famous was his story that he became the subject of a biography, and a film *The Great Impostor*, with Tony Curtis in the title role. A more recent publicisation of a true story is that of the conman Frank W. Abagnale, Jr., portrayed in the film *Catch Me if You Can*, starring Leonards DiCaprio and Tom Hanks.

Contemporary variants may include the one-time politician and novelist, Jeffrey Archer, whose curriculum vitae failed to fit his modus vivendi, and the writer Laurens van der Post, whose biographical fabrications have been documented, and who seems not to have made good distinctions between literal and imaginative truths (Jones, 2001). The novelist Anthony Burgess was a pathological liar, and Iris Murdoch had a fantasy brother that her lifelong friend never suspected was an invention. At the more sinister end of this spectrum must be counted those who succeed by their falsehoods in entrapping people and murdering them, such as Neville Heath. The interested reader is referred to Sarah Burton's (2001) engaging catalogue of such characters in her book *Impostors; Six Kinds of Liar.*

Lying

It seems clear from the above descriptions that a spectrum of behaviours exist, which all involve deceit, which affect different populations of people, ranging from those who successfully tread the boards of society until they are rumbled (but how many more are not?) to frank psychopathologies. In a medicolegal context, the role of lying, as a deliberate ploy to obtain financial gain, has to be set alongside the universal tendency to deceive which is inherent in human behaviour. This touches directly on the issue of conscious awareness of the deceit, which is discussed in a later chapter. It also links to the subject of memory, how we remember and what we remember and why, which is the subject of the next chapter. Before considering how malingering and the factitious disorder spectrum can be detected, a consideration of lying in a more general context is considered. The interested reader is referred to the texts by Ford (1996) and Ekman (1992).

We are surrounded by lies. No one really believes the more sensational claims of the tabloid newspapers, or the adverts that bombard our senses daily, or the silky words of today's political toad trying to be tomorrow's popular prince ('Watch my lips . . .'). Sir Robert Armstrong, when under cross-examination in the supreme court in New South Wales, replied that he had not under oath told a lie, but had been 'economical with the truth'. And yet, we all do it, or at least we behave as if we do. It is as if we were conceived to be deceived. As T. S. Eliot wrote: 'Human kind cannot bear very much reality'. We go on listening to adverts, buying newspapers and taking notice of our politicians. Surveys suggest that up to 90% of people admit to being deceitful, and indeed, anyone who says they have never told a lie is lying by definition. Lying about the amount of alcohol we consume, the number of cigarettes we smoke, the number of sexual partners we have had, the amount we eat and so forth is a part of the fabric of our lives. One in three people produce dishonest curriculum vitae. Physicians often lie to their patients. This may be with good intention, to give encouragement that some new treatment may soon be discovered for an illness, or that the prognosis is better than it really is, but even so they know the information to be false.

Thus the spectrum of lying is broad and multicoloured, by time, place and person. The commonest form however is self-deceit, and in this deceit we also lie to others. Denial is one of the best-known unconscious psychological defence mechanisms. Reading such deceptions is difficult, but for some it becomes a job in itself, for example for forensic psychiatrists, police detectives and poker players.

Ford defines various forms of lies in Table 4.2. This emphasises the broad spectrum of lying, from the mundane to the pathological, and all forms contribute to the spectrum of behaviours to be evaluated in a forensic or medicolegal setting. Further, some other well-described psychological defence mechanisms contribute

Table 4.2 A Classification of lying

Type of lie	Motive
White lies	To lubricate social relationships
Humorous lies	To amuse the listener
Altruistic lies	To reduce suffering
Defensive lies	To protect the self
Aggressive lies	To hurt someone else
Pathological lies	Bring no obvious gain to the liar
Pseudologia fantastica	Often associated with psychiatric illness

Adapted from the text of Ford (1996).

to the distortion of reality by the ego, and to self-deception. These include dissoci-ation (see Chapter 8), intellectualisation and rationalisation. Emotions are isolated from the fact of external reality and reasons for behaviour are cognitively contrived. In addition to these is repression the process of blocking out from consciousness emotionally painful experiences. Denial of our own deception becomes a link to repression; it is a form of adaptive self-deception.

Quite why lying should be a universal attribute is unclear but, as several authors have pointed out, simulation and deceit are very common in a wide species of animals, from butterflies to baby chimpanzees, and at a biological evolutionary level have some survival value. However, whether such behaviours in preverbal animals can really be equated with human lying is a very debatable point, especially since lying is essentially a verbal attribute, a link discussed further below. There may well be neuroanatomical circuits linked with these behaviours, and it is well known that the frontal lobes of the brain have much to do with social control and monitoring of ongoing behaviours. There are case reports of patients with frontal damage developing pathological lying, and other forms of verbal deception, such as confabulation, are seen with damage to cerebral circuits involving the frontal lobes and midbrain neuronal pathways. It has already been noted how certain cognitive styles, associated especially with histrionic and antisocial personality disorders, lend themselves to verbal exaggerations and selective memorisation.

Lying implies a degree of reality testing, and an awareness of the concept of deceit. However, many of the subtle forms of lying derive from social, personality and developmental factors. Developmental factors must include the way parents respond to a growing child's deceits, in that lying is universal in children, and Pinocchio's nose is a barometer. Essentially, children's ideas about what a lie is do not conform to those of an adult until about age 10. They are poor at detecting lies, and use lies as part of play and fantasy. The intention to deceive is lacking. Lying may be more acceptable in certain subcultures, and may be driven by home circumstances, such as living in an environment of abuse where lying may have protective value, and serve to enhance self-esteem.

Lying is obviously central to the concept of malingering, and both relate to exaggeration, the enhancement of expression for whatever motive. In medicolegal practice, financial gain is seen as the external motive for malingering, and yet Collie (1917) pointed out how susceptible our minds are to suggestion, thoughts running along lines of least resistance. The injured workman automatically attributes an accident at work to his disability, he rejects alternatives, and interprets reality only in accordance with his core beliefs. A theory of what happened becomes a belief that it happened.

The views of authors such as Kamman have been noted. Good (1942) described the malingerer as a psychopath who had no feelings of guilt about his malingering. He consciously assumes and exploits his symptoms of illness, but the form the symptom takes is determined by unconscious defence mechanisms and the personality style, blurring the boundaries between the conscious and the unconscious. Henry Miller (1961) was one of the more outspoken antagonists who was against such conceptual confusions. He based his conclusions on a review of 47 head-injury cases, who developed psychoneurotic symptoms, and were seeking compensation. He found that such complaints were twice as common in industrial as opposed to road traffic accidents, especially if the employers were large industrial organisations or nationalised industries; that they were twice as common in men as opposed to women, in contrast to the usual excess of females with these disorders outside legal practice; that there was an inverse relationship between the severity of the head injury and the severity of the neurosis; and that the symptoms were more prominent in social classes IV and V. With regards to malingering he opined: 'Many of those concerned with compensation work . . . are convinced that [malingering] is far from uncommon in these cases, and deplore the inability of doctors to recognise the condition or their hesitancy in expressing an opinion in this connection to which they will freely admit in private conversation'.

The detection of deceit and malingering

In spite of the spectrum of presentations within the penumbra of factitious illness and malingering, some authors have laid down firm guidelines for detecting malingering. Hurst (1940) suggested that there were only two conditions that led to the diagnosis of malingering with any certainty. One was to catch the person *in flagrante delicto*. Patients are literally caught in the act they say they cannot do, when they think they are alone and unseen. The following is a quote from Hamilton (1904):

An apparently helpless man, who with great difficulty took the witness chair, and after testifying to the absolutely paralysed condition of his right arm, was quietly asked by the defendant's council how high he could raise his hand *before* his accident, and without a moment's hesitation he thrust it high above his head.

The same thing happened in another case. The plaintiff, who received a verdict of $5000 for a collection of vague symptoms and alleged injuries, and who in the courtroom was the picture of helplessness, made a violent and apparently muscular demonstration of joy when the jury announced her good fortune.

Collie (1917) recommended surprise visits to plaintiffs' homes, when warm boots or clothes might reveal the fictional bed-bound state of the patient.

As Richard Asher (1972) observed: 'The pride of a doctor who has caught a malingerer is alike to that of a fisherman who has landed an enormous fish and his stories (like those of fishermen) may become somewhat exaggerated in the telling'. It is not therefore proposed here to relate many instances of malingering, either personally observed or reported. Needless to say, anyone experienced in medicolegal practice will be aware of not only the frequency of exaggeration, but also frank malingering, although many express a reluctance to discuss the issue.

The case described by Punton (1903) revealed overt criminal behaviour. The man would deliberately loosen the floorboards of trains and streetcars, and then fall over them, sustaining alleged injury and seek compensation. He admitted that he employed the best of doctors to examine him, as they were the most easily fooled, but the insurance companies were better satisfied with their opinions!

There are many variants of this con, and they are well reviewed by Malleson (2003). He devoted a whole chapter of his book *Whiplash and Other Useful Injuries* to 'jumpers' and 'add-ons' – people who leap on buses or tramcars involved in accidents, or even stage faked accidents in order to seek compensation. It makes very revealing reading.

The following was reported in the *Guardian* (19 August 1993). Accidents in buses were contrived in a sting operation in New Jersey and cameras were placed inside and outside the vehicles. Immediately after the accident people were observed scrambling on to the bus before the police arrived, and all later claimed to have been injured in the accident!

Graham (2002) recounts his experience with cases after a minor bus crash. Within 24 hours, the number of patients claiming whiplash injury allegedly due to the crash exceeded by a factor of four the capacity of the vehicle. In other instances he cites claims that are made for passengers in a car involved in a crash who were never even in the car!

In another well-publicised case, several members of the same family claimed compensation for paralysis from spinal injury and brain damage leading to coma, but investigation revealed the claimants to be leading normal and healthy lives.

Graham pointed out that these claims could only have progressed with the collusion of medical experts, and warns, 'the medical expert should be aware that he is not exempt from the consequences of perjury' (p. 25).

Reginald Kelly was fond of the anecdote of the man who won substantial compensation for a supposed paralysis, but whom the defence suspected of malingering. After the case he was told he would be followed until he was exposed, to which he replied 'you had better follow me to Lourdes then!'

The second certainty of the diagnosis of malingering, suggested by Hurst (1940), was when patients actually confessed they were shamming. This is extremely uncommon! However, sometimes malingerers are shopped by their relatives, friends or work colleagues.

Huddleston (1932) suggested that it was possible to detect malingerers by their attitude:

The out and out malingerer is usually detectable by various bits of evidence: peculiar attitudes towards the examination – generally suspicious, sometimes sullen, sometimes 'smart-alecky' – a certain avoidance of too close scrutiny, often an unusual solicitude for his rights . . . generally a mental incapacity to be quite consistent in his complaints. The malingerer shows a tendency to overact his part'.

Bassett Jones and Llewellyn (1917) urged us to look at the eyes:

It is in and around the eyes that we may discern most clearly the natural language of slyness, cunning, craft or other sparks of deceit. The conscious malingerer is uneasy, fearful of detection, his unrest betraying itself by the restless wavering of the eyes, their furtive glance through veiled or drooping lids.

Engel (1970) commented:

In general the malingerer is aloof, suspicious, hostile, secretive, unfriendly, and more concerned about his symptoms; the patient with conversion is more dependent, appealing, clinging, and although clearly acting out the sick role, shows less than the expected concern about the symptom . . . The malingerer may be reluctant to co-operate in diagnostic procedures which unmask him; the conversion patient is eager for confirmation of an organic explanation for his symptoms . . . Because the skilful malingerer applies his intellectual knowledge of the disease in the simulation, the end result is more likely to resemble the real thing. Careful observation, especially when the patient is unaware that he is being observed, often will reveal that the patient is not as disabled as he claims. Unlike the patient with conversion, the malingerer must work to maintain his ruse. Hence, he cannot always resist the temptation to relax the deception, especially when he believes himself to be alone (p. 667).

Henry Miller (1961) described a typical patient with 'accident neurosis' (a term he coined) at the consultation thus:

If he is being examined at the request of the insurance company he frequently arrives late. He is invariably accompanied, often by a member of his family, who does not wait to be invited into the consulting room, but who resolutely enters with him, and more often than not takes an active part in the consultation, speaking for him, prompting him, and reminding him of symptoms that may for the moment have slipped his memory. The patient's attitude is one of martyred gloom, but he is also very much on the defensive, and exudes hostility, especially at any suggestion that his condition may be improving . . . The most consistent clinical feature is the subject's unshakeable conviction of unfitness for work, a conviction quite unrelated to overt disability even if his symptomatology is accepted at its face value. At a later stage the patient will declare his fitness for light work, which is not often available . . . The equanimity with which these patients will accept the tedium of months or even years of idleness, apparently unmitigated by any pleasurable diversion, is remarkable.

Another cardinal feature is an absolute refusal to admit any degree of symptomatic improvement.

Resnick (1984), who believes that malingering should be suspected in the examination of all patients, gives the following characteristics to help distinguish conversion disorder from malingering:

1. The malingerer often presents as suspicious, uncooperative, resentful, aloof, secretive and unfriendly. Patients with conversion disorder are more likely to be cooperative, and be described as appealing, clinging and dependent.
2. The malingerer may try to avoid examination, unless it is required as a condition for receiving some financial benefit. The patient with conversion disorder welcomes examinations.
3. While the malingerer may decline to cooperate with recommended diagnostic and therapeutic procedures, patients with conversion disorder are typically eager for an organic explanation for their symptoms.
4. The malingerer is more likely than the patient with conversion disorder to refuse employment that could be handled in spite of some disability.
5. The malingerer is likely to give every detail of the accident and its sequelae; the patient with conversion disorder is more likely to give an account that contains gaps, inaccuracies and vague generalised complaints.

Scott (1991) comments on the following behaviours in the orthopaedic patient:

The patient enters the consulting room slowly and apparently in great pain . . . The patient wears at least two or more of the following items: dark glasses, a collar and a wrist support. On disrobing a surgical corset is revealed and possibly also tubigrip supports on the knees. One or more sticks are used. If a single stick it is used on the inappropriate side, the side on which the pain exists . . . it is wise when observing the patient's gait not to walk too close to the patient who has a tendency to collapse on the examiner, perhaps to make the maximum impression on him.

The most striking features of the malingerer's history are his astonishing recall of every last detail of the accident, which may have happened a long time ago; coupled with this is an amazing vagueness when questioned in detail about the influence his present daily routine has on his symptoms. This detailed questioning makes the patient initially uneasy, then irritable and finally aggressive.

Graham (2002) pays attention to the three Gs – grimacing, grunts and groans – which are present during minimal activity, but often absent with more vigorous parts of the physical examination.

Faust (1995) points out how easy it is to deceive sympathetic individuals, especially when they are inclined to assume sincerity. He stresses the importance of considering the degree to which the examinee has a motive to deceive, making the obvious but overlooked point that in a compensation setting there is going to be more malingering than outside such circumstances. Physical examination is not enough, and the detection of malingering requires the collation of collateral information which may not become available until late in the legal process.

Ekman (1992) describes many ways of detecting lying. His own studies revealed how poor most observers are at detecting deliberate lying, but he believes clues to deceit can be learned. Attention to the words used, what is said and the facial expression are important, since liars control what they say and how they say it carefully. Slips of the tongue, pauses, hesitations, voice pitch, pace of speech, blink rate, signs of autonomic arousal and body gestures may all be used to suggest deceit to the experienced examiner.

It has to be acknowledged that most of these criteria, which seem to have stemmed from clinical experience and perhaps a bias in patient selection, have never been subjected to any experimental verification, and depend on clinical acumen. There must therefore be considerable caution used when identifying possible malingering. None the less, since much of psychiatric practice is based on the evaluation of subjective symptoms, and making judgements about patients' personalities and behaviours, perhaps they cannot be dismissed too lightly.

The detection of malingering is aided in practice by a number of other techniques. These include information gathered by private investigators, the use of psychological tests and mechanical measurements obtained by the use of, for example, lie detectors. The latter are not relevant to medicolegal practice, and are not discussed further, but the interested reader is referred to Ekman (1992) and Rogers (1997). Since many of the psychological tests used are related to memory function, these are described in more detail in the next chapter, while some other psychological tests that may be helpful, such as the Abnormal Illness Behaviour Questionnaire, are referred to in Chapter 6.

Observation of claimants may include inpatient evaluations by a multidisciplinary team and covert surveillance by video taping of claimants, when they are not expecting to be observed. The behaviour on the ward may be distinctly inconsistent, symptoms coming and going depending on whether or not patients think they are being watched. Malingered signs are difficult to sustain for prolonged periods. Patients may refuse examinations, be hostile to the staff generally and be secretive, hiding medications and the like, either to reproduce symptoms or for their own personal use. Sometimes swift self-discharge occurs as soon as the patient realises the purpose of the admission, namely to 'get to the bottom of your problems'.

Video taping of claimants is frequently employed by defence solicitors, even when malingering is not suspected. This can be very valuable, especially if the observations are carried out close to the time of medical examinations when the patient's complaints are documented. The physician should not refrain from recommending such observations if he or she believes it will aid in the understanding of the claimant's unexplained symptoms.

Legal aspects of malingering

Malingering is rarely to be found in the legal context; specific definitions are only found in military law (Jones, 2003). Apparently there are no reported cases in which this concept has been considered by the civil courts. While the concept of 'functional overlay' is often found in judgements, the onus seems to be on the defendant to provide evidence that any claimant is a malingerer, and most cases are compromised before any case gets to court (Spence et al., 2003). This chapter has expressed the view that classifying somebody as a malingerer is essentially a legal rather than a medical matter, a view upheld by Jones (2003), who points out that if there is no medical explanation for what is going on (either physical or psychiatric), then experts should go no further, and it should be up to the judge to assess the truthfulness of the claimant and to pronounce on malingering. An allegation of malingering is essentially that of fraud, and in a legal setting such an allegation must be supported by admissible evidence.

Spence and colleagues (2003) examined two standard electronic legal databases (Lexis and Westlaw), which reported on cases since at least 1945, and came up with approximately 250 where 'malingering' was mentioned in the judgement.

Jones (2003) reported that a large proportion of these cases were back or whiplash injuries, that the cases typically involved disputes between medical experts (Jones commented that 'orthopaedic surgeons take a more robust view of the abilities of claimants than psychiatrists do'!).

Further, it was noted that where an allegation of malingering had been made, it was only in a small proportion that the court concluded the claimant was in fact a malingerer and usually euphemistically referred to the claimant as exaggerating symptoms, either consciously or unconsciously. In summary, Jones (2003) noted the very small number out of the total of personal injury cases in which malingering was mentioned in the judgements, and thought there were three possible explanations. The first was that malingering was not common: this possibility has already been commented on in this chapter. The second was that, as only cases that raise important questions of law are reported, and since being a malingerer is 'a question of fact' rather than 'a question of law', relevant cases from a medical point of view simply may not have been required for the law reports. The third relates to the seriousness of the allegation of malingering, essentially as one of fraud. Often judges, even faced with evidence, for example, from video tapes that claimants can do things they claim not to be able to do, prefer to avoid the term 'malingerer', and embody their judgements with euphemisms.

Conclusions

Lying is a universal human attribute, ingrained into our social repertoire from childhood days. The spectrum ranges from white lies, through to exaggeration to various forms of pathological lying. Further, certain personalities embed these styles in ways that influence not only their appreciation of reality, but also their reporting of it. Common features of those who deceive in relation to illness include early childhood trauma, growing up in a disorganised dysfunctional family, claims of abuse and the development of patterns of behaviour referred to as hysterical, borderline or antisocial. These are associated with the somatoform disorders, and AIB, hence the perceived overlap of these disorders with the social construct of malingering.

In medicolegal practice, for those who encourage the use of manuals such as DSM-IV, malingering should be suspected in any encounter (criterion 1), and be reinforced by the diagnosis of an antisocial personality disorder. However, the spectrum of personalities associated with exaggeration and imprecision is broadened beyond DSM-IV, as has been discussed in Chapter 2.

Clear distinctions between malingering and other forms of AIB are often difficult to define in a clinical setting, but cannot reside totally on the naive division of conscious versus unconscious motives (Table 4.1). A summary of the features of some of the disorders discussed in this and the previous chapter is given in Table 4.3.

Proof of malingering is hard to get, but to maintain the suspicion must be acceptable medical practice. The demonstration of exaggeration does not in itself necessarily imply malingering, and neither does the demonstration of lying. However these will cast much doubt on the credibility and reliability of the claimant and may be a pointer in the direction of a malingered claim.

Table 4.3 Some features of disorders discussed in Chapters 3 and 4

	Hypochondriasis	Somatisation disorder	Conversion disorder	Factitious disorder	Münchausen's syndrome	Malingering	Somatic delusional disorder
Gender (M)	F>M	F>M	F>M	F>M	M>F	M>F	M=F
Monosymptomatic (M) or poly-symptomatic (P)	P: 5% M	P	M often	M or P	>M	M or P	M or P
Personality disorder	Low: as other psychiatric disorders	High: borderline, histrionic, antisocial	High: histrionic, dependent	?	High: especially antisocial	High: especially antisocial	No
Associated psychiatric disorder	Depression/anxiety	Depression/anxiety	High: depression/anxiety	No	No	Pseudodepression and psychosis	Depression or psychosis
External incentive	No	No	No	No	Yes	Yes	No
Special features	High anxiety		Belle indifférence		Peregrination	Compensation setting	Delusional conviction

Assessing claimants in a medicolegal setting is entirely different to non-legal settings, a fundamental point which is not acknowledged by many experts, and ignored by advocates and often judges. A firm diagnosis of posttraumatic dystonia or fibromyalgia, or the suggestion of 'a little bit of brain damage' in a claimant evaluated by an inexperienced examiner, or one unfamiliar with the medicolegal terrain, will send a cock-a-hoop solicitor with the claimant all the way to the High Court. The claim may have substance, but if it falls at the last hurdle, on grounds of suspected malingering, the psychological damage to the claimant may be severe. There is (or should be) embarrassement all round, and the experts involved in supporting the claim become that bit wiser.

REFERENCES

Ackroyd, P. (2001). *London, the Biography*. London: Vintage.

American Psychiatric Association (1994). *Diagnostic and Statistical Manual of Mental Disorders*, 4th edn. Washington, DC: American Psychiatric Association.

Asher, R. (1972). *Talking Sense – a selection of his papers*. London: Pitman Medical.

Bassett Jones, A. and Llewellyn, L. J. (1917). *Malingering or the Simulation of Disease*. London: William Heinemann.

Bursten, B. (1965). On Munchausen's syndrome. *Archives of General Psychiatry*, **13**, 261–8.

Burton, S. (2001). *Impostors; Six Kinds of Liar*. London: Penguin Books.

Cassidy, J. D., Carroll, L. J., Coté, P. *et al*. (2000). Effect of eliminating compensation for pain and suffering on the outcome of insurance claims for whiplash injury. *New England Journal of Medicine*, **342**, 1179–86.

Clark, C. R. (1997). Sociopathy, malingering and defensiveness. In Rogers R., *Clinical Assessment of Malingering and Deception*, ed. R. Rogers, pp. 68–84. New York: Guilford Press.

Collie, J. (1917). *Malingering and Feigned Sickness*. London: Edward Arnold.

Dembe, A. E. (1996). *Occupation and Disease*. New Haven: Yale University Press.

Eissler, K. R. (1986). *Freud as an Expert Witness*. Translated by C. Trollope. Connecticut: International Universities Press.

Ekman, P. (1992). *Telling Lies: Clues to Deceit in the Marketplace, Politics and Marriage*. New York: WW Norton.

Engel, G. L. (1970). Conversion symptoms. In: *Signs and Symptoms*, Vth edn, ed. C. M. McBryde and R. S. Blacklow, pp. 650–68. New York: Lippincott/Williams & Wilkins.

Faust, D. (1995). The detection of deception. In *Malingering and Conversion Disorders*, ed. M. I. Weintraub, pp. 255–66. Philadelphia: WB Saunders.

Ford, C. V. (1996). *Lies! Lies! Lies! The Psychology of Deceit*. Washington, DC: American Psychiatric Press.

Gavin, H. (1843). *On Feigned and Factitious Diseases, Chiefly of Soldiers and Seamen*. London: J. Churchill.

Good, R. (1942). Malingering. *British Medical Journal*, **ii**, 359.

Graham, D. F. (2002). Neck and back injury claims – malingering. *Journal of Personal Injury Law*, March, 17–35.

Halligan, P. W., Bass, C. and Oakley, D. A. (2003). Willful deception as illness behaviour. In: *Malingering and Illness Deception*, pp. 3–28. Oxford: Oxford University Press.

Hamilton, A. M. (1904). *Railway and Other Accidents*. London: Baillière Tindall.

Hawkins, J. R., Jones, K. S., Sim, M. and Tibbets, R. W. (1956). Deliberate disability. *British Medical Journal*, I, 361–7.

Huddleston, J. H. (1932). *Accidents, Neuroses and Compensation*. Baltimore, MD: Williams and Wilkins.

Hurst, A. F. (1940). *Medical Diseases of War*. London: Edward Arnold.

Jones, J. D. F. (2001). *Storyteller; The many lives of Laurens van der Post*. London: John Murray.

Jones, M. A. (2003). Law Lies and Videotape: Malingering as a legal phenomenon. In: *Malingering and Illness Deception*, ed. P. W. Halligan, C. Bass and D. Oakley, pp. 207–17. Oxford: Oxford University Press.

Kamman, G. R. (1951). Traumatic neurosis, compensation neurosis or attitude pathosis? *Archives of Neurology and Psychiatry*, **65**, 593.

Malleson, A. (2003). *Whiplash and Other Useful Illnesses*. Quebec: McGilt Queens University.

Meadow, R. (1977). Munchausen's syndrome by proxy: the hinterland of child abuse. *Archives of Disease in Childhood*, **57**, 92–8.

Miller, H. (1961). Accident neurosis. *British Medical Journal*, I, 919–25, 992–8.

Mock, H. E. (1930). Rehabilitation of the disabled. *Journal of the American Medical Association*, **95**, 31.

Page, H. (1885). *Injuries of the Spine and Spinal Cord without Apparent Mechanical Lesions*. London: J. and A. Churchill.

Punton, J. (1903). Quoted in Ford, C. V. (1983), p. 130.

Putnam, J. J. (1881). Recent investigations into patients of so-called concussion of the spine. *Boston Medical and Surgical Journal*, **109**, 217.

Resnick, P. (1984). The detection of malingered mental illness. *Behavioural Sciences and the Law*, **2**, 21–38.

Rogers, R. (ed.) (1997). *Clinical Assessment of Malingering and Deception*. New York: Guilford Press.

Rogers, R. and Neuman, C. S. (2003). Conceptual issues and explanatory models of malingering. In: *Malingering and Illness Deception*, ed. P. W. Halligan, C. Bass and D. A. Oakley, pp. 69–80. Oxford: Oxford University Press.

Ross, T. A. (1941). *Lectures on War Neuroses*. London: Edward Arnold.

Schilder, P. (1940). Neuroses following head and brain injuries. In *Injuries of the Skull, Brain and Spinal Cord*, ed. S. Brock, pp. 275–307. Philadelphia: Williams and Wilkins.

Scott, J. H. S. (1991). Litigant's backache. In: *A Practical Guide to Medicine and the Law*, ed. J. P. Jackson, pp. 189–97. Springer Verlag.

Sierles, F. S. (1984). Correlates of malingering. *Behavioural Sciences and the Law*, **2**, 113–18.

Spence, S., Farrow, T. and Leung, D. (2003). Lying as an executive function. In: *Malingering and Illness Deception*, ed. P. W. Halligan, C. Bass and D. A. Cakley, pp. 253–264. Oxford: Oxford University Press.

Times, Sunday 29 December 2002.

Travin, S. and Protter, B. (1984). Malingering and malingering-like behaviour: some clinical and conceptual issues. *Psychiatric Quarterly*, **53**, 3.

Trimble, M. R. (1981). *Post-traumatic Neurosis, from Railway Spine to the Whiplash*. Chichester: John Wiley.

Turner, M. (1999). Malingering, hysteria, and the factitious disorders. *Cognitive Neuropsychiatry*, **4**, 193–201.

World Health Organization (1993). *The ICD–10 Classification of Mental and Behavioural Disorders*. Geneva: World Health Organization.

5

Memory in a medicolegal context

So heightened and important an occasion can lead to its excited recollection being worked over again and again. THE KEY MOMENTS ARE PICKED OUT AND DWELT ON. Some of the events are elided; others are shaped into a more satisfactory pattern, another sequence. New causal connections are established. The result of this process becomes fixed; it becomes the memory of the event.

(Edmonds and Eidinow, 2001, pp. 222–3)

As most lawyers know, eyewitnesses often err ... If an event suggests some tempting interpretation, then this interpretation, more often than not, is allowed to distort what has actually been seen.

(p. 217)

Introduction

Memory is central to the legal process, and yet is rarely considered except in the limited context of forensic cases, where amnesia for crimes is claimed. So often testimony is given on the basis of two fundamental principles, that the witness or expert is telling the truth, and that they have perfect recall of that which they are being asked about. The very term 'witness' excites a meaning of a camera-like ordering of memories laid down at a point in time relevant to the trial.

The issue of what is truth, and how that may relate to reality is closely linked to memory, but human memory, as will be explored in this chapter, is simply unreliable. When Maurice Chevalier crooned, 'I remember it well', he clearly didn't. As Milan Kundera puts it; 'remembering is a form of forgetting'.

Memory is friable like a spider's web, initially seeming robust and purposeful, but easily damaged by an indelicate touch. It frays under the burden of nature, and eventually coalesces with others to form the agglutinated cobwebs of fantasy, which hang around corners of the mind long after the spider has left.

Our memories, like the eggs we eat for breakfast, are also fryable. Any chef can alter the final shape and taste of what is served up; the more skilful the cook, the more appetising the meal. In medicolegal practice, there are many cooks egging the pudding!

In times past, memory was assumed to be a property of the structure of the mind, which reflected the structure of the world. Associationist psychology assumed each psychic experience to be atomic, composed of elements, which shuffled around the brain, memories passively attaching themselves to others dependent on environmental inputs. Such dormant traces of the past were then retrieved intact, and there was no place for any complex active psychologically bound retrieval process. For the direct realist, the act of remembering was being in direct touch with the past. This absurdity was further championed by the behaviourist school of psychology, which not only believed that all human behaviour could be explained by principles of conditioning, but assumed that nothing of any substance lay in the billions of cerebral neurones which could intervene between a stimulus and any subsequent response!

There are several related processes of memory in action. An event must be perceived, and it has been noted in Chapter 2 how perceptions are modified in fundamental ways by personality. There is then a consolidation phase, where some representation of the event is laid down in the brain. No one today has an idea how this is achieved, but representationists will accept that remembering refers indirectly to a trace of the past, which 'represents' the latter. Historically we have moved from notions of animal spirits and pores in the brain to neurotransmitters and receptors as substrates for memory, but the ideas remain similar, and representations are considered as brain states. The more a channel of activation is used, the more facile it becomes, and the more likely is its pattern to be 'remembered'. Then there is the process of recall, the elegant reconstruction of the past that for us textures every moment of daily existence, and which in verbal report is given to another. All along the way, the fixed chain of associations is broken. The poet philosopher Samuel Taylor Coleridge (1817/1885) put it thus:

it . . . results inevitably, that the will, the reason, the judgement, and the understanding, instead of being the determining causes of the association, must needs be represented as its creatures (p. 215).

For the majority of the twentieth century, a so-called modular view of the brain was extant. This assumed that certain brain regions related to specific brain functions, and that somehow the neurones at one site were the site, and only site of containment of that function. Various parts of the brain were specialised to perform certain functions, speech for example being contained and confined to certain parts of the left cerebral hemisphere.

Current models emphasise an alternative. These connectionist theories acknowledge that the brain relies on parallel (as opposed to sequential) processing, in which information is stored as a pattern of activation in multiple connected processing units, widely distributed within the brain. Learning is viewed as a change in connection valences between units in multilayered networks of neurones over time. However, what is 'represented' and exactly what memory 'traces' are remains entirely illusive. As Wittgenstein (1980) mocked; 'Whatever the event does leave behind, it isn't the memory'. Some theories even do away with the concept of memory traces altogether; others rely on computer metaphors for explanation. However, even resorting to computer analogies fails. Memory is not a replica, it is not subject to linear physics, it is plastic and dynamic, but it is also tightly bound in with semantics. Semantic constraints give meaning and provide creativity. As the biologist Gerald Edelman remarks, 'every act of memory is an act of imagination'.

Memory classification

Memory has been subject to many different classifications, perhaps a reflection on the tricky nature of the subject. In fact, as the above introduction reveals, over time analogies with prevailing technology have guided our theories. Further, much of memory theory has been based upon data from patients with brain damage, which, while being one legitimate source of knowledge, may reflect poorly on memory processes in the intact brain.

As a generalisation, three major dichotomies of memory have been identified. These are intrinsic (implicit) and extrinsic (explicit), short-term and long-term, and verbal and non-verbal.

Implicit (procedural) learning refers to that which takes place without conscious awareness, the kind of memory we all integrate into our daily lives, often reflected in motor sequences. Explicit memory in contrast is intentional and conscious. Short-term memory refers to that of limited storage capacity, usually of a matter of seconds, the kind of quick skill needed to recall a telephone number read to us from directory enquiries. Long-term memory is any memory that falls outside short-term memory, and has several subdivisions. Semantic memory is memory for facts, words and knowledge, which tends to be stable throughout adult life, unless there is obvious damage to the left temporal lobe.

These subdivisions will not be elaborated on further, but they do serve to highlight some confusion in the current scientific structuring of our knowledge about memory. In part an attempt has been made to localise anatomical structures to the different types of memory, but this too remains unresolved for many components.

From a medicolegal context, the kind of memories most discussed are long-term, in particular autobiographical (mainly episodic) memories, and the main neuroanatomical underpinnings are in a neuronal system which involves the medial temporal and diencephalic structures of the brain and the frontal lobes.

Accident-related amnesia

The relevance of understanding amnesias following accidents to the theme of somatisation is twofold. First, accidents are often associated with head injuries, and the contribution of the latter to the overall picture of somatisation may be relevant. Second, amnesias, even following head injuries, are not necessarily neurological in origin, and may be psychologically induced.

The usual way to assess the severity of a head injury is by the length of the post-traumatic amnesia (PTA). The first enquiry is about the pretraumatic or retrograde amnesia (RA), what the person remembers up to the immediate time of the accident. PTA is defined as the point in time after an accident when the patient can give a clear and consecutive account of what is happening around him or her (Symonds and Russell, 1943). This does not include islands of memory, which may be recalled, for example if a patient is moved at the site of the accident and experiences pain or some other very emotional event. Neither does it include false memories, evoked by delirium, an amalgam of hallucinations and delusions which may cloud the immediate post-head-injury state, or the much commoner confabulations, with misrecalls of experiences, that emerge in a confusional state (Whitty and Zangwill, 1977).

In general, the RA is shorter than the PTA, and a very prolonged RA in the presence of a short PTA suggests a psychogenic amnesia. It is unusual to find a RA lasting longer than a week. There is not much correlation between the RA and the PTA, and the PTA is usually taken as the more relevant indicator of the severity of the head injury.

These amnesias do not necessarily correlate with the duration of any loss of consciousness, and different scales are used to monitor the latter, such as the Glasgow Coma Scale, which assesses eye opening (none to spontaneous), motor responses (none to obeying commands) and verbal responses (none to oriented). This is usually scored with a maximum of 15 points.

With time the RA tends to shrink, with items from the more distant past recovering first (Russell and Nathan, 1946). However, an RA may persist after the resolution of the PTA, although generally PTA, once present, tends to remain unchanged.

There are a number of problems in the assessment of these amnesias, especially their retrospective assessment. These are compounded in medicolegal settings. First, patients are often given sedative medications in an ambulance, or on arrival at a hospital, and these may be sufficient to cloud memory. Second, on admission to hospital, patients may sleep, and it is often only on awakening that they will have regained clear consciousness. Both situations lead to a false prolongation of the PTA. In some patients, with repeated questioning about the length of the PTA over time for the purpose of medicolegal reports, the deficit seems to get longer – there are no physiological explanations for this effect, but the influence of others in encouraging this distortion is suggested (Gronwall and Wrightson, 1980).

It is very important to understand that amnesia is common in patients who suffer from psychological shock at the time of the accident. Indeed, psychogenic amnesia for the traumatic moments is one of the cardinal symptoms of a posttraumatic stress disorder (PTSD). It is related to dissociation (see below), and seems to be a predictor of the later development of PTSD. However, it is not uncommon in medicolegal settings to evaluate a patient who has had a head injury and reports a PTA which in reality can be readily explained by a psychological rather than neurological process.

Following head injuries, patients may continue to complain of memory difficulties. This may be due to ongoing neurological impairment, either as a reversible postconcussion syndrome, or as a less reversible outcome of damage to the cerebral structures that are essential to laying down and retrieving memories. Alternatively, the memory problems may be due to the development of psychiatric disorders (such as anxiety, depression or alcohol or drug abuse), be a feature of a dissociative disorder or a somatoform disorder, or be a part of the pseudodementia spectrum.

These anterograde amnesias (AA) can be difficult to assess, even with neuropsychological test batteries. Where there has been obvious cerebral damage, especially of a focal nature, this may be quite easily confirmed by neuropsychological tests. However, in the kind of cases considered here, patients complain of memory deficits years after a head injury, assessment of the RA and PTA has been difficult and controversial, and psychological factors are clearly seen to be clouding the results of neuropsychological assessment. Often memory and other neuropsychological functions have been tested serially, and an initial improvement at say 1 year has been noted, only for performance to deteriorate later. In general, after mild head injuries, deficits rarely last more than 3 months and the majority of recovery takes place in the first 12 months (Kapur, 1988; Goldstein and Levin, 1991). While there are some neurological causes for late deterioration, such as hydrocephalus, which must be ruled out, an understanding of such problems requires familiarity with the syndromes of psychogenic amnesia.

Psychogenic amnesia

Psychogenic amnesia, referred to in both ICD-10 (World Health Organization, 1993) and DSM-IV (American Psychiatric Association, 1994) as dissociative amnesia, is also cited as a diagnostic criterion for PTSD. It represents a variety of dissociative disorder, discussed in more detail below, and refers to loss of recall of important personal information (episodic memory), too extensive to be explained

Table 5.1 Psychogenic amnesias listed in order
of chronicity

Situational amnesia
Posttraumatic stress disorder[a]
Ganser's syndrome[b]
Psychogenic fugue
Hysterical dementia
Depressive dementia
Multiple personality disorder[b]
Histrionic personality disorder[a]

[a] Amnesia is commonly but not invariably present.
[b] The nosology of these syndromes is least certain.
Reproduced from Mace and Trimble (1991), with
permission.

by ordinary forgetfulness, and not explained by underlying neurological damage. It can be an isolated episode, it can be recurrent, and it can be chronic.

The main syndromes are listed in Table 5.1. Those towards the bottom of the list are more chronic than those at the top. The syndromes marked with superscript *a* indicate that amnesia is not necessarily present in these disorders, and that the nosological validity of the syndrome has been the subject of continual doubt.

Some of the disorders appear to be regularly associated with memory problems, particularly for example depressive dementia, with impairment of new learning, or psychogenic fugues. In the latter there is an initial retrograde, possibly global, amnesia, which is classically followed by a residual amnesia for the period of wandering following recovery from the initial amnesia.

Others, particularly those that have been referred to as hysterical amnesias, can exhibit a wide range of presentations. They may include general amnesias (with a lifelong retrograde loss) to more localised amnesias (with a circumscribed episodic memory loss), to selective amnesias, with loss restricted to material that is systematically linked by association to a traumatic event. There are also continuous amnesias, with an inability to recall experienced events, that continue from the time of an accident up to the time of medical examination.

Not a lot of attention has been paid to the variability of the time course of these various forms of amnesia, but differences in duration are likely to be of considerable significance for questions of pathogenesis, diagnosis and treatment. Kopelman (1999) put forward a tentative classification of the psychogenic amnesias that highlighted a division between impairments that were discretely episodic, and those that were sustained, a primary distinction he also made when classifying 'organic amnesias'. It is important to recognise, however, that while some psychogenic amnesias are characteristically protracted (depressive dementia may last for years if untreated), and others brief (situational amnesias), others can be highly variable in their course.

The disruption of biographical memory for identity in psychogenic fugue, as an example, may persist for a matter of hours only, or may go on for years. In the case reported by Pratt (1977), a 45-year-old man was brought into hospital for an investigation of 'fits'. He had an amnesia lasting for the previous 15 years, being unaware of his personal identity, or of any biographical details of his previous life. As he claimed to have no name, he selected one from a shop opposite the hospital, James Williamson. He gradually started to relearn general information, and then was found by his brother. His real name, remarkably, turned out to be William Jameson. Three years later, when his mother was ill, he met his wife and three children, and, at his mother's deathbed, the memory of his former life returned in full.

Situational amnesia

This describes brief memory failures of apparently psychological origin, and represents the most common variety of psychogenic amnesia. It is seen in all ages, and is not necessarily associated with other forms of psychopathology. For example, if the short-lived memory impairment is linked to a particular emotional situation, it may be brief and self-limiting, as in PTSD. More commonly its onset and offset encompass an event that is perceived as traumatic, and the memory may be lost for all events within the given period, or, occasionally, for a group of memories that are thematically linked to the trauma.

It is unclear whether a disorder of memory such as this represents a failure of retrieval of stored memories, as would be consistent with a theoretical construction of the psychoanalytic concept of repression, or whether it is a problem with encoding new information. In the latter case, the episodic nature of the personal anterograde amnesia found in these cases might be explained by a temporary disruption of encoding as a consequence of high arousal precipitated by the emotional triggering event. This theory has been tested in the sense that sometimes these amnesias are seen to be reversible, either spontaneously, or with the use of suggestion or hypnosis or abreaction. However, the results are highly variable.

Psychogenic fugue

This has the status of being a distinct syndrome in DSM-IV. In a psychogenic fugue, an amnesia arises during, and can be subsequently limited to, a period in which there is evidence of behavioural changes. These take the form of wandering, in a superficially purposeful way, during which time subjects are unable to recall their

Table 5.2 Clinical assessment of fugue states

Psychogenic fugue	Postictal fugue
Identifiable emotional precipitant (may be preceded by fit or head injury)	Unlikely to be patient's first presentation of epilepsy
'Wandering' is socially appropriate	Perambulation accompanied by evident confusion
Recovery of orientation usually gradual	Recovery rapid
EEG usually normal	EEG abnormal

EEG, electroencephalogram.

past. As a consequence, the patient may assume a different identity. The episodes are usually brief, lasting a matter of hours, but if the initial amnesia for identity persists, the new identity may be consolidated and retained, as in the remarkable case quoted above by Pratt.

Psychogenic fugues usually follow some obvious precipitating trauma, although a history of prior head injury is not uncommon. Clinically they are often associated with a depressive disorder, and for a long time have been suggested to act as a means of coping with active suicidal impulses.

Psychogenic fugues need to be distinguished from epileptic automatisms, those events that occur following an epileptic seizure where wandering may occur; help with the differential diagnosis is given in Table 5.2. A further important diagnostic distinction is between psychogenic fugues and the consequences of alcoholism, namely alcoholic blackouts. Unfortunately, alcoholism, head injury, secondary seizures and depressive fugues tend to afflict a similar population, emphasising the need for great care in diagnosis.

Pseudodementia

This term applies to persisting symptoms of memory loss and intellectual impairment that mimic neurological dementias, but which are attributed to the presence of an independent psychiatric disorder. Depression, schizophrenia, hysteria and personality disorders have all been implicated, and although the term 'pseudodementia' is not academically satisfying, the importance of the diagnosis is that, unlike the majority of cases of neurological dementia, pseudodementia is a reversible cognitive state, particularly if underlying it there is a depressive or anxiety-related condition.

While depression is usually characterised by the overriding change of the affect, in some patients failures of memory and concentration come to dominate the clinical picture such that the depression becomes ignored. Careful history-taking is relevant,

Table 5.3 Differentiation of depressive dementia from organic (Alzheimer-type) dementia

Depressive dementia	Degenerative dementia
History	
Family history of affective disorder	Family history of dementia
Past episodes of affective illness or resolving episodes of cognitive impairment	Recent history of subtle personality change
Rapid onset	Insidious onset
Associated features	
Biological and cognitive symptoms of depression	Symptoms of cortical involvement (i.e. dysphasias, dyspraxias, etc.)
Behaviour	
Patient complains of memory loss (and other inadequacies)	Insight linked to denial and catastrophic reactions
Orienting skills largely intact	Visible problems with topographic memory
Mental state	
Affect depressed	Affect shallow even if depressed
Poor performance on cognitive tests through lack of participation (i.e. 'don't know' responses)	Poor performance through incorrect responses which reflect objective difficulty of test
Course	
Resolving with treatment for affective symptoms	Exacerbated by CNS depressants

CNS, central nervous system.

as always, but the distinction between a depressive pseudodementia and the onset of a dementia due to neurological disease can be difficult. Neuropsychological testing becomes important, since the pattern of neuropsychological responses in patients with pseudodementia (see below) is often characteristic, as indeed it may be in neurological dementias.

Table 5.3 gives a summary of some of the clinical differences between depressive dementia and degenerative dementia. Valuable information is often obtained from a carer or close relative, which allows the distinction between the two disorders to be clarified further. Behavioural observations in unfamiliar situations and at home can be invaluable.

Another variety of pseudodementia is hysterical dementia. In this condition there are clinical features of a neurological disorder (dementia) which appear to correspond more to an idea in the mind of the patient as to what dementia should be like than any known underlying neurological problem. This often takes the form

Table 5.4 Comparison of two modes of persistent psychogenic amnesia

Hysterical dementia	Depressive dementia
Onset	
(Both rapid and may follow emotional precipitants) Hysterical dementia more likely to follow a physical trauma	
Incidence	
Rare; all adults	Common, especially elderly depressives
Past history	
Conversion symptoms	Affective episodes
Course	
Highly unpredictable	Remitting and recurring with affective disorder
Presentation	
Lack of expressed concern, ready demonstrations of inability to remember	Protestations of memory loss (in excess of actual difficulties)
Associated findings	
(Often) conversion symptoms (e.g. dysphasias, anaesthesias)	Other features of depression, viz. agitation, retardation, fatigue
Memory loss	
Bizarre in pattern (e.g. global retrograde with loss of personal identity; continuous amnesia with defective immediate recall)	Patchy anterograde with some difficulty learning new material
Test performance	
Highly variable, may produce paradoxically bad responses	Particularly bad on tests requiring effort after active recall

Reproduced from Mace and Trimble (1991, p. 445), with permission.

of a quite literally transparent imitation of patients with low intelligence, and psychological testing reveals gross internal inconsistencies; often the scores of patients are entirely incompatible with any kind of existence at all. Distinctions between depressive dementia and hysterical dementia are shown in Table 5.4. A clinical problem is that mood changes often appear to bring on or herald the onset of the hysterical dementia, and a combination of affective disorder, conversion symptoms and cognitive impairment is frequently seen. This happens in a medicolegal setting when, following a relatively trivial head injury, patients (often of middle age) develop a depressive illness, during which complaints of concentration and memory difficulties arise. They then come to believe (often because they are incorrectly informed by those advising them) that they have suffered from cerebral injury and brain damage. The depression gradually resolves, but the cognitive picture disintegrates further, to that of a classical hysterical dementia.

Hysterical amnesia

Unusual patterns of memory deficit that cannot be attributed to neurological problems and which seem encapsulated to a memory problem are sometimes encountered. Again, such cases sometimes involve episodes of unconsciousness (through head injury, for example), and can persist for many years.

A variant is referred to as the Ganser syndrome; the importance of this condition is that, when originally described by Ganser, it was associated with prisoners who were thought to have considerable secondary gain from the development of the symptoms.

It has one key symptom, namely *Vorbeireden*, when patients respond to questions with answers that are consistently wrong and often patently absurd, but which approximate to the true answer and therefore closely betray a knowledge of the required response. A typical question such as: how many legs does a spider have? is answered as seven. The Ganser syndrome is often heralded by some kind of physical trauma, and can be quite sudden in its eventual remission. Interestingly, in the original reports, patients often initially had some clouding of consciousness, and the role of psychogenesis in this particular disorder has always been one of considerable debate.

Personality disorders

The relationship between personality disorders and memory has been discussed in Chapter 2, and this debate is not repeated here. However, it is important to recognise that it is very important to take into account personality style when assessing patients who have amnesic deficits, since not only are some, for example the obsessional, more likely to complain about very small degrees of memory impairment than others, but, as noted, the memories of patients with borderline and histrionic personalities may simply lack detail, be poorly focused and reflect global, emotional-driven impressions.

Dissociation

It is unfortunate that this word is so imprecise in meaning, denoting at the same time symptoms (dissociative amnesia, dissociative fugue), syndromes (dissociative disorders) and a mechanism. DSM-IV refers to dissociation as a disruption in the usually integrated functions of consciousness, memory, identity and perception (American Psychiatric Association, 1994, p. 477). The disorders listed are dissociative amnesia, dissociative fugue, dissociative identity disorder and depersonalisation disorder. The relevant syndromes have already been described. However, the overlaps between them and hysterical conversion disorders and malingering must seem clear. Dissociation has become a central mechanism for the explanation of medically unexplained symptoms (see Chapter 8), and for most, if not all, of the psychogenic amnestic syndromes. In addition, dissociation seems associated in some way with physical and sexual abuse. Further, pathological dissociation blends with physiological dissociation, a cerebral mechanism available to us all, and used at various stages and certain times of life, which lies at the heart of the unconsciousness/consciousness debate. The mechanisms underlying dissociation are discussed in more detail in Chapter 8. Suffice it to comment here that some of the newer theories emphasise normal as opposed to abnormal psychological processes.

The term 'dissociation' has been too widely applied and, for example, it is now cited as the reason why we can drive a car and talk at the same time, the car-driving being automatic and 'dissociated' from immediate conscious awareness. However, in such settings, the act can be brought to awareness by a switch of attention; there is nothing unusual or remotely pathological about the situation. Dissociation is better reserved for events that are excluded from consciousness and inaccessible to voluntary recall (Nemiah, 1991; Cardeña, 1994). Information ordinarily accessible to the individual is not therefore dissociated. This use includes amnesia associated with some other psychological experiences such as hypnosis, and neurological states such as blind-sight. In blind-sight, patients with occipital lesions who state they are blind can be shown to have visual discriminating ability by appropriate tests, locating visual stimuli in space, but being unaware of their accuracy. This removes the definition of dissociation from every less than conscious act we perform in the course of daily activities. Depersonalisation and derealisation states are also referred to under the rubric of dissociation, but seem qualitatively distinct from the above, and perhaps should be regarded separately. The psychological construct mostly referred to in relation to dissociation is repression.

In clinical and research practice, several scales and assessment schedules have been developed to measure dissociation, including the Dissociative Experiences Scale (DES) (Bernstein and Putnam, 1986), and the Structured Clinical Interview for DSM Dissociative Disorders (SCID-D) (Steinberg, 1992). However, these have no place in the medicolegal assessment of patients.

False memories

As already noted, memory is friable, deniable and unreliable. We may have continuous perceptions, but our memory is of sequences and not of a continuous chain of events, laid down and replayed as if a video camera had recorded a scene. Neither is memory replicated as in a computer, in some recognised code. Memory is a property of a non-linear system, based on synaptic changes in the brain, and as such is plastic, associative and degenerative. Furthermore, our perceptions are not veridical, but context- and state-dependent. An event leaves a trace in memory but, as Wittgenstein remarked, whatever the event leaves behind, it is not memory. The sediment is multilayered, biographically laden, murky. We simply do not carry around sets of mental pictures in our heads which we can call up with ease; we tell more than we can remember. There is no logical reason to believe in a direct causal connection between an event remembered and the remembered event. Memory works by selection, semantic constraints give meaning, and it is a creative process.

In recent times the phenomenon of false memories has become popular, but it can be seen that at one level, all our memories are false. That is simply the way of the nervous system. In clinical practice, false memories present in a variety of settings, from confabulation to 'recovered' memories of child abuse to pseudologia fantastica (Kopelman, 1999).

With confabulation patients spontaneously report false events as if true, and can be easily persuaded to confirm things that have never happened (such as 'we have met before, haven't we? Remember when . . .'). It is commonly met in patients with organic amnesias, especially when frontal lobe function is compromised. There seems no self-control of the output, there is defective self-monitoring of performance, but in addition social constraints alter patients' responses.

False confessions are another type of false memory, in which eventually the confessors themselves believe in the reality of their supposed deeds. Four types of person are involved (Gudjonsson and MacKeith, 1990). There are those who have a craving for publicity; those who wish to protect a real criminal; those with such guilt about some other misdemeanour that they feel some vindication from it by confessing to another crime; and those with a psychiatric disorder of reality testing, bordering on the pseudologia fantastica. Gudjonsson and MacKeith (1990) also refer to the memory-distrust syndrome, in which people so much distrust their own memories that they come to rely on external information to guide their memory.

At the centre of the discussions on false retrieval stands the controversy over recovered memories, especially for earlier abuse, notably sexual abuse. People come to believe or seem to believe in events that they claim happened earlier in their lives that simply never happened. Such memories are said to remain dormant, apparently having been 'repressed' for years, but can be evoked by appropriate methods (such as psychotherapy or hypnosis). The debate has been considerable, and it is ongoing. It is acknowledged that sexual abuse is not uncommon, and that such abuse may be a forerunner of later psychopathology. Further, there are countless cases of patients who were sexually abused and later developed symptoms or sought therapy, but who never forgot the abuse. However, in studies that have been set up to examine the issue of recovered memories, verifying the earlier episode(s) of abuse has always been a stumbling block. The arguments go back to Freud, who initially developed his theories on the basis that his patients had been sexually abused, and that this was intimate to the development of their conversion symptoms. His 'seduction hypothesis' implied that memories of actual events were 'repressed', and remained unresolved. For Janet they were 'dissociated' from normal consciousness. Such memories remained inaccessible, unless insight was gained in therapy (psychoanalysis). Freud then revised this to consider that what was repressed was not the memory of actual seductions, but fantasised sexual experiences, on which basis he developed his psychological theories of the development of the infant mind.

In spite of all the recent brouhaha over the issue of false memories, the scientific evidence that people recover veridical memories of earlier abuse after long periods of amnesia is lacking. In many cases, it is only single case histories that are given, and often the alleged abuse seems to have taken place before the brain has developed sufficiently to lay down effective episodic memory traces (which occurs between the ages of 4 and 6). Implicit rather than episodic memory is suggested as a possible mechanism, body memories being evoked via the sensorimotor system, but there is no evidence that implicit memories translate to episodic ones.

A working party set up by the Royal College of Psychiatrists (UK) examined the issue in considerable detail (Brandon *et al.*, 1998). The false-memory syndrome was defined as 'a condition in which a person's identity and interpersonal relationships are centred around a memory of a traumatic experience which is objectively false but in which the person strongly believes . . . The memory tends to take on a life of its own, encapsulated and resistant to correction' (Brandon *et al.*, 1998, p. 297).

The report concluded that: 'no evidence exists for the repression and recovery of verified, severely traumatic events, and their role in symptom formation has yet to be proved' (p. 303). Recovered memories were narratives rather than memories *per se*, becoming increasingly elaborate with time. A firmly held belief rather than a clear memory was the key.

The report pointed out that there is evidence from psychological experiments that 'flashbulb memories', that is, memories for events of such significance as the assassination of President Kennedy, are very unreliable, but are also held with conviction. For example, a group of students were asked where they were when the spacecraft Challenger blew up, one day after the event. Two and a half years later they were asked the same question. None of the later memories were entirely accurate, and in a third they were wildly inaccurate (Neisser and Harsch, 1992).

The Royal College report noted that: 'suggestibility and confabulation increase with the length of time between the event and later attempts to recall it. Repeated questioning over time and the authority of the questioner also heighten suggestibility' (Brandon *et al.*, 1998, p. 299). Subjects in laboratory studies can be shown to incorporate deliberately suggested false memories into their biographies, and with imagination of supposed events, 'imagination inflation' occurs in some individuals. Simply imagining an event can increase someone's belief that an event actually happened (Loftus, 1997).

Such comments and conclusions have considerable relevance for understanding PTSD and amnesias in the medicolegal setting, and reflect on the fragility of the whole process of history-taking in the clinical setting, especially several years after an event has occurred. In PTSD, there is evidence that memory amplification occurs with time. Southwick *et al.* (1997) gave questionnaires 1 month and 2 years after return from combat to 59 traumatised National Guard reservists involved in Operation Desert Storm of the Gulf War. Inconsistencies of recall for events of a highly traumatic nature were found in most subjects, and amplification of memory for the events was the norm.

False memories are created when actual memories are combined with the suggestions of others, and among those others are doctors, therapists and lawyers. In this way, postaccident information becomes integrated into subsequent accounts of the event, and influences clinical symptomatology. The accident becomes a *leitmotiv* around which the melody assembles; there is a metamorphosis of fragments, and a constant transformation.

The way that proper investigation of these difficult matters is hampered by lay interference is reflected through lobby groups, such as the False Memory Syndrome Foundation (USA) and the British False Memory Society (BFMS), both supporting accused families, and alternative organisations (including recovered memory therapists, whose bible is *The Courage to Heal* by Bass and Davis, 1994) supporting the apparently traumatised victims. Such polarisations are encouraged by the incredibility of some recollections. These include abduction by aliens, ritual satanic abuse and being stuck in the maternal fallopian tubes. The novel *Fragments* by Wilkomirski, which described childhood experiences in a concentration camp, was found to be fake, but the author still persisted with his story (DelMonte, 2001).

The above controversies and investigations have led to a questioning of the concepts of repression and dissociation, and of the reality of some of the associated clinical syndromes, including the false-memory syndrome and dissociative (multiple) identity disorder. Several respected investigators believe the latter to be iatrogenic, arising in suggestible patients along with the expectations of the investigating therapist (Merskey, 1995).

The problem of false memory extends then well beyond the false-memory syndrome, and should be seen as very important in the evaluation of all histories taken in a medicolegal setting; memory is simply unreliable! It is also relevant in the context of false denials in a forensic setting, and in the concept of 'faking good' in a civilian setting. This brings us back to the area of exaggeration and malingering, and how they may be detected with neuropsychological tests.

Malingering and memory – neuropsychological tests

In forensic psychiatry, claims for amnesia of a criminal event are common. Thus 20–40% of criminals deny recall of their alleged crime. In this context, it has to be remembered that to be convicted of a crime, it must be shown that the person committed a voluntary act, and has a *mens rea*, or guilty mind. A sane person, not acting voluntarily, must be acquitted. Leaving aside the issue of automatism, since the case of *Podola* ([1959] 3 WLR 718; [1959] 3 All ER 418), in which it was contended that, following a head injury, the accused had total amnesia for the offence, and was therefore unable to construct his own defence or instruct counsel, amnesia is no bar to a trial (Padola was found to be feigning, and the latter decision was taken by the Court of Appeal).

Nevertheless, claims for amnesia are common. Sometimes a medical cause comes to light, such as an alcoholic blackout, an epileptic seizure or a psychotic paramnesia. More often, mechanisms of dissociation are invoked, and an association with depressed mood has been shown (Kopelman, 1987). Since many crimes for which amnesia is claimed involve homicide, and since they are committed in states of high arousal, often associated with alcohol use, some neurophysiological mechanism may be suggested in some cases. However, the issue of simulation is invariably raised, and techniques to detect malingered memory complaints have been developed. A number of these have been used in assessing patients in civil cases.

Assessment of memory

There are a number of standard memory tests employed by neuropsychologists which have been developed essentially to detect mnestic problems secondary to neurological damage. These were initially tested on patients with obvious neurological disease or damage, and the results taken over into routine clinical practice. However, while they may have reliability and validity in certain settings, most have not been validated in a medicolegal setting.

Their interpretation is often unclear, but properly is the provenance of neuropsychologists, namely those psychologists who have special training in the neurosciences, and have practised with brain-damaged patients. It must be appreciated that as such, neuropsychological testing represents an interaction between a person (patient or claimant) and the neuropsychologist. The interaction is dependent on many factors, including the mental state and cooperability of the former, and interpretation of the results in the setting of psychiatric illness represents a significant challenge. The results are dependent on the effort and will of the subject, neither of which are measurable, and are subject to external incentives.

In recent years it has become appreciated that memory problems secondary to neurological damage occur following interruption of certain cortical–subcortical brain circuits, especially involving the hippocampus, the thalamus and the

Table 5.5 Some standardised
tests of memory

Wechsler Memory Scale (Revised)
California Verbal Learning Test
Auditory-Verbal Learning Test
Recognition Memory Tests

Table 5.6 Some standardised clinical
and neuropsychological tests of
frontal executive functions

Word and figure fluency
Proverb and metaphor interpretion
Three-step hand position test (Luria)
Copying tasks (multiple loops)
Rhythm-tapping tasks
Cognitive estimates
Maze tests
Block design test
Stroop test
Wisconsin card-sorting test
Weigl colour-form sorting test

white-matter fibres connecting these structures. However, it is also known that adequate functioning of memory involves nuclei such as the amygdala, which are involved particularly in the emotional tone of memory, and the prefrontal cortices. The latter are just as susceptible to damage following head trauma as are the anterior temporal lobe structures (including the amygdala and the hippocampus), and are particularly involved in working memory – that component of memory that holds online ongoing tasks, allowing successful completion. The frontal lobes, representing a very significant portion of the overall brain volume, are referred to as executive, and their function, amongst others, involves planning and execution of moment-to-moment activities. In this context, some comments are made here about testing of 'executive' function, especially in the medicolegal setting.

A list of standard tests used to test memory is shown in Table 5.5, some tasks of executive function are shown in Table 5.6 and some neuropsychological tests helpful for detecting dissimulation are shown in Table 5.7.

Usually a battery of memory tests is given, and attempts are made to assess the main subcategories of memory, namely verbal and non-verbal, immediate and delayed and the skills of recognition and recall. However, memory is liable to be

Table 5.7 Some tests used to identify malingering

Rey 15-Item Memory Test – see text

Recognition Memory Tests – see text

Perceptual Learning Tasks – recognition of fragments of words or pictures following previous exposure to the complete item[a]

Stem Completion Tasks – finding an appropriate word ending when only given the stem after previous exposure to the complete item[a]

Coin-In-The-Hand Test – examiner has a coin in the hand and shows it to the patient, the coin is then placed behind the examiner's back and the patient is asked to indicate which hand it is in following distraction[b]

---

[a] Amnesics can easily do this task.

[b] Malingerers tend to go for the wrong hand.

interfered with by attentional factors, and if attention is disturbed, then the process of laying down memory and of recall will also be disturbed.

It is usual to obtain some estimate of the person's preaccident or premorbid intelligence. Some indication of this comes from an analysis of school and other achievement records, but the National Adult Reading Test is a standard. This test of reading ability (a part of semantic memory) is based on the clinical fact that, in brain damage, verbal skills are more robust than others, and verbal ability corresponds well with overall IQ.

The Wechsler Memory Scale includes a number of separate subtests, which tap into several memory components, including concentration, and summary indices are derived, which, like IQ scores, have a mean of 100. Included within are tasks of logical memory, in which subjects are asked to recall the content of two stories read to them (immediately and after a 30-minute delay), and a Verbal Paired Associates test in which the task is to learn word pairs (baby–cries), and then to recall the second one when only the first is presented. The association can be simple or hard (obey–inch).

Other tests measure a person's ability to learn over several trials. One is the California Verbal Learning Test, in which 16 words are given, the list being repeated five times. Then a second list is given, serving to interfere with the first list, after which recall of the first list is requested. Since the words from the first list come from four semantic categories, it is possible then to ask the responder to recall words by category – testing cued as opposed to free recall. A simpler variant is the Auditory-Verbal Learning Task, a 15-item five-trial test, from which recall (immediate and delayed), and recognition memory can be tapped.

Forced-choice tests are popular, in which recognition of words or non-verbal material (pictures or faces) is noted after initial presentations and after representation intermixed with distracter (new) items (Warrington, 1985, 1996). Chance alone would lead to the correct recognition 50% of the time.

Over time, many other memory tasks have been developed, for example, to tap into biographical memory, remote memory (questions covering several decades of verifiable information, such as famous people), and tests for procedural (intrinsic) knowledge, but these are not usually tested in the medicolegal setting.

Malingering and memory

The difficulties of interpreting the results of memory tests are compounded in medicolegal practice by several factors. First, as emphasised, the majority of tests have not been validated in this setting. This can prove an easy trap for the neophyte (or the ignorant) since it is not possible to assume that the results from patients with demonstrable brain damage can be carried over into a context where there may be considerable argument about the possibility of cerebral damage, even though the neuropsychological tests support the proposition. It must be noted that brain damage should never be assumed from neuropsychological tests alone.

Confounding factors include the presence of psychiatric illness, such as anxiety, depression or a psychosis. In all three settings, but particularly in psychosis, the results simply become unreliable. The problem of pseudodementia has already been noted. Embraced under that concept is a range of clinical presentations, from an underlying depression to the Ganser syndrome, to frank malingering. Somatoform disorders are relevant here, especially on account of the potential for dissociation.

Because of the ever-present possibility of malingering, especially in a forensic setting, much effort has gone into trying to detect malingered memory disorders using standardised tests. The results have been variable, but some tests are used regularly in personal injury cases where complaints of memory are present, and the possibility of brain damage raised.

As a generalisation, tests to detect malingering disguise simple tasks to seem more complicated. The tasks are often ones that are known to be achievable by patients with a severe neurological amnesia and, usually, the results from the claimant are so bizarre or bad that they would not be compatible with everyday existence! In fact, malingerers often produce test results rather worse than volunteers asked to simulate.

As a general point, claimants who are disoriented for time, place and person, but who are living in the community, with or without help, are simulating. Severe failure of autobiographical memory (can't-remember-anything syndrome) is only seen in the end stages of advanced dementia. Extreme variability is also very suspect, namely the claimant who says that he or she can be totally lost and disoriented, with no memory at all for days, and at other times is quite intact. It is always important to examine the tested neuropsychological profile and seek incongruities with the claimant's described lifestyle. Also the profile of responding should be checked for incongruities of test performance. For example, it is relevant to look both for errors of magnitude (greater than expected in a brain-injured patient) and errors in the pattern of responding.

Test for simulation tap into aspects of memory which are known to be intact in severely amnestic patients. Such patients perform normally or nearly normally on such tasks simulators fail, because the latter assume they should fail! In fact, it is quite unusual for a neurologically amnestic patient to show no learning, and so on a learning task (such as the Auditory Verbal Learning Task) recall over a succession of trials is expected, as is some retention of target words.

The forced-choice procedure is valuable, since it gives a 50/50 chance level, and the probability of the patient being amnesic can be calculated from the results. Since there are two alternatives, random responding gives 50% correct answers, and those who perform below chance must be deliberately giving incorrect responses, knowing the correct ones. Even severe amnesics perform better than chance, and simulators have been shown to perform below chance level on such recognition memory tests (Brandt et al., 1985).

Incongruity of performance may be noted, comparing results on more difficult (effort-requiring) and less difficult (automatic) components of a task or a battery. In general, digit span forward is longer than digit span backward; immediate recall is better than delayed recall; recognition is easier than recall. Some tests, such as the Trails test, have two components, one easier than the other. In this task, patients have to join up scattered dots. In part A, they are numbered consecutively, in part B there are numbers and letters, and the task changes from joining up sequenced numbers (1–2–3, etc.) to numbers and letters (1–A–2–B, etc.). Trails B is harder than Trails A. In another task, Raven's Progressive Matrices, simulators may perform badly on the easier items (Gudjonsson and Shackleton, 1986).

The Wechsler Memory Scale has been used to detect malingering, when the general memory score is higher than the attention–concentration index. On the California Verbal Learning Task, simulators have been shown to perform worse than controls, showing inconsistencies, such as demonstrating a practice effect with non-verbal, but not with verbal tasks. The Rey 15-item Memory Test (Rey, 1964) is commonly given. The subject is shown, for 10 seconds, 15 letters, numbers and shapes, arranged in five rows of three items per row. The items are patterned, and easy to recall. Participants are asked to reproduce the array, which is quite simple, and achieved by neurologically impaired patients (Lee et al., 1992).

Schmand et al. (1998) reported on the Amsterdam Short Term Memory Test. In their study they gave patients with a whiplash injury and cognitive complaints a task, which has 30 items. Each item has five printed words from the same semantic category, which are read aloud and remembered. A simple arithmetical task is

Table 5.8 A threshold model for feigned amnesia

In an appropriate context, feigning should be fully investigated in cases of memory impairment in which any of the following indicators are present:

1. Impairment of attention or immediate memory that is much worse than impairment of overall learning and memory
2. Standardised scores on tests of recognition memory that are lower than standardised scores on tests of free recall
3. Reports of dense retrograde amnesia in the absence of other neurological abnormality
4. Reports of dense retrograde amnesia together with intact new learning and memory
5. Gross inconsistency between test performance and everyday functioning
6. Gross inconsistency across tests or testing occasions
7. Evasive, uncooperative or unusual test-taking behaviour

Reproduced from Cercy *et al.* (1997), with permission.

Table 5.9 Clinical decision model for the determination of feigned amnesia

---

In an appropriate context, feigned amnesia can be determined by either of the following:

1. Forced-choice recognition memory test performance that is worse than chance
2. Multiple indicators from Table 5.8, and strong corroborative evidence of feigned amnesia, including admission of feigning when given feedback on indicators in Table 5.8, or unequivocal independent evidence

---

then given as a distracter, and five words of the same semantic categories are then presented. The subject has to indicate the three words that were also in the first series. The maximum score was then 90 (3 times 30), and head-injured patients with neurological amnesias do well, scoring between 87 and 90. Low scores were found twice as frequently in litigation cases, and suggest malingering.

In practice there is no single neuropsychological test of malingering, and it is a developing pattern of findings and results which raises suspicion (Powell, 2004). Disproportionate deficits, bizarre responses, unexpected results and inconsistencies are all contributory.

A threshold model for feigned amnesia is given in Table 5.8 (Cercy *et al.*, 1997), and a clinical decision model recommended by the same authors in Table 5.9.

Frontal lobe syndromes

Executive function is often referred to in the context of frontal lobe activity. The important role of the frontal lobes in regulating behaviour has been appreciated for many years, but only in the past two decades have neuropsychologists paid much attention to detecting frontal deficits on neuropsychological tests. A number have been developed, and several more are being evaluated.

Early clinical reports, such as that of the American Phineas Gage who, after his frontal lobes were shattered by a metal bar in an accident, underwent a marked personality change, emphasised the role of the frontal cortex in behaviour (Harlow, 1868). There are various pathologies that lead to frontal lobe damage, including brain tumours, cerebrovascular accidents, some degenerative diseases like frontal lobe dementia and cerebral trauma. Over time various frontal syndromes have been defined; the clinical characteristics of the three principal syndromes are shown in Table 5.10. In reality, many patients, particularly following frontal lobe damage from head trauma, show an admixture of symptomatology.

One of the specific behaviour deficits seen after frontal lobe damage relates to attention, with patients showing distractibility and poor attention. They present with poor memory, which is sometimes referred to as 'forgetting to remember'. This retrieval problem is different from the amnesia of temporal lobe origin and may be reflected in paramnesic errors such as reduplicative paramnesia. The thinking of frontal lobe patients tends to be concrete and they may show perseveration and stereotypy of their responses. The perseveration, with an inability to switch from one line of thinking to another, leads to difficulties with arithmetical calculations such as serial 7s or carry-over subtractions. Aphasia is sometimes seen in association with anterior frontal lesions, referred to as dynamic aphasia. Patients have well preserved motor speech, and no anomia; repetition is intact, but they show difficulty in propositionising, and active speech is severely impaired.

Other features of frontal lobe syndromes include reduced activity, particularly with a diminution of spontaneous activity, lack of drive, inability to plan ahead and lack of concern. Sometimes associated with this are bouts of restless, aimless uncoordinated behaviour. The affect is often disturbed, with apathy and emotional blunting, and the patient showing an indifference to the world around him or her. Clinically this picture can closely resemble that of a major depressive illness with psychomotor retardation.

In contrast, on other occasions euphoria and disinhibition are described. This euphoria is not that of a mania, however, and has a rather empty quality to it. This disinhibition can lead to markedly abnormal behaviour, often associated with outbursts of irritability and aggression.

Some authors have distinguished between lesions of the lateral frontal cortex, linked more to the motor structures of the brain, leading to disturbances of movement and action with perseveration and inertia, and lesions of the orbital areas, interlinked with the emotional (limbic system) areas of the brain, leading to disinhibition and changes of affect. The term 'pseudopsychopathic' has been used to describe the clinical features of this latter syndrome (Blumer and Benson, 1975).

Table 5.10 Clinical characteristics of the three principal
frontal lobe syndromes

Orbitofrontal syndrome (disinhibited)
Disinhibited, impulsive behaviour ('pseudopsychopathic')
Inappropriate jocular affect, euphoria
Emotional lability
Poor judgement and insight
Distractibility
Environmental dependence

Frontal convexity syndrome (apathetic)
Apathetic (occasional brief angry or aggressive outbursts common)
Indifference
Psychomotor retardation
Motor perseveration and impersistence
Loss of set
Stimulus boundedness
Discrepant motor and verbal behaviour
Motor-programming deficits
   Three-step hand sequence
   Alternating programmes
   Reciprocal programmes
   Rhythm-tapping
   Multiple tapping
   Multiple loops
Poor word-list generation
Poor abstraction and categorisation
Segmented approach to visuospatial analysis

Anterior cingulate
Impaired motivation
Akinetic mutism
Apathy
Poverty of speech
Indifference to pain

Adapted from Cummings (1985, p. 58) and Mega and Cummings
(1994), with permission.

A third syndrome, the medial frontal–cingulate syndrome, is also described,
marked by akinesia, sometimes mutism, but also with gait disturbances and sometimes incontinence.

After large frontal lobe lesions, especially with involvement of medial structures,
the so-called apathetico-akinetico-abulic syndrome may occur, in which patients

Table 5.11 Some useful tests of frontal lobe function

Word fluency and figure fluency

Abstract thinking (If I have 18 books and two bookshelves, and I want twice as many books on one shelf as the other, how many books on each shelf?)

Proverb and metaphor interpretation

Wisconsin Card-Sorting Task

Other sorting tasks

Block design

Maze test

Hand position test (three-step hand sequence)

Copying tasks (multiple loops)

Rhythm-tapping tasks

Cognitive estimates

lie around passively, being unaroused, doing little, being unable to complete tasks or follow commands. Abulia refers to the syndrome of lack of will, and is not uncommonly seen in patients with a variety of neuropsychiatric disorders, often with pathology in the frontal lobes and basal ganglia of the brain.

Clinical signs that may be associated with frontal lobe damage include sensory inattention to the contralateral sensory field, abnormalities of visual searching, echo phenomena such as echolalia and echopraxia, confabulation, hyperphagia and changes in cognitive function.

Detection of frontal lobe damage can be difficult, and special techniques are used to identify this. Often the standard neurological examination will be normal, as may be results from standardised neuropsychological tests such as the Wechsler Adult Intelligence Scale (WAIS). Of the various tasks that can be used to help demonstrate frontal pathology clinically, those given in Table 5.11 are recommended. However, not all patients with frontal damage show abnormalities on testing, and not all tests are exclusively found to be abnormal in frontal lobe pathology.

Cognitive tasks include the word fluency task, in which a patient is asked to generate as many words as possible beginning with a single letter in a minute (most people achieve around 15 or above). The figure task depends on patients reproducing specified drawings as rapidly as possible in a designated period of time. Proverb and metaphor interpretation can be remarkably concrete. Problem-solving, for example, carry-over additions or subtractions, can be tested by simple questions. Serial 7s is difficult to perform, particularly with subtraction where the decimal figure is changing (for example from the 70s to the 60s or the 60s to the 50s). Cognitive estimates are also used, asking patients to answer questions with no exact answers, such as 'how fast does a racehorse run?'

Specific laboratory-based tasks of abstract reasoning include the Wisconsin Card-Sorting Task and other sorting tasks. The essential nature of these is to arrange a variety of objects into groups depending on one common abstract property, for example, colour. In the Wisconsin Card-Sorting Task patients are given a pack of cards with symbols on them, which differ in form, colour and numbers. Four stimulus cards are available, and the patient has to place each response card in front of one of the four stimulus cards. The tester tells the patient if he or she is right or wrong, and the patient has to use that information to place the next card in front of the next stimulus card. The sorting is done arbitrarily into colour, form or number, and the patient's task is to shift the set from one type of stimulus response to another based on the information provided. Patients with frontal lobe lesions cannot overcome previously established responses, and show a high frequency of perseverative errors.

Patients with frontal lobe lesions do badly on maze learning tasks, and on block design tasks because of their inability to plan and organise their behaviour. The Tower of London task has patients rearranging beads on vertical rods to match a template, using as few moves as possible, which also involves planning skills.

Patients with frontal lobe abnormalities may show perseveration of motor tasks when carrying out sequences of motor actions. Skilled movements are no longer performed smoothly, and previously automated actions such as handwriting or playing a musical instrument may be impaired. Tests such as asking the patient to follow a succession of hand positions (with the hand first placed flat, then on the side and then in a fist on a flat surface, the Luria hand position task) or being asked to tap aloud a complex rhythm (for example, two loud and three soft beats) are incoordinate. Perseveration may be tested by asking the patient to draw, for example, a circle or copy a complex pattern with recurring shapes in it, which alternate with one another. The patient perseverates on the pattern.

One feature of many of the above tasks is the discrepancy between the patient's knowing what to do, and being able to verbalise the instructions, and the patient's failure when it comes to carrying out the motor act.

It is well established that, during head injury, because the frontal (and temporal) lobes are normally held rigidly by the bony anterior fossae of the calvarium, that they can be damaged when brain movement lags behind movement of the skull following impact. Although diffuse axonal injury with white matter damage is one sequel, the anterior temporal and frontal lobes are particularly susceptible to damage, and so-called contrecoup lesions are commonest at these sites.

In assessing patients who have had a head injury, where frontal lobe abnormalities may be suspected, there are numerous complications, particularly if magnetic resonance imaging scans and neurological testing fail to reveal any abnormalities. It is well known that damage to the frontal lobes can lead to depressive illness and, as noted, one of the presentations of frontal lobe damage is as a pseudopsychopathic syndrome. But, the differential diagnosis may also include pre-existing personality disorders or depression and interpretation of the behavioural features and neuropsychological findings must therefore be carried out with considerable care.

Neuropsychological functioning in borderline personality disorder

The identification of frontal lobe syndromes is now fairly routine in neuropsychiatric practice, although often much reliance is placed on neuropsychological testing, especially in patients following minor head injuries. In the context of the syndromes defined in this book, especially variants of pseudodementia, interpretation however is much more complex. Thus, the concept that frontal lobe function may be perverse in patients with primary psychiatric disorders such as schizophrenia, and in patients with personality disorders, is often not appreciated. To discuss the neuropsychological complications of the psychoses is beyond the scope of this chapter, but it is noted here again that the interpretation of neuropsychological tests in psychotic patients is very hazardous, and that frontal deficits are now an accepted part of the schizophrenia syndrome. Further, aberrant frontal lobe testing is often seen in patients with a depressive pseudodementia, in which condition other indices of frontal function, for example, as seen with functional brain imaging, may also be abnormal (Trimble, 1996).

Some studies have investigated neuropsychological functioning in patients with borderline personality disorder. Most of the studies have found that this is associated with significant deficits on a number of neuropsychological measures compared to what one would expect from 'normally' functioning individuals. Taken together, the results of the studies reveal a relatively consistent pattern of neuropsychological abnormalities.

A deficit in delayed memory (i.e. retrieval of newly learned information after a delay) has been found in three studies (O'Leary et al., 1991; Burgess, 1992; Swirsky-Sacchetti et al., 1993) comparing adult borderline patients with age- and sex-matched normal controls. Burgess (1992) observed a similar delayed memory deficit in borderline patients compared to those with major depression or schizophrenia. A deficit in immediate memory (i.e. retrieval of newly learned information without a delay) was found by only O'Leary et al. (1991), despite being assessed in a number of other studies.

Borderline patients have been found to perform significantly worse than matched controls on the Rey–Osterrieth Complex Figure (ROCF), a task designed to assess visual discrimination and filtering (O'Leary et al., 1991; Swirsky-Sacchetti et al., 1993; van Reekum et al., 1993). van Reekum et al. (1996) actually found a trend indicating inferior performance on the ROCF by borderline patients compared to traumatic brain-injured controls, although this difference did not reach significance.

Executive function deficits

The most consistent area of neuropsychological disturbance in patients with borderline personality disorder is within the frontal executive domain, with most studies findings deficits in this area. Burgess (1992) found that borderline patients were more likely to make errors of omission on tasks requiring planning/sequencing than matched normal controls; a difference in omission errors was also found between borderline personality disorder patients and schizophrenic controls (Burgess, 1991). However, Burgess (1991) also found that borderline personality disorder patients were significantly better than schizophrenics at performing a three-step command, and on the similarities subtest of the WAIS. In contrast, Burgess (1992) found that borderline personality disorder patients made more errors on serial 7s and similarity/dependence comparison tasks, were less able to perform the Luria hand position task, made more concrete mistakes when interpreting proverbs and were more likely to perseverate than matched controls. A deficit on the Luria hand position task was also found by Swirsky-Sacchetti *et al.* (1993), who observed increased interference on the colour–word Stroop task in borderline personality disorder patients compared to matched controls.

van Reekum *et al.* (1993) reported a deficit on the Wisconsin Card-Sorting Task in their group of borderline personality disorder patients, although this deficit was not quantified in comparison to a control group; moreover, 6 of the 7 patients showing a deficit on the task had suffered 'definite brain injury'. In a repeat study, with significant methodological improvements, van Reekum *et al.* (1996) failed to find a significant difference on the Wisconsin Card-Sorting Task between borderline personality disorder and traumatic brain injury controls; it is nevertheless apparent that this reflected on the poor Wisconsin Card-Sorting Task performance of the control group in this study rather than on the ability of borderline personality disorder patients to perform this task well. Indeed, the similarity between the borderline personality disorder and the brain-injured patients in this study led the authors to conclude that frontal executive dysfunction is an important part of the borderline personality disorder syndrome (van Reekum *et al.*, 1996).

While some others have failed to note such a significant deficit in Wisconsin Card-Sorting Task performance in these patients compared to normal controls (O'Leary *et al.*, 1991; Swirsky-Sacchetti *et al.*, 1993), Paris *et al.* (1999) found that children with borderline personality disorder perform significantly worse on the Wisconsin Card-Sorting Task compared to age-matched non-borderline personality-disorder psychiatric controls, even after controlling for conduct disorder and intelligence.

Paris *et al.* (1999) also found that borderline personality disorder children performed significantly worse than controls on a continuous performance task designed to assess vigilance and sustained attention.

Finally, there is some evidence to suggest that patients with borderline personality disorder have impoverished cognitive flexibility, as illustrated by their inferior performance on the Trails B task reported by van Reekum *et al.* (1993).

In summary, while the evidence concerning the neuropsychological profile of patients with this personality profile is limited both methodologically and in terms of number of studies, the majority of the available evidence suggests that patients with borderline personality disorder have deficits in delayed memory, visual discrimination/filtering and executive functions, all of which may be regarded as involving the frontal lobes. It is also possible that deficits in delayed memory and visual discrimination/filtering performance in these patients are partly a reflection of disturbed executive processing. While it is nevertheless unclear what the precise nature of the borderline personality disorder executive deficit might be, the importance of these studies from a medicolegal point of view is clear. Not all abnormalities of neuropsychological testing can be attributed to underlying cerebral damage, even following head trauma, and interpretation of neuropsychological tests, especially of memory and executive functions in the presence of psychiatric illness and at least some forms of personality disorders, is frankly unreliable.

Conclusions

One review of the literature (Pankratz and Binder, 1997) estimated that 20–60% of patients with mild head injury in a compensation setting show improbably poor performances on neuropsychological tests, for example performing worse on forced-choice tests than patients with noted brain dysfunction. This chapter has reviewed the phenomenon of memory and its testing, especially when viewed in a medicolegal context. While there are no definitive neuropsychological tests of malingering, the literature has emphasised the frequency with which neuropsychological test performance can be anomalous or incongruous in patients in medicolegal settings, and the important role of personality variables and psychiatric illness in such findings. Further, the mistaken assumption that memory provides a robust replay of life's experiences has repeatedly been emphasised. It has been known for a long time that when people repeatedly recall a story, it becomes more distorted with the retelling.

Memory is imagination, recall is always in part confabulation, meaning and motivation monitor mnesis. The reliance that is usually placed on a claimant's (or defendant's) memory of past events in a court setting is naive to the extreme, and defies much of what we know about memory from contemporary neuroscience research, but also from common sense. As this chapter and Chapter 2 have revealed, psychological processes, including neuropsychological performance, are intimately entwined within the personality structure of us all.

REFERENCES

American Psychiatric Association Press (1994). *Diagnostic and Statistical Manual of Mental Disorders*, 4th edn (DSM-IV). Washington, DC: APA Press.

Bass, E. and Davis, L. (1994). *The Courage to Heal.* New York: Harper Collins.

Bernstein, E. M. and Putnam, F. W. (1986). Development, reliability, and validity of a dissociation scale. *Journal of Nervous and Mental Disease*, **174**, 197–202.

Blumer, D. and Benson, D. F. (1975). Personality changes with frontal and temporal lobe lesions. In *Psychiatric Aspects of Neurologic Disease*, eds. D. F. Benson and D. Blumer, pp. 151–69. New York: Grune & Stratton.

Brandon, S., Boakes, J., Glaser, D. and Green, R. (1998). Recovered memories of childhood sexual abuse. Implications for clinical practice. *British Journal of Psychiatry*, **172**, 296–307.

Brandt, J., Rubinsky, E. and Lassen, G. (1985). Uncovering malingered amnesia. *Annals of the New York Academy of Sciences*, **444**, 502–3.

Burgess, J. W. (1991). The relationship of depression and cognitive impairment to self-injury in borderline personality disorder, major depression and schizophrenia. *Psychiatry Research*, **38**, 77–87.

(1992). Neurocognitive impairment in dramatic personalities: histrionic, narcissistic, borderline and antisocial disorders. *Psychiatry Research*, **42**, 283–90.

Cardeña, E. (1994). The domain of dissociation. In *Dissociation, Clinical and Theoretical Perspectives*, pp. 15–31. ed. S. J. Lynn and J. W. Rhue. New York: Guilford Press.

Cercy, S. P. Schretlen, D. J. and Brandt, J. (1997). Simulated amnesia and the pseudo-memory phenomena. In *Clinical Assessment of Malingering and Deception*, ed. R. Rogers, pp. 85–107. New York: Guilford Press.

Coleridge, S. T. (1817/1885). *Biographia Literaria.* Oxford: Oxford University Press.

Cummings, J. (1985). *Clinical Neuropsychiatry.* Orlands, Florida: Grune & Stratton.

DelMonte, M. M. (2001). Fact or fantasy. A review of recovered memories of childhood sexual abuse. *Irish Medical Journal*, **18**, 99–105.

Edmonds, D. and Eidinow, J. (2001). *Wittgenstein's Poker.* London: Faber & Faber.

Goldstein, F. C. and Levin, H. S. (1991). Memory disorders after closed head injury. In *Memory Disorders*, ed. T. Yanagihara and R. C. Petersen, pp. 255–78. New York: Marcel Dekker.

Gronwall, D. and Wrightson, P. (1980). Duration of post-traumatic amnesia after mild head injury. *Journal of Clinical Neuropsychology*, **2**, 51–60.

Gudjonsson, G. H. and MacKeith, J. A. (1990). Retracted confessions: legal, psychological and psychiatric aspects. *Medicine, Science and the Law*, **28**, 329–35.

Gudjonsson, G. H. and Shackleton, H. (1986). The pattern of scores on Raven's matrices during "faking bad" and "non-faking" performance. *British Journal of Clinical Psychology*, **25**, 35–41.

Harlow, J. M. (1868). Recovery from the passage of an iron bar through the head. *Publications of the Massachusetts Medical Society*, **2**, 329–46.

Kapur, N. (1988). *Memory Disorders in Clinical Practice*. London: Butterworths.

Kopelman, M. D. (1987). Crime and amnesia. *Behavioural Sciences and the Law*, **5**, 323–42.

Kopelman, M. D. (1999). Varieties of false memory. *Cognitive Neuropsychology*, **16**, 197–214.

Lee, G. P., Loring, D. W. and Martin, R. C. (1992). Rey's 15-item visual memory test for the detection of malingering: normative observations on patients with neurological disorders. *Psychological Assessment*, **4**, 43–6.

Loftus, E. F. (1997). Creating false memories. *Scientific American*, September, 51–5.

Mace, C. J. and Trimble, M. R. (1991). Psychogenic Amnesias. In *Memory Disorders*, eds. T. Yanagihara and R. C. Petersen, pp. 429–56. New York: Marcel Dekker.

Mega, M. S. and Cummings, J. L. (1994). Frontal-subcortical circuits and neuropsychiatric disorders. *Journal of Neuropsychiatry and Clinical Neurosciences*, **6**, 358–70.

Merskey, H. (1995). Multiple personality disorder and false memory syndrome. *British Journal of Psychiatry*, **166**, 281–3.

Neisser, V. and Harsch, N. (1992). Phantom flashbulbs: false recollections of hearing the news about Challenger. In *Affect and Accuracy in Recall*, ed. E. Winograd and E. Neisser, pp. 9–31. Cambridge: Cambridge University Press.

Nemiah, J. (1991). Dissociation, conversion, and somatisation. In *American Psychiatric Press, Review of Psychiatry*, vol. 10, ed. A. Tasman and S. M. Goldfinger, pp. 248–60. Washington, DC: APA Press.

O'Leary, K. M., Brouwers, P. M. S. W., Gardner, D. L. and Cowdry, R. W. (1991). Neuropsychological testing of patients with borderline personality disorder. *American Journal of Psychiatry*, **148**, 106–11.

Pankratz, L. and Binder, L. M. (1997). Malingering on neuropsychological measures. In *Clinical Assessment of Malingering and Deception*, ed. R. Rogers, pp. 223–36. New York: Guilford Press.

Paris, J., Zelkowitz, P., Guzder, J., Joseph, S. and Feldman, R. (1999). Neuropsychological factors associated with borderline pathology in children. *Journal of the American Academy of Child and Adolescent Psychiatry*, **38**, 770–4.

Powell, G. E. (2004). Neuropsychology and the law. In *Clinical Neuropsychology*, ed. L. H. Goldstein and J. McNeil. Chichester: John Wiley (in press).

Pratt, R. T. C. (1977). Psychogenic loss of memory. In *Amnesia*, 2nd edn, ed. C. W. M. Whitty and O. L. Zangwill, pp. 224–32. London: Butterworths.

Rey, A. (1964). *L'examen Clinique en Psychologie*. Paris: Presses Universitaires de France.

Russell, W. R. and Nathan, P. (1946). Traumatic amnesia. *Brain*, **69**, 183–7.

Schmand, B., Lindeboom, J., Scagen, S. *et al.* (1998). Cognitive complaints in patients after whiplash injury; the impact of malingering. *Journal of Neurology, Neurosurgery and Psychiatry*, **64**, 339–43.

Southwick, S. M., Morgan, C. A., Nicolaou, A. L. and Charney, D. S. (1997). Consistency of memory for combat-related traumatic events in veterans of operation desert storm. *American Journal of Psychiatry*, **154**, 173–7.

Steinberg, M. (1992). *The Interviewer's Guide to the Structured Clinical Interview for DSM-IV Dissociative Disorders*. Washington, DC: APA Press.

Swirsky-Sacchetti, T., Gorton, G., Samuel, S. *et al.* (1993). Neuropsychological function in borderline personality disorder. *Journal of Clinical Psychology*, **49**, 385–96.

Symonds, C. P. and Russell, W. R. (1943). Accidental head injuries: prognosis in service patients. *Lancet*, **I**, 1–10.

Trimble, M. R. (1996). *Biological Psychiatry*, 2nd edn. Chichester: John Wiley.

van Reekum, R., Conway, C. A., Gansler, D., White, R. and Bachman, D. L. (1993). Neurobehavioural study of borderline personality disorder. *Journal of Psychiatry in Neuroscience*, **18**, 121–9.

van Reekum, R., Links, P. S., Finlayson, M. A. J. *et al.* (1996). Repeat neurobehavioural study of borderline personality disorder. *Journal of Psychiatry in Neuroscience*, **21**, 13–20.

Warrington, E. K. (1985). A disconnection analysis of amnesia. *Annals of the New York Academy of Science*, **444**, 72–7.

Warrington, E. (1996). *Camden Recognition Memory Test*. London: Psychology Press Books.

Whitty, C. W. M. and Zangwill, O. L. (1977). Traumatic amnesia. In *Amnesia*, 2nd edn, ed. Whitty, C. W. M. and Zangwill O, pp. 92–108. London: Butterworths.

World Health Organization (1993). *The ICD-10 Classification of Mental and Behavioural Disorders*. Geneva: World Health Organization.

Assessment, treatment and prognosis

Feste . . . words are very rascals, since bonds disgraced them.

Viola: Thy reason, man?

Feste: Troth, sir, I can yield you none without words, and words are grown so false, I am loath to prove reason with them. (William Shakespeare, *Twelfth Night*, III, i, 18–24).

Introduction

In earlier chapters, several methods of assessing patients with the spectrum of disorders discussed in this book have been noted. Clinical evaluation is foremost, and relies on the now rather maligned value of experience. Maligned, not in the sense that experience is devalued as one way of gathering information (the empirical method), but because it is notoriously subjective, and bias-ridden in interpretation. Clinicians often use their own idiosyncratic diagnostic inclusion criteria, and sometimes eccentric diagnoses, without even considering inclusion and exclusion criteria. These matters have already been discussed in some detail. In the light of such problems, it has become fashionable in recent years to rake up the importance of the diagnostic manuals such as DSM-IV (American Psychiatric Association, 1994) or ICD-10 (World Health Organization, 1992), and to urge for assessment using ratings scales, which supposedly possess objectivity.

Neuropsychological assessments for the evaluation of psychogenic amnesias and malingering have been discussed, whereas in this chapter, some of the rating scales used more specifically in the evaluation of somatoform disorders are presented.

The use of rating scales in medicolegal practice

It is important to understand that rating scales, like diagnostic manuals, are created by groups of people, with a view either to concretising (essencing) or measuring the intensity of a condition. In psychiatric practice, they are largely subjective, in the sense that they are filled out by people/patients, who are asked to mark on the relevant form in the relevant place the way they feel, or what they have been doing either now, or at some specified time in the past (e.g. 'the last week'). Their responses are marked, a total score and subscores may be calculated, and then the results are used for comparative purposes. Either the score is compared to a previous score from the same person, or the score is compared to population norms, usually matched for things such as gender and age. It is assumed that, because science is measurement, to have a measure is scientific, and that such a measurement has meaning in the clinical context.

There are two crucial features of rating scales that need to be determined before they can have much value. One is validity, the other is reliability.

There are several meanings of validity, but essentially this seeks the obvious: does the scale measure that which it purports to measure? It seeks an absence of bias, and assumes a gold standard against which the scale can be evaluated. Validity reflects on the degree of confidence that we can ascribe to the result of the assessment, and the numerical value obtained. This in turn dictates that the scale has validity in the context in which it has been evaluated, and it cannot be used with the same validity in other settings.

Several types of validity are described, including face validity, content validity, construct validity and criterion validity. The first is actually totally subjective: does the scale contain items that appear to measure what the scale intends to measure? The second refers to the question content, do the questions asked sample adequately the construct under consideration? This, too, is largely subjective. Construct validity is determined by assessing whether the scale shows relationships with other measures predicted to assess the same construct. Criterion validity requires that the scale discriminates between groups of people who are dissimilar on criteria that are external to the scale itself. The latter two tests of validity thus require evaluation with other scales or other groups of patients.

Reliability asks only that the scale shall be precise and consistent when applied to the same people under the same conditions. It is assessed purely by statistical analysis, and usually both test–retest reliability and interobserver reliability are evaluated. In the former, the scale is tested in the same person on two or more occasions, under identical conditions. The interobserver reliability refers to the need for two or more raters to obtain the same results on the same person at the same observation time. This applies essentially to scales that are not filled in subjectively by people, but rely on observer ratings.

Validity and reliability are but two of the considerations necessary for a rating scale to be of use in practice. It goes without saying that an unreliable scale cannot be valid. Often, and even more important are considerations relating to whether those filling out the scale understand the questions and the mode of reply. Can they read, do they know the meaning of the words, can they be bothered to wade through often many questions that seem to them irrelevant? All such factors need to be considered when advocating the use of a rating scale in any particular setting.

In fact, most behavioural rating scales have been introduced for research purposes, and have then been taken over by clinicians, as if somehow to bolster their clinical judgements. This immediately raises issues of validity. In practice they are more beloved by psychologists than psychiatrists, particularly because of the mistaken belief that they can be used to make clinical diagnoses. In fact, this is the one thing they cannot do! They do not make diagnoses, since that by definition is a clinical matter, and linked to medical training and experience.

They may perhaps be more legitimately used to help quantify the extent of symptomatology, after a diagnosis has been made, or to track the severity of a syndrome over time. Unfortunately, severity has many dimensions, and change in the patient may occur over time but not be reflected in the scales or vice versa. This reflects on the third issue of rating scale development – sensitivity. In fact, very few of the scales in use have been specifically evaluated over time to test their sensitivity to change.

The issue of response sets has also to be overcome, namely that some people prefer to reply 'yes' rather than 'no' to questions, or that they overtune their responses to be the most socially desirable. Several scales have embedded within them questions that form a lie scale, to estimate the extent to which it is likely that the respondent is doing more than just gilding the lily.

There are some scales that have different functions, for example those that assess personality traits in a population, and some that seek to be more objective and less subjective, so-called structured or semistructured interviews. In the latter, patients are asked selected questions only, and they can be probed to see if they understand the questions. Their replies lead on to the next set of questions, often with a complex loop of interrogation, but with very specific end-points. This increases reliability, which is further bolstered by having the raters especially trained in the interview method. In practice, such schedules are mainly used in research, and have not found use in medicolegal work.

In the following section, only a few rating scales that are used in the assessment of somatoform disorders are briefly described; more comprehensive reviews are available and referenced. However, it should be repeated that these scales have been developed for research, they are not widely used in general medical practice and, crucially, they have not been developed for use in a medicolegal context. Some, as with the memory assessments already discussed, have been adopted for medicolegal purposes, but issues of reliability and validity remain outstanding. In fact, this issue is central to the use of all of the psychiatric/psychological rating scales that are used in medicolegal practice. It is a fact that the scales often portrayed in medicolegal reports as demonstrating this or that diagnosis of this or that severity simply have not been assessed for validity and reliability specifically in the medicolegal context. Rating scales, especially of a subjective nature, filled out by claimants, simply can have no claim to be veridical, and can be utterly misleading. This applies to rating scales for posttraumatic stress disorder (PTSD), as much as it does for rating scales of anxiety and depression. Without validity in the context of its use, a rating scale is open to misrepresentation, and to pretend otherwise is disingenuous.

Rating of somatoform and related disorders

Somatoform disorders

The main scales in use are listed in Table 6.1. They include some general scales of psychopathology, such as the Minnesota Multiphasic Personality Inventory (MMPI), from which relevant subscales are constructed, to more specific ones. The ones cited relate to the assessment of somatisation, dissociation and fatigue. To reiterate, with few exceptions, these have never been evaluated in a medicolegal context, have been developed primarily for research, and should not be used to make medical diagnoses.

One of the most used rating scales over time has been the MMPI, although it finds value mainly in the USA, where it was first standardised and validated. It is a personality scale, and respondents reply to 550 questions about personality characteristics either in the affirmative or with denial. For only some of the questions is the 'true' response the pathological one, and some of the subscales derived are sensitive to overreporting of traits. Among the subscales are ones for hypochondriasis (Hs) and hysteria (Hy), but the scale has also been used in the context of malingering.

The Hy and Hs scales have been used for many years along with the depression (D) scale as an index of neuroticism – the so-called neurotic triad (with high scores on Hs and Hy, and low D) – forming on the printout of the scores an inverted U pattern, the low D situated between the high Hs and Hy scores. The F scale is used as an index of malingering, and is widely used in the USA as a psychological indicator of malingered psychiatric illness. The questions ask about behaviours associated in the lay mind with serious psychopathology, which in practice patients with severe psychiatric illness do not have. In other words, malingerers 'fake bad'. Other indices to suggest simulation have also been derived, based on the pattern of endorsement of items (obvious as opposed to subtle ones endorsed by those with psychopathology), and empirical tables have been generated which profile exaggeration of responses (Faust, 1995).

Another widely used scale in the USA which has subscales that are used in assessing somatoform disorders is the Symptom Check List 90 (SCL-90; Derogatis *et al.*, 1974), which lists 12 common somatic symptoms.

Table 6.1 Rating scales used to assess somatoform disorders

Somatisation	
Minnesota Multiphasic Personality Inventory (MMPI)	Subscales Hy, Hs, F Malingering
Primary Care Evaluation of Mental Disorders (PRIME-MD)	Somatisation disorder
Illness Behaviour Questionnaire (IBQ)	Abnormal illness behaviour, hypochondriasis, malingering
Whiteley Index of Hypochondriasis	Hypochondriasis
Somatosensory Amplification Scale	Sensitivity to body sensations, hypochondriasis
Health Attitude Survey	Somatisation
Symptom Check List 90 (SCL-90)	Somatisation
Somatic Symptom Index (SSI)	Somatisation
Dissociation	
Dissociative Experiences Scale (DES)	Amnestic and dissociative states
Structured Clinical Interview for DSM – Dissociative Disorders (SCID-D)	Dissociation and related diagnoses
Fatigue	
Fatigue Scale	Fatigue
Fatigue Assessment Instrument	Fatigue
Profile of Fatigue-Related Symptoms	Fatigue
Mental Fatigue Scale	Fatigue
Multidimensional Fatigue Inventory	Fatigue

The Whitely Index of Hypochondriasis is a 14-item questionnaire, which taps into attitudes of health and illness, rather than symptoms, and fits well with the DSM-IV diagnostic criteria for hypochondriasis. It has been used in community studies to assess the prevalence of abnormal illness behaviour (AIB), and has been found to correlate with 'doctor shopping' and with prognosis at 1-year follow-up (Pilowsky, 1997).

An expanded form of the Whitely Index, the Illness Behaviour Questionnaire (IBQ), was developed by Pilowsky (1997). It was originally developed in a pain clinic, mainly for studies of patients with somatoform pain disorders. It is a 62-item inventory, with seven subscales, namely: General Hypochondriasis (GH), Disease Conviction (DC), Psychological versus Somatic perception of illness (P–S), Affective Inhibition (AI), Affective Disturbance (AD), Denial (D) and Irritability (I). Second-order factors were also derived for Affective State (AS) and Disease Affirmation (DA). The latter indicates a feeling of certainty that the symptoms are physically based and a rejection of psychological interpretations.

Table 6.2 The item for disease affirmation in the Illness
Behaviour Questionnaire

Do you think there is something seriously wrong with your body? (Yes)

Does your illness interfere with your life a great deal? (Yes)

If the doctor told you he could find nothing wrong with you, would
  you believe him? (No)

Do you find you are often aware of various things happening in your
  body? (Yes)

Are you sleeping well? (No)

Do you find that you are bothered by many different symptoms? (Yes)

Do you ever think of your illness as a punishment for something you
  have done wrong in the past? (No)

Are you bothered by many pains and aches? (Yes)

Do you think there is something the matter with your mind? (No)

Is your bad health the biggest difficulty of your life? (Yes)

Do you think your symptoms may be caused by worry? (No)

Psychogenic pain patients are particularly discriminated by the DC scale, and
have a high score on DA. Patients with hysteria, when compared with patients with
a neurological cause for their symptoms, score higher on AI, and in comparison
to psychiatric patients score higher on D (Wilson-Barnett and Trimble, 1985). In a
gastroenterological setting, patients with no organic cause for their complaints and
an accompanying psychiatric disorder score higher on DC, GH and AI and lower
on P–S compared with an organic group (Colgan *et al.*, 1988).

In patients with chronic low back pain, those displaying several Waddell's signs
showed higher scoring on scales for DC, I, DA and AS, and had higher Whitely
Index scores. In other words, the presence of Waddell's signs reflect on abnormal
attitudes to health, and disturbed affect. A group of patients were examined with
the IBQ before and after surgery for their back pain, and the score on the DA scale
was strongly predictive of the outcome of the surgery (Waddell *et al.*, 1989).

Other relevant studies have been conducted in whiplash patients, chronic fatigue
and simulated illness. DA and somatic focusing predicted patients with chronic and
very chronic whiplash symptoms, and a poor outcome in chronic fatigue was also
predicted by the DA scale (Pilowsky, 1997). The items reflecting on DA are shown
in Table 6.2.

Clayer *et al.* (1984) tried to adopt the IBQ to detect simulation. They gave the
scale to several groups, one of which was asked to fill it out as if they were consciously
exaggerating their illness; another came from a pain clinic and had pain considered to be neurotically determined. They derived a 21-item scale (the Conscious

Exaggeration or CE subscale), which they reported separated conscious exaggerators from neurotics and normals.

The Primary Care Evaluation of Mental Disorders (PRIME-MD; Spitzer *et al.*, 1994) has a subsection which covers 15 common physical symptoms, which patients report to community physicians. Three or more positive responses lead on to a further section of the PRIME-MD, which is a structured interview. Higher scores correlate with mood disorders and functional impairment, and patients endorsing seven or more symptoms have a reasonably high probability of meeting criteria for a multisomatoform disorder (Kroenke *et al.*, 1988).

The Somatosensory Amplification Scale is a 10-item measure of how people may magnify bodily sensations (Barsky and Wyshak, 1990), and the Health Attitude Survey (Noyes *et al.*, 1999) consists of 27 items, which focus on interaction with doctors, satisfaction with care and psychological distress, rather than on symptoms.

Assessment of somatisation can be derived from semistructured interviews such as the Somatic Symptom Index (SSI) of the Diagnostic Interview Schedule (DIS; Robins and Helzer, 1982). The DIS lists 38 somatic symptoms, and uses probes to assess severity, and has inclusion/exclusion criteria. The SSI represents an abridged construct, in which somatoform disorder can be identified using lower cut-off values on the DIS than those required for somatisation (Escobar *et al.*, 1989). Males scoring higher than four and females more than six symptoms have been shown to have more associated psychopathology, to be more disabled and to overuse medical facilities in comparison with those below the cut-offs. Apparently, simply meeting these criteria for somatoform problems has predictive value.

Abbreviated screening instruments have also been tested, such as a checklist of seven key symptoms. These are: breathlessness, menstrual cramps, perineal or oral burning, difficulty swallowing or a persistent lump in the throat, extended amnesia, frequent vomiting and frequent pain in the fingers or toes. This checklist has a specificity of 94% for somatisation disorder for a score of three or more symptoms (Othmer and DeSouza, 1987).

Dissociation

There are several scales used to assess dissociation, but the most widely used are the Dissociation Experiences Scale (DES), and the Structured Clinical Interview for DSM – Dissociative Disorders (SCID-D).

The SCID-D is a structured interview derived from DSM criteria. It is a 250-item interview, rating the existence of five key dissociative symptoms, namely amnesia, depersonalisation, derealisation, identity confusion and identity alteration. A shorter screening version, the Mini-SCID-D, is also available.

The DES is a 28-item self-report scale that has been widely used in research, which probes the frequency of amnestic experiences, depersonalisation and derealisation, and imaginative involvement (Bernstein and Putnam, 1986). It can be completed quickly, and is a useful screening tool, unlike the SCID-D, the latter which can also be used for diagnostic purposes. Although widely used, the DES has been criticised, especially since many of the included items suggest 'non-pathological' dissociation. A shorter scale, the DES Taxon has been developed to measure the more pathological symptoms (Waller and Ross, 1997).

Treatments

'It is hard to imagine any illness for which more unproven remedies have been advocated with greater enthusiasm than chronic fatigue syndrome' (Wessely *et al.*, 1998, p. 370).

This pronouncement, from one of the leading researchers in the field of somatisation, reflects on the poor quality of evaluation of treatments for this spectrum of disorders, and the wide nature of the remedies applied. Since the symptoms of the somatoform disorders are diverse, the remedies applied might also be expected to be diverse, which is the case.

Because patients and their doctors are somatically fixated, initially the treatments are symptom-directed – stomach remedies for abdominal pains, analgesics for rheumatism, inhalers for asthma, etc. As the number of symptoms escalates, so does the number of medicaments. The patient becomes a walking pharmacopoeia, yet still complains of symptoms, as yet more medicaments are suggested. A patient with somatoform disorder may be on anything from 10 to 20 different prescriptions, among them toxic addictive drugs such as opiate analgesics. The case of chronic fatigue is compounded by the fads of enthusiasts who advocate further remedies based on fantasised views of the cause of the disorder, anecdotal reports being taken as the scientific foundation for efficacy. Wessely *et al.* note how positive harm emerges from obscure advice. One of the most commonly advocated cures for fatigue is rest (aggressive rest therapy!), which is not only counterproductive in chronic fatigue syndrome (CFS), but is the exact opposite of what has been shown to be beneficial.

As a general statement it is a fact that there are relatively very few studies of the effects of treatment for any of the somatoform disorders, and most reports are anecdotes and single case studies. Controlled trials, the gold standard for evaluating therapies, are conspicuously absent from the literature. Advice is plentiful, but often leads patients off to another round of failed, sometimes expensive, treatment, with further reinforcement of their somatic conviction. Psychiatric interventions are avoided, psychological interpretations are denied and physical treatments are vigorously pursued.

The reason why so little work has been carried out on treatments for these disorders reflects several problems that are specific to somatising patients. They go to a wide variety of physicians, who individually miss the broad picture of the somatisation, concentrating only on the symptoms pertaining to their special area of interest. Doctors are simply reluctant to recognise and diagnose these conditions, preferring endlessly to seek the quark but missing the quirk. Psychiatrists, many of whom are unfamiliar with such patients, frequently miss the diagnosis, especially if overt depression, for example, is not present. Unless familiar with epilepsy, they see a pseudoseizure but feel unable to progress further, worrying that they have seen an epileptic seizure. In reality, to capture fully the diagnostic flavour of these patients, psychiatrists have to be familiar with, and confident about, general medicine. Since many patients present with unexplained neurological symptoms, an intimate knowledge of neurology is also important.

In spite of the above problems, there are a few centres that have set up specialist services to deal with somatising patients, which has allowed collections of patients to accrue, and research to be carried out. The majority of controlled studies have been on CFS, perhaps because of its identifiablity, its frequency and the publicity surrounding it.

Those treating these disorders tend to advocate multidisciplinary treatment, with both physical and psychological interventions, and the judicious use of medications where indicated. Often, however, the first step is to wean patients off their tablets, to which they are strongly attached!

The few available studies in CFS are reviewed by Wessely et al. (1998), and they rely heavily on antidepressant drugs and cognitive-behaviour therapy (CBT). Since depression is often comorbid in patients with somatoform disorders, it is not surprising that patients are treated with these drugs. Since many of the older antidepressants, the tricyclic drugs, provoke somatic symptoms as side-effects, they are now less preferred to the newer, safer selective serotonin reuptake inhibitors (SSRIs). Only two studies against placebo in CFS are reported, both with fluoxetine (Prozac), but the results were not convincingly in favour of the active drug.

Wessely et al. tabulated eight studies of antidepressants in fibromyalgia. Most used the tricyclic drug amitriptyline, but two used the SSRIs. The latter were both negative, while several of the amitriptyline studies suggested benefit above placebo rates for patients. The dose of amitriptyline was quite small (less than 50 mg), hardly likely to produce an antidepressant effect, but perhaps enough to enhance sleep, and aid analgesia.

A key factor in the success of CBT is the acceptance by patients that psychological factors may be relevant in their disorder, and that non-physically based treatments may aid their recovery. To quote Wessely et al. (1998) again: 'A belief in viral persistence, some unknown agent sitting in nerves or muscles and always ready to flare up, leads to rest and avoidance. These beliefs have been shown to be indicators of a poor prognosis in CFS in every study in which they have been examined'

(p. 383). This sentiment cuts across the whole spectrum of somatoform disorders, and is the basis for CBT, but also reflects on the dilemma for those advising claimants in a medicolegal setting.

Thus, if patients believe that they have this and that physical symptom because they have been injured, and that they suffer from some ghastly disorder such as fibromyalgia or CFS, and that their prognosis is at best 'guarded', not only will they remain unwell, but they will also not make themselves available for treatment. It all harks back to concussion of the spine, and reminds us that, in a medicolegal setting, claimants, their advisors and their experts can collude simply to occlude the possibilities of enlightenment.

The basis of CBT is to adjust patients' beliefs about themselves and their illness, in other words to put a check on AIB, and to get them to think positively rather than negatively about their future. Time and time again in medicolegal reports, it is possible to read only of gloom and doom, of poor prognoses, of statements that people will never return to an active life. This is so counterproductive to the idea of rehabilitation that it is no wonder that many units will not consider taking patients for treatment while the legal process continues, the latter being seen as a perpetuating factor for the symptoms (referred to here as lexigenic illness).

There are several controlled trials of CBT in CFS, some reporting negative and others positive results. The more convincing studies use explanation, education and exercise to rehabilitate patients and show a significant benefit for CBT over alternatives, such as a regimen of relaxation (Sharpe et al., 1996; Deale et al., 1997). In a recent evaluation of 44 trials of various therapies, including more than 2800 patients, exercise and CBT were overall found to be the most effective therapy for CFS (Editorial, 2001).

The final summary of the Working Group on CFS/ME (2002) is that three specific strategies seem important to treatment; graded exercise, CBT and pacing. Daily levels of activity should be agreed and set by the patients and their therapists, and increased as the treatment progresses, and adjuncts such as simple analgesics and psychotropic drugs used as necessary. It also notes that the emphasis should be on improvement and adjustment rather than on cure!

Goldenberg et al. (1989, 1994) have used CBT in patients with fibromyalgia, and shown a significant improvement across a range of symptoms, and they recommend a stress-reduction CBT as an adjunct for therapy. Others have used graded exercise, with generally positive results. Recently, Richards and Scott (2002) reported that graded aerobic exercise was significantly better than relaxation in both self-rating of fibromyalgia symptoms and in the number of tender points counted on examination, and benefits were maintained at 12 months.

Klimes et al. (1990) adopted a similar strategy with patients diagnosed as having atypical non-cardiac chest pain of at least 3 months' duration. They reported significant improvements when compared with controls, and the treatment was quite acceptable to patients.

In a controlled trial of CBT in patients with medically unexplained symptoms, Speckens *et al.* (1995) reported that six to 16 sessions of CBT were effective in reducing symptoms, and that gains were maintained through to a 12-month follow-up.

In an analysis of the various treatments used for Briquet's syndrome, Scallett *et al.* (1976) reviewed 23 papers on management, but noted little difference between various methods.

Wessely *et al.* have laid down helpful and effective guidelines about the treatment methods they use in the management of CFS, and these are helpful for the spectrum of somatoform disorders. They refer to a 'biopsychosocial' approach, broad-spectrum in design but flexible in praxis. In general, management of these disorders requires specialised knowledge, and should be carried out by a team which is knowledgeable not only about somatoform disorders, but also the presentations that they mirror. In a neurological setting this requires both psychiatric and neurological training and expertise. It is very important that those involved in management have the courage of their convictions that they are dealing with medically unexplained symptoms, and that their interpretation of the history of somatisation is correct. It is important that a multidisciplinary approach is taken, involving psychiatrists, neurologists, psychologists, physiotherapists, nursing staff, occupational therapists and other experienced staff whose individual expertise is brought to the case as necessary. Obviously, not all such staff or input are required for all patients, and many cases of somatoform disorder, so common in general practice, resolve with reassurance, good advice and psychotropic drugs as necessary. However, as patients approach the more severe end of the spectrum, and especially with somatisation disorder, the input required is clearly more extensive.

To adopt one approach rather than another, to hold rigid ideas about the precise cause of the symptoms, to limit flexibility and to be confrontational, will all reduce the effectiveness of achieving a therapeutic liaison with the patient. Patients are often so somatically fixated that initially a purely pragmatic physical approach is needed before a therapeutic alliance with the patient can be made, and psychological inroads attempted. Arguments with the patient over whether or not the symptoms are 'organic' or not are rarely fruitful, and requests for further 'tests' should be logically but firmly resisted.

Wessely *et al.* list attitudes that are helpful for the treatment of CFS, shown in Table 6.3. They emphasise the importance of CBT, the value of which is applicable across the whole spectrum of somatoform presentations. However, the targets for treatment are broad (Table 6.4). Antidepressants, preferably not tricyclic, should be used, even in the absence of overt depression, although it is often important to

Table 6.3 Attitudes required for effective treatment of patients with somatoform disorders

Unqualified acceptance of the validity of the patient's illness experience
Willingness to listen to patients' views and take them seriously
A positive attitude to therapy
Ability to tolerate slow progress and setbacks
Willingness to let the patient take the credit for success

Reproduced from Wessely *et al.* (1998), with permission.

Table 6.4 Targets for treatment

Important misunderstandings about the illness	Education
Depression/anxiety disorders	Antidepressants
Major disturbance in activity/rest/sleep pattern	Behavioural therapy
Psychological conflicts and problems	Psychotherapy
Physical deconditioning	Graded activity

Reproduced from Wessely *et al.* (1998), with permission.

emphasise to the patient that they are being used as modifiers of brain and nerve function, rather than as antidepressants *per se.* In a meta-analysis of antidepressant therapy for medically unexplained symptoms (94 trials involving 6595 patients), 69% of the studies suggested benefit for at least one outcome measure (O'Malley *et al.*, 1999). Side-effects should be minimised by starting low and going slow, and compliance encouraged by the use of non-sedating antidepressants that can be given on a once-daily basis.

Hypnosis and abreaction

In the past, the use of hypnosis and Sodium Amytal abreaction were popular, especially for the more acute-onset monosymptomatic cases, for example with paralysis. The rise of these treatments has been documented in earlier chapters; hypnosis was used by Charcot and the French school, while abreaction, in which a small dose of Sodium Amytal is injected intravenously, became popular in soldiers breaking down in the Second World War. While no trials as we know them today, controlled and comparative, have been done, it is clear that such treatments were very effective in a subgroup of patients, and are perhaps quite underused today. Both rely on the use of psychological persuasion, and to some extent collusion between the patient and the therapist. The role of suggestion in the development of symptoms has been discussed, and the psychological techniques advocated here, from CBT to abreaction are all making use of suggestions to patients about their symptoms and how to obtain symptom relief. Treatments such as hypnosis and abreaction provide instant 'high-dose' suggestion. In both, patients, while in a certain state of consciousness, are encouraged to bring to life any psychologically traumatic events and the associated emotions that may be related to their symptoms. With the suggestion of symptom improvement while being abreacted, quick relief may be obtained, the paralysed limb moving or the aphonic vocal cords adducting; such progress must be grasped and promoted with vigour. These treatments are however not advocated for patients with obvious personality disorders, or for those with somatisation disorder.

Where, when and how?

The question of where to carry out treatment, when to give it, and how long it takes obviously is highly patient-dependent. More severe cases need the structure and routine of inpatient care, but many patients, especially those with monosymptomatic conversion disorders, somatised depression, panic disorder with somatic presentations and pseudoseizures, are treated as outpatients. There are a few centres that specialise in these disorders, and ideally patients are best referred to groups with such expertise. The problem is that there are few such units, but the number of patients, even if limited to the more severe cases, is vast. At present those reaching specialised treatment are merely the tip of the iceberg. Many patients simply remain undiagnosed, swooning and somatising, swallowing medications they do not need for diseases they do not have.

Patients diagnosed, even if untreated, perhaps because of their refusal to embark on such regimens as outlined, should be followed up, preferably by a specialist who knows their history. The main point of contact should be the general practitioner (GP), who can grasp the entirety of the patient's history, and try to refrain from satisfying the patient's importuning requests to have further specialist opinions and investigations. Goldberg and colleagues (1989) have specifically devised a treatment protocol for GPs to use for somatising patients, central to which is refocusing the patients' way of viewing their illness, and discreetly attempting to relate physical symptoms to psychosocial problems.

However, specialist follow-up is also desirable, not only to share the burden of care with the GP, but also to provide patients with a 'specialist' who knows their case. To see a different junior doctor every time such patients come to a clinic is quite unhelpful, and likely to lead on to more worries about the nature of the symptoms, new investigations and much opportunity for patients to manipulate the situation.

The appointments need not be often, but should be regular, and requests to increase such contacts should be resisted unless obviously necessary.

Prognosis

T. A. Ross, writing between the two World Wars, described his follow-up experience of 1200 personally examined patients with all different kinds of neuroses. Many patients had been treated at the Cassell Hospital for Functional Nervous Disorders, founded initially in 1919 to care for soldiers suffering from shellshock and their civilian counterparts. They received a combination of hypnotism, persuasion and psychoanalysis. Within his sample, he examined the outcome of those with traumatic neuroses and compensation neuroses. He had some harsh things to say about the latter. He said: 'There is certainly no other neurosis where the patient is so free from receiving advice from his friends to pull himself together and to get on with his business, which is a curious reflection on the attitude of the family towards these disorders' (Ross, 1936).

He did not think that traumatic neurosis ever occurred in the absence of some compensation, noting that 'trauma itself does not cause neurosis . . . though the history of trauma occurred, the neurosis depended on the exploitation of that trauma' (Ross, 1936, p. 89). He described a personal series of eight patients with traumatic neurosis, whom he tried to treat and then followed. Two did 'absolutely badly', but the outcome of the rest, he hinted, was compensation-directed: 'If the legal profession, bench, bar and solicitors could grasp the conception of neurosis, and if it were possible that legislators could become capable of being educated to see that not trauma, but advantage to be gained by a history of trauma, was what made these people ill, this form of illness would disappear' (p. 92).

Since that time, there have been a number of follow-up studies (Tables 6.5 and 6.6). These do not include follow-up of patients with acute-onset symptoms who generally have a good prognosis, nor special conditions such as CFS, pseudoseizures or fibromyalgia, which are dealt with separately.

Table 6.5 reviews some of the earlier studies in what might be referred to as the pre-Slater era. Slater published his often-quoted paper in 1965, where he made the point that the diagnosis of hysteria was a disguise for ignorance, a delusion and a snare. He noted that, of 85 patients diagnosed as having hysteria, initially 19 had a combination with some organic (not necessarily neurological) pathology. At follow-up, 12 had died, four from suicide, and neurological illness had developed in 22, which was undetected at the time of the initial assessment. Only 19 were free of symptoms at follow-up. He was basically telling his neurological colleagues that they were unable to diagnose neurological illness and that the term 'hysteria' was simply a fertile source of clinical error.

Table 6.5 Follow-up studies of patients with various forms of somatoform disorder – earlier studies

Study	Number[a]	Female (%)	Length of follow-up (years)	Disabled (%)	Psychiatric/organic illness[b]	Dead[c]
Carter (1949)	90/100	60	4–6	21	4/0	1 (1)
Ziegler et al. (1960)	62/66	94	20–25	57	48/14	2 (1)
Ljungberg (1957)	381/401	61	7–23	38 (1 year) 20 (15 years)	5/4	11 (6)
Guze and Perley (1963)	29/37	84	3–10	85	6/18	0
Slater (1965)	85/99	53	7–10	85	13/58	12 (4)

[a] Number followed/total sample.
[b] Percentage with psychiatric/organic disorder at follow-up.
[c] Actual number of patients committing suicide in brackets.

This evoked ripostes from eminent neurologists such as Sir Francis Walshe and Sir Charles Symonds, defending the diagnostic acumen of neurologists. Walshe (1965) reasserted that hysteria was a psychological construct, and Symonds (1970), bringing to bear his extensive wartime experience and use of hypnosis, considered compensation a valid factor to be considered, and that the symptoms of hysteria were driven by factors 'partly conscious'.

These early follow-up studies emphasised several important points. The majority of patients were female, although outcome seems to be the same for both sexes. A percentage of the total do go on to develop other recognisable medical, especially neurological, disorders. In a time before non-invasive brain imaging, and before the era of sophistication in neurological science that we have today, this is hardly surprising. Slater probably overplayed his cards somewhat with these data, but some other early series from the same hospital also noted a high comorbidity with neurological illness. Merskey and Buhrich (1975) reported that 61 of 89 patients with conversion symptoms also had organic disease, with epilepsy being the commonest. However, they included a control group, which also had a similar percentage of patients with neurological disorder. In other words, selection played an important part in the results; these data originated from a neurological specialist centre. As noted already, selection of symptoms may sometimes be based on modelling by the patient from prior knowledge, hence the possible association between epilepsy and pseudoseizures. Merskey (1995) has argued, however, that there is more to the link between neurological disorders and hysteria than just modelling, and, in any case, the association with underlying organicity has been less discussed in recent

Table 6.6 Further follow-up studies of hysteria

Study	Number[a]	Female (%)	Length of years	Disabled (%)	Psychiatric/organic illness[b]	Dead[c]
Lewis (1975)	98	74	7–12	45	11/1	8 (1)
Chandrasekaran et al. (1994)	38	38	5	37	?/0	0
Krull and Schifferdecker (1990)	220	64	1–11	60	Not given	None
Couprie et al. (1995)	56	64	4.5 (mean)	41	4/?	0
Kent et al. (1995)	70/98	87	4.5 (mean)	81 somatisation 50 conversion	43/7	5 (1)
Mace and Trimble (1996)	73/79	78	8–11	41	64/15	3
Crimlisk et al. (1998)	64/73	48	5–7	70	75/5	7 (1?)
Stone et al. (2002)	42–60	81	12	>50	?/1	1

[a] Number followed/total sample.
[b] Percentage with psychiatric/organic disorder at follow-up.
[c] Actual number of patients committing suicide in brackets.

years, in part based on further follow-up studies, and in part as a reaction to the conclusions of Slater.

Leaving aside the issue of organicity, these studies emphasise the considerable morbidity associated with the diagnosis – anywhere between 21% and 85% of patients were disabled in long-term follow-up. The better prognoses, such as those in the study of Carter (1949), dealt mainly with monosymptomatic patients, and Lungberg's (1957) study implies that a fifth of patients remain disabled in the long term. He reported that prognosis was better for those with 'non-deviating personalities', and those with astasia-abasia, paralyses, amnesias and aphonia had more favourable prognoses in this and in Carter's study.

In contrast to Slater, Lewis (1975) revived neurological respectability. He followed up 98 patients with a diagnosis of hysteria at the Maudsley Hospital, a specialist psychiatric centre. Although 45% remained disabled, only a small percentage went on to develop other disorders (Table 6.6). This led Lewis to his pronouncement that hysteria would outlive its obiturists.

Another approach came from the St Louis school, which redefined hysteria as a chronic disorder, giving it the eponym Briquet's hysteria. By definition this was a condition with a poor prognosis; symptoms went on over many years, with only a minority achieving any kind of permanent remission. In a follow-up of patients given a diagnosis of Briquet's syndrome, two-thirds retained this same diagnosis after 6–12 years, emphasising the long-term stability of the syndrome (Guze *et al.*, 1986).

More recent follow-up studies are shown in Table 6.6. Kent *et al.* (1995) confirmed that, in contrast to a diagnosis of conversion disorder, patients with somatisation disorder tended to retain the diagnosis at follow-up and have more long-term morbidity. They identified a relatively high frequency of depression at follow-up, associated with both diagnoses.

Chandrasekaran *et al.* (1994), in a study from India, noted that outcome was related to personality variables, especially what they referred to as the hysterical personality, which had a very poor prognosis.

The study by Couprie *et al.* (1995) noted that patients who had responded well to hospital inpatient treatment had a better prognosis than those who were recalcitrant to treatment. The only other prognostic factor was age – those over 40 at follow-up fared worst. Krull and Schifferdecker (1990) noted poorer prognoses in patients with monopareses, bladder dysfunction and pain, and who had hysterical or asthenic personality traits. Wish for a pension was also noted to be associated with a poorer prognosis.

Mace and Trimble (1996) published data on 73 patients who had been carefully examined 10 years previously, both neurologically and psychiatrically. These patients had received a diagnosis of either conversion disorder or hysteria, and all came from the same hospital where Slater previously carried out his study. Complete remission of symptoms was noted in 30%, but symptoms were progressive in 18%. Overall, this group, which represented a tertiary referral centre sample of patients with a spectrum of medically unexplained symptoms, had a rather poor prognosis. A poor outcome correlated positively with the number of medical consultations the patients had had over the years of follow-up (GP visits, outpatient visits, weeks in hospital and 'other' National Health Service consultations), and was predicted by age, length of previous history, the use of non-psychotropic medication and an auxilliary psychiatric diagnosis. Most of the latter were affective in nature, but 23% of the sample had personality disorders. Three patients had a diagnosis of Briquet's syndrome, and none improved.

Crimlisk and colleagues (1998) followed up a somewhat different sample, from the same hospital. This group had unexplained motor symptoms, which included dystonias, pseudohemi- and paraplegias and tremors. However, most subjects were not monosymptomatic, and 20% fulfilled ICD-10 criteria for somatisation disorder. Patients with pseudoseizures were specifically excluded. Of the total sample, at follow-up, 70% were either on sick leave or had retired on grounds of ill health.

Incidentally, over a fifth of the group had worked in medical or paramedical areas. Only two patients were shown to have had previously undetected neurological problems.

Predictors of a good outcome in this study were a short duration of symptoms at initial assessment (<1 year), a psychiatric diagnosis for affective disorder or schizophrenia and a change in marital status during the follow-up period. Bad prognostics were being in receipt of financial benefits at the time of admission, and pending litigation.

Other studies of the long-term outcome of psychogenic movement disorders paint the same picture of chronic morbidity, poor remission rates and high rates of continuing unemployment (Feinstein *et al.*, 2001; Garza *et al.*, 2001). In a recent 12-year follow up of patients with unilateral non-neurological weakness and sensory disturbance, Stone *et al.* (2003), noted that 83% of 42 patients were still reporting symptoms, and 52% had considerable ongoing limitations to their daily lifestyle. In this series, only one patient developed a new neurological diagnosis.

Special groups
Children

There are few data on children. The presentation with acute onset unexplained medical symptoms in childhood is a very common medical event; recurrent head or abdominal pains are typical. Often, with the greater transparency of childhood, the identifying stress can easily be noted, and the symptoms usually resolve within a short time. However, a number of children have their healthy appendices removed, or are given a diagnosis of asthma or migraine or some such condition, and in a smaller number, their histories reveal the early buds of what will later flower into a somatisation disorder.

Turgay (1990) reported on the treatment outcome of 89 children and adolescents with conversion disorder, and noted that the majority responded favourably to a short course of dynamic insight-oriented individual or family therapy treatment. In his opinion, a good response in this age group was related to young age, a healthy personality with a lack of internal conflict and inflexible neurotic defences, acceptance by the family of the psychological nature of the illness and healthy family compliance.

CFS

The prognosis for CFS has been reviewed by Wessely *et al.* (1998). They point out the diagnostic stability over time, and the general anecdotal impression that the disorder is chronic and unremitting. They quote seven more formal follow-up studies, which give rates of improvement at around a half to two-thirds, but rates

Table 6.7 Prognosis in chronic fatigue syndrome

1. Between 20% and 50% of patients seen in specialist care improve in the medium term, but fewer than 10% return to premorbid functioning
2. The prognosis is better in children and in primary care
3. The principal predictors of poor outcome are intensity of illness beliefs and psychiatric morbidity
4. There is no increase in mortality (with the possible exception of suicide)

Reproduced from Wessely *et al.* (1998, p. 151), with permission.

of full recovery were disappointing at between 3 and 13%. Their summary points are given in Table 6.7.

Other disorders

The outlook for a diagnosis of fibromyalgia is not much better. In one study (Ledingham *et al.*, 1993), 72 patients with primary fibromyalgia syndrome were followed over 4 years. Ninety-seven per cent still had symptoms, and in 60% it was worse than at initial presentation. Functional disability was high, as was the reporting of symptoms of anxiety and depression. In another study, Felson and Goldenberg (1986) also reported that moderate or severe symptoms were persistent after a mean of 4.3 years' follow-up. In these studies, no evidence for the development of an alternative medical condition emerged with time, and the commonest comorbid diagnosis was depression.

Pseudoseizures have been the subject of several independent studies, which are beyond the scope of this book. Many patients with pseudoseizures are polysymptomatic, and a subgroup have somatisation disorder, thus outcome data reflect such heterogeneity. Many have associated epilepsy, which influences prognosis, and often the 'pseudoseizure' is really a misdiagnosed psychiatric disorder such as panic disorder, which will respond well to appropriate cognitive interventions. In a recent megareview of the data, the range of patients becoming seizure-free ranged from 19% to 87%. As with the other conditions considered here, there are a group who do well, responding to interventions with resolution of symptoms, and those who fail to respond, and become chronic. A figure of 60% continuing with this seizure type at 5 years has been estimated (Bowman, 2001). Better prognosis is associated with recent onset, clear-cut precipitating factors and acceptance of the diagnosis. Again, the poor prognostic factors were previous psychiatric diagnoses – notably for dissociative and personality disorders – and sexual abuse. In one study, pending litigation was implicated with a poor outcome (Ettinger *et al.*, 1999).

Table 6.8 Prognostic factors for outcome of conversion symptoms

Good outcome	Poor outcome
Acute onset	Chronic disorder
Monosymptomatic	Polysymptomatic
Depression/anxiety	Personality disorder
Change in marital status	High consultation rates
Acceptance of a psychological cause of the symptoms	Involvement in litigation
	Receipt of financial benefits
Good compliance	

A summary of the predictors of good and bad prognoses culled from the above studies is shown in Table 6.8. These make good pragmatic sense and follow clinical intuition. A good prognosis is associated with patients who can accept a psychological interpretation for their problems, and have had symptoms of recent onset. 'Recent onset' is not very precise, but suggests under a year. The presence of a treatable psychiatric disorder associated with the somatic symptoms is important, especially depression, as is compliance with treatment.

The association of somatic symptoms with personality disorders with a bad prognosis has been found in every study that has looked for it, and the persistence of a somatic focus (AIB) is also a bad sign. Involvement in litigation, a factor often ignored in follow-up studies, is also noted to be significant in several studies. While those quoted so far have not derived from a population necessarily involved in litigation, there are prognostic studies that have been carried out specifically on litigants. Although these have not investigated somatising patients as such, several studies have been of patients with a spectrum of neurotic presentations.

Follow-up studies of litigants

None of the above quoted studies specifically studied litigants, although those commenting on litigation seem to suggest that those patients involved in litigation have a worse prognosis compared with those who were not plaintiffs. The literature examining only litigants obviously represents a very biased group, biased further in terms of the investigator reporting the data. All studies are subjective series, and they tend to have been collected either by someone who generally represented claimants or by another who assessed mainly defence cases.

The lines were first drawn by the Erichsen versus Page dispute, discussed already. Similar viewpoints emerged in the last century, again as the result of follow-up studies. Purves-Stewart (1928) observed that, after settlement of litigation, patients ceased to be patients, and he drew the obvious conclusions. In a review of the literature up to 1953, Pokorny and Moore (1953) commented that most authors seemed to agree that the factor of compensation adversely affected recovery. These suggestions were powerfully supported by the neurologist Miller, who, in a series of papers, quoted in Chapter 4, noted social differences in the population of patients who sustained industrial as opposed to other accidents, and presented data on 50 of his patients, all with disabling nervous symptoms in a compensation setting. Two years after settlement of their claim, only two were disabled. Miller (1961) opined that their illness: 'is not the result of the accident but a concomitant of the compensation and a manifestation of the hope of financial gain'. Hinting at the obvious, he went on: 'To accept these cases uncritically as incidences of hysteria is to concede a general unconsciousness of motivation which strains my credulity. Indeed, what evidence is available on this issue points rather in the opposite direction'.

For Miller, then, the outcome was a reflection of the setting in which the accident occurred. It related to a 'lack of social responsibility'; the response of the injured workman to a brick falling on his head being not 'where am I'? but 'whose brick is it'?

The rebuttal came from another formidable British neurologist, Reginald Kelly (1972, 1975; Kelly and Smith, 1981). He criticised Miller's data, noting the retrospective nature of the biased sample, and the unfavourable doctor–patient relationship under which they had been gathered. Kelly studied 152 cases of head injury patients prospectively; some 75% had neurotic symptoms. Thirty-four patients were injured at home or in sports accidents, and so no compensation was forthcoming in this group.

Many of the claimants had returned to work before the settlement of their case, and no relationship was noted between the severity of the head injury and the severity of the neurosis. In contrast to Miller's sample, two-thirds came from managerial or professional classes.

Fifty-one claimants with posttraumatic neurotic symptoms were still disabled at the time of settlement. Recovery was much greater in those referred to him personally (93%) than in those referred from insurance companies (23%). Of 26 who had not been working on the day of settlement, 22 had not returned at follow-up, a mean of nearly 3 years later. Kelly concluded that failure to have returned to work by the time of the settlement carried a bad prognosis. He attributed these poor results to a failure of aggressive medical interventions early on after the accident.

The patients assessed by both Miller and Kelly were all head-injury cases, of varying severity, although Miller did select people with 'gross neurotic symptoms'. The argument was taken up further by two Australian psychiatrists, Mendelson (1988) and Goldney (1988), with a broader spectrum of patients.

Mendelson reviewed the literature on follow-up studies, and also provided his own series. Thompson (1965) reported on 190 patients with postaccident psychoneurosis after settlement, and noted that only 15% were improved. In contrast, Culpan and Taylor (1973) found that most of 60 patients with posttraumatic psychiatric symptoms had returned to work by settlement, and at follow-up 21% were more or less disabled.

In his own series, Mendelson reported on 101 litigants with psychiatric symptoms who had been involved in industrial or motor vehicle accidents who were assessed at an average 15.7 months after settlement. All had been working before their accidents. Thirty-five were back at work by the time of their settlement, but of those followed up, 83% were not working. Age was again noted as significant; younger patients (mean age 34) had a more favourable prognosis than older ones (mean age 47).

Mendelson noted in reality the paucity of follow-up studies, often carried out on a small number of cases. None the less, he concluded from 11 publications that between 50 and 85% of claimants failed to return to work after settlement, *pace* Miller. His view was that financial compensation alone does not explain these data, and that psychological, cultural and interpersonal factors were also relevant to outcome.

Goldney's rebuttal was essentially his own literature review, and a rebuke to Mendelson for selectively quoting from the studies. He drew attention to the rather high percentage of patients who are lost to follow-up in most of these studies. In his view, 'not cured by verdict' was not proven!

Aside from Mendelson's review, a small number of other studies have appeared. Tarsh and Royston (1985) followed up 35 litigants with severe somatic symptoms, with no underlying physical explanation. The follow-up was personal, often in the patients' homes, and family members were also interviewed. Most came from social classes IV and V; 75% had received injury at work. Only two returned to work before settlement, and only eight after, therefore employment in this group was the exception rather than the rule. At least one-third were certain to continue to live lives of invalidism, totally dependent on other family members.

Other conditions – neck and back injuries

The above studies have to do with the more general field of posttraumatic neurosis, many of them being carried out before the invention of PTSD, and only that of Tarsh and Royston (1985) specifically addresses the outcome of somatoform disorders in a medicolegal setting. There is a literature related to follow-up of neck and back injuries, also reviewed by Mendelson.

Gotten's work has already been referred to (Chapter 3); he felt more people were disabled by the diagnosis than by the injury itself!

Balla and Moraitis (1970) studied 82 Greek patients living in Australia with neck and back injuries who were involved in litigation. There was a preponderance of males. They noted that about 50% of the patients returned to work before any settlement (albeit often to a lower status), but of those not working, 74% remained unemployed at an average 2-year follow-up. They commented on the large numbers of doctors often involved in treating these patients; 70% had consulted over six. Nearly 25% were involved in more than one accident-related claim. Unusual physical signs were frequent, and pain often extended beyond anatomical expectations. Patients treated with a brace and those having surgery had a poorer prognosis. They thought that immobility was a possible factor in prolonging symptoms.

Hohl (1974) followed up a group of 146 patients with neck injuries following road traffic accidents, who were said to have had no preaccident symptoms. Fifty per cent with no legal claims were free of symptoms. All the rest had settled, and those who settled quickly (less than 18 months) had a much higher rate of complete recovery (83%) compared with those whose claims took longer (38%).

Woodyard (1982) followed up 584 litigants through GP records; the majority were injured at work. Of those with 'minor' injuries, return to work was less likely for an older age group and for unskilled workers, and those with back injuries had the worse prognosis.

In the study of Michler et al. (1993), over half of patients complaining of chronic whiplash symptoms and seeking compensation had had similar symptoms before their accidents, but in 57% this was denied, and only discovered by analysis of medical records. Studies from countries where compensation for whiplash symptoms is unavailable and chronic whiplash seems non-existent have already been discussed.

There are several follow-up studies pertaining to low-back injuries, but most stem from an era before magnetic resonance imaging scanning was available. Few address the impact of compensation factors in patients with non-lesional back pain. Krusen and Ford (1958) followed up over 500 patients with low-back injuries, and noted that, of those receiving compensation, only 56% were 'improved' as opposed to 89% of those with no compensation. Similar poorer rates of improvement in patients with low-back injuries in a compensation setting were reported by Arnhoff et al. (1977) and Sander and Meyers (1986).

Conclusions

Wade (2001), who did a Medline search for trials of rehabilitation in patients with conversion disorders, ended up by mainly reviewing anecdotes. He concluded that: 'at present, no good evidence to support any specific intervention for patients with hysterical conversion disorder can be found . . . and indeed there is no evidence to show that any intervention has any effect' (p. 334).

While on an individual basis, this conclusion is harsh, since there clearly are patients who respond well to appropriate interventions, it does reflect on the general lack of scientific interest in this area, and the failure to harness appropriate multi-disciplinary approaches to management.

Some symptoms have a good prognosis, especially those of acute onset, in the setting of stress, and associated with a recognisable psychiatric disorder, such as depression. However, the outlook for chronic disorders is bleaker, especially if the patient is polysymptomatic and associated personality disorders are present. Social factors act to maintain and promote symptoms, as discussed in more detail in chapter 8.

It seems to be the case that if people with the spectrum of disorders discussed above are not back at some kind of work by the time of settlement of their legal claim, they have a limited prospect of gaining employment, and that among factors contributing to a negative prognosis is the litigation process itself, and what is referred to here as lexigenic morbidity.

This chapter serves as a reminder that rating scales of behaviour and psychopathology have little value in medicolegal settings, because of issues of validity and reliability, and that clinical skills are paramount in assessment. Intimate knowledge of psychiatry, neurology and a broader sweep of general medicine are prerequisites for the evaluation of complicated somatising patients.

REFERENCES

American Psychiatric Association (1994). *Diagnostic and Statistic Manual of Mental Disorders*, 4th edn (DSM-IV). Washington, DC: APA Press.

Arnhoff, F. N., Triplett, H. B. and Pokorney, B. (1977). Follow-up status of patients treated with nerve blocks for low back pain. *Anaesthesiology*, **46**, 170–8.

Balla, J. I. and Moraitis, S. (1970). Knights in armour: a follow up study of injuries after legal settlement. *Medical Journal of Australia*, **2**, 355–61.

Barsky, A. J. and Wyshak, G. (1990). Hypochondriasis and somatosensory amplification. *British Journal of Psychiatry*, **157**, 404–9.

Bernstein, E. M. and Putnam, F. W. (1986). Development, reliability and validity of a dissociation scale. *Journal of Nervous and Mental Disease*, **174**, 727–35.

Bowman, E. S. (2001). Psychopathology and outcome in pseudoseizures. In eds A. B. Ettinger and A. M. Kanner, pp. 355–78. *Psychiatric Issues in Epilepsy*, New York: Lippincott/Williams and Wilkins.

Carter, A. B. (1949). The prognosis of certain hysterical symptoms. *British Medical Journal*, I, 1076–9.

Chandrasekaran, R., Goswami, U., Sivakumar, V. *et al.* (1994). Hysterical neurosis – a follow up study. *Acta Psychiatrica Scandinavica*, **89**, 78–80.

Clayer, J. R., Bookless, C. and Ross, M. W. (1984). Neurosis and conscious symptom exaggeration: its differentiation by the illness behaviour questionnaire. *Journal of Psychosomatic Research*, **28**, 237–41.

Colgan, S., Creed, F. and Klass, H. (1988). Symptom complaints, psychiatric disorder and abnormal illness behaviour in patients with upper abdominal pain. *Psychological Medicine*, **18**, 887–92.

Couprie, W., Wijdicks, E. F. M., Rooijmans, H. G. M. and van Gijn, J. (1995). Outcome in conversion disorder: a follow up study. *Journal of Neurology, Neurosurgery and Psychiatry*, **58**, 750–2.

Crimlisk, H. L., Bhatia, K., Cope, H. *et al.* (1998). Slater revisited: six year follow-up study of patients with medically unexplained symptoms. *British Medical Journal*, **316**, 582–6.

Culpan, R. and Taylor, C. (1973). Psychiatric disorders following road traffic and industrial injuries. *Australia and New Zealand Journal of Psychiatry*, **7**, 32–9.

Deale, A., Chalder, T., Marks, I. and Wessely, S. A. (1997). A randomised controlled trial of cognitive behaviour therapy versus relaxation therapy for chronic fatigue syndrome. *American Journal of Psychiatry*, **154**, 408–14.

Derogatis, L. R., Rickels, K., Ulenhuth, E. H. *et al.* (1974). The Hopkins symptom check list. In *Psychological Measurements in Psychopharmacology: Modern Problems in Pharmacopsychiatry*, vol. 7, pp. 79–110. Basel: eds P. Pichot, R. Olivier-Martin and S. Karger.

Editorial (2001). *Journal of the American Medical Association*, **286**, 1360–8.

Escobar, J. I., Rubio-stipec, M., Canino, G. and Karno, M. (1989). Somatic Symptom Index (SSI): a new and abridged somatization construct. *Journal of Nervous and Mental Disease*, **177**, 140–6.

Ettinger, A. B., Dhoon, A., Weisbrot, D. M. and Devinsky, O. (1999). Predictive factors for outcome of nonepileptic seizures after diagnosis. *Journal of Neuropsychiatry and Clinical Neuroscience*, **11**, 458–63.

Faust, D. (1995). The detection of deception. In *Malingering and Conversion Disorders*, pp. 225–66. ed. M. I. Weintraub, Philadelphia: WB Saunders.

Feinstein, A., Stergiopoulos, V., Fine, J. and Lang, A. E. (2001). Psychiatric outcome in patients with a psychogenic movement disorder. *Neuropsychiatry, Neuropsychology and Behavioural Neurology*, **14**, 169–76.

Felson, D. and Goldenberg, D. (1986). The natural history of fibromyalgia. *Arthritis and Rheumatism*, **29**, 1522–6.

Garza, J. A., Louis, E. D. and Ford, B. (2001). Long-term outcome of psychogenic movement disorders. *53rd Annual Meeting of the American Academy of Neurology*, p. 02.084 (abstract). Washington: APA Press.

Goldenberg, D. P., Gask, L. and O'Dowd, T. (1989). The treatment of somatisation – teaching techniques of reattribution. *Journal of Psychosomatic Research*, **33**, 686–96.

Goldenberg, D. L., Kaplan, K. H., Nadeau, M. G. *et al.* (1994). A controlled study of a stress reduction, cognitive behavioural treatment program in fibromyalgia. *Journal of Muskuloskeletal Pain*, **2**, 53–65.

Goldney, R. D. (1988). "Not cured by verdict". A re-evaluation of the literature. *Australian Journal of Forensic Sciences*, **20**, 295–300.

Guze, S. B. and Perley, M. J. (1963). Observations on the natural history of hysteria. *American Journal of Psychiatry*, **119**, 960–5.

Guze, S. B., Cloninger, C. R., Martin, R. L. and Clayton, P. J. (1986). A follow-up and family study of Briquet's syndrome. *British Journal of Psychiatry*, **149**, 17–23.

Hohl, M. (1974). Soft tissue injuries of the neck in automobile accidents: factors influencing prognosis. *Journal of Bone and Joint Surgery (Am)*, **56-a**, 1675–82.

Kelly, R. (1972). The post-traumatic syndrome. *Pahlevi Medical Journal*, **3**, 530–47.

(1975). The post-traumatic syndrome: an iatrogenic disease. *Forensic Science*, **6**, 17–24.

Kelly, R. and Smith, B. N. (1981). Post traumatic syndrome: another myth discredited. *Journal of the Royal Society of Medicine*, **74**, 275–7.

Kent, D. A., Tomasson, K. and Coryell, W. (1995). Course and outcome of conversion and somatisation disorders. A four year follow-up. *Psychosomatics*, **36**, 138–44.

Klimes, I., Mayou, R. A., Pearce, M. J., Coles, L. and Fagg, J. R. (1990). Psychological treatment for atypical non-cardiac chest pain: a controlled evaluation. *Psychological Medicine*, **20**, 605–11.

Kroenke, K., Spitzer, R. L., de Gruy, F. V. and Swindle, R. (1988). A symptom check list to screen for somatoform disorders in primary care. *Psychosomatics*, **39**, 263–72.

Krull, F. and Schifferdecker, M. (1990). Inpatient treatment for conversion disorder: a clinical investigation of outcome. *Psychotherapy and Psychosomatics*, **53**, 138–44.

Krusen, E. M. and Ford, D. E. (1958). Compensation factor in low back injuries. *Journal of the American Medical Association*, **166**, 1128–33.

Ledingham, J., Doherty, S. and Doherty, M. (1993). Primary fibromyalgia syndrome: an outcome study. *British Journal of Rheumatism*, **32**, 139–42.

Lewis, A. (1975). The survival of hysteria. *Psychological Medicine*, **5**, 9–12.

Lungberg, L. (1957). Hysteria, a clinical, prognostic and genetic study. *Acta Psychiatrica Scandanavica*, **32** (suppl. 112).

Mace, C. and Trimble, M. R. (1996). Ten year prognosis of conversion disorder. *British Journal of Psychiatry*, **169**, 282–8.

Mendelson, G. (1988). *Psychiatric Aspects of Personal Injury Claims*. Illinois: Charles C. Thomas.

Merskey, H. (1995). *The Analysis of Hysteria*. London: Gaskell Press.

Merskey, H. and Buhrich, N. A. (1975). Hysteria and organic brain disease. *British Journal of Medical Psychology*, **48**, 259–366.

Michler, R. P., Bovim, G. and Schrader, H. (1993). Physicians' statements concerning whiplash injuries. Significance of supplementary information. *Tiolsskrift for den Norske Laegeforening*, **113**, 1104–6.

Miller, H., (1961). Accident neurosis. *British Medical Journal*, **I**, 919–25, 992–8.

Noyes, R., Langbehn, D. R., Happell, R. L. *et al.* (1999). Health attitude survey: a scale for assessing somatising patients. *Psychosomatics*, **40**, 470–8.

O'Malley, P. G., Jackson, J. L., Santoro, J. *et al.* (1999). Antidepressant therapy for unexplained symptoms and syndromes. *Journal of Family Practice*, **48**, 980–90.

Othmer, E. and DeSouza, C. (1987). A screening test for somatisation disorder. *American Journal of Psychiatry*, **142**, 1146–9.

Pilowsky, I. (1997). *Abnormal Illness Behaviour*. Chichester: John Wiley.

Pokorny, A. D. and Moore, E. J. (1953). Neurosis and compensation: chronic psychiatric disorders following injury or stress in compensable situations. 1. Review of the literature. *Archives of Industrial Hygiene and Occupational Medicine*, **8**, 547–63.

Purves-Stewart, J. (1928). Discussion on traumatic neurasthenia and the litigation neurosis. *Proceedings of the Royal Society of Medicine*, **21**, 359–61.

Richards, S. C. M. and Scott, D. L. (2002). Prescribed exercise in people with fibromyalgia: parallel group randomized controlled study. *British Medical Journal*, **325**, 185–7.

Robins, L. and Helzer, J. (1982). Diagnostic Interview Schedule. *Archives of General Psychiatry*, **39**, 1442–5.

Ross, T. A. (1936). *An Enquiry into the Prognosis in the Neurosis*. London: Cambridge University Press.

Sander, R. A. and Meyers, J. E. (1986). The relationship of disability to compensation status. *Spine*, **11**, 141–3.

Scallett, A., Cloninger, R. and Othmer, E. (1976). The management of chronic hysteria: a review and double-blind trial of electrosleep and other relaxation methods. *Diseases of the Nervous System*, **37**, 347–53.

Sharpe, M., Hawton, K., Simkin, S. *et al.* (1996). Cognitive therapy for chronic fatigue syndrome: a randomised controlled trial. *British Medical Journal*, **312**, 22–6.

Slater, E. (1965). The prognosis of certain hysterical reactions. *British Medical Journal*, **I**, 1076–9.

Speckens, A. E. M. Van Hemert, A. M., Spinhoven, P. *et al.* (1995). Cognitive behavior therapy for medically unexplained physical symptoms: a randomised controlled trial. *British Medical Journal*, **311**, 1328–32.

Spitzer, R. L., Williams J. B., Kroenke, K. *et al.* (1994). Utility of a new procedure for diagnosing mental disorders in primary care. The PRIME-MD 1000 study. *Journal of the American Medical Association*, **272**, 1749–56.

Stone, J., Rothwell, P. M., Warlow, C. P. and Sharpe, M. (2003). The 12 year prognosis of unilateral functional weakness and sensory disturbance. *Journal of Neurology, Neurosurgery and Psychiatry*, **74**, 591–6.

Symonds, C. (1970). Address given at the National Hospital for Nervous Diseases, 27, 2, 1970. Text in: Merskey, H. (1995). *The Analysis of Hysteria*, 2nd edn, pp. 407–13. London: Gaskell Press.

Tarsh, M. J. and Royston, C. (1985). A follow-up study of accident neurosis. *British Journal of Psychiatry*, **146**, 18–25.

Thompson, G. N. (1965). Post traumatic psychoneurosis. *American Journal of Psychiatry*, **121**, 1043–8.

Turgay, A. (1990). Conversion disorder in children and adolescents. *Proceedings of the 143rd American Psychiatric Association Annual Meeting*, session 52, paper 156. Washington, DC: American Psychiatric Association.

Waddell, G., Pilowsky, I. and Bond, M. R. (1989). Clinical assessment and interpretation of abnormal illness behaviour in low back pain. *Pain*, **39**, 41–53.

Wade, D. T. (2001). Rehabilitation for hysterical conversion states. In *Contemporary Approaches to the Study of Hysteria*. Oxford: Oxford University Press. eds P. Halligan, C. Bass and J. C. Marshall, pp. 330–46.

Waller, N. G. and Ross, C. A. (1977). The prevalence and biometric structure of pathological dissociation in the general population. *Journal of Abnormal Psychology*, **106**, 499–510.

Walshe, F. (1965). Diagnosis of hysteria. *British Medical Journal*, **ii**, 1451–4.

Wessely, S., Hotopf, M. and Sharpe, M. (1998). *Chronic Fatigue and its Syndromes*. Oxford: Oxford University Press.

Wilson-Barnett, J. and Trimble, M. R. (1985). An investigation of hysteria using the Illness Behaviour Questionnaire. *British Journal of Psychiatry*, **146**, 601–8.

Working Group on CFS/ME (2002). *Report of the Working Group on CFS/ME*. London: Department of Health.

Woodyard, J. E. (1982). Injury compensation claims and prognosis. *Journal of the Society of Occupational Medicine*, **30**, 2–5.

World Health Organization (1992). *The ICD IO Classification of Mental and Behavioural Disorders*. Geneva: World Health Organization.

Ziegler, F. J., Imboden, J. B. and Meyer, E. (1960). Contemporary conversion reactions: a clinical study. *American Journal of Psychiatry*, **116**, 901–10.

7

Somatoform disorders in a medicolegal context

Lest men suspect your tale to be untrue
Keep probability – some say – in view . . .

(John Gay, Fables)

Facts are only the steam which obscures the mirror of truth.

(Ronald Knox, Bishop of Much Wenlock)

Introduction

It should not be forgotten that the basis of civil law is revenge, a motive as old as human history. Just before Titus kills his beloved, ravaged daughter Lavinia, he utters:

A reason mighty, strong and effectual;
A pattern, precedent, and lively warrant
For me, most wretched to perform alike (Shakespeare, *Titus Andronicus*, V, iii, 42)

The revenger here has his own way, out of a failure of the imperial law, appealing, as all revengers do, to the precedent of mythical tragedies stemming back to the House of Atreus. When Agamemnon cries of the 'ancient violence that longs to breed' (Aeschylus, *Agamemnon*, line 755), it is only intercession of the law in the form of Athena, representing the balance of passion and intellect, that decides between the Furies and Apollo on the fate of Orestes, finally acquitting him of murder. Precedent at this point moves from the realm of the gods to humans, from the congenital to the legal. Precedent became the bedrock of common law, Titus' appeal echoing down to Sir Edward Coke's introduction in the seventeenth century of a system of rules in English justice whereby past decisions bind the present. Everything about the law is retrospective. Gulliver had something to say about precedent: 'whatever hath been done before, may legally be done again: And therefore [lawyers] take special Care to record all the Decisions formerly made against common Justice and the general Reason of Mankind. These, under the Name of *Precedents*, they produce as Authorities to justify the most iniquitous Opinions' (Swift, 1998/1726, p. 242).

It is a fact of life that it is the responsibility of all citizens that, whenever they can reasonably foresee harm to another, they have a duty to exercise reasonable care to avoid causing that harm. A tort is a civil wrong, leading to a liability for damages. Negligence is the commonest tort in terms of the number of cases brought before the courts, and it has four central elements. These are a duty to take care, a breach of that duty, damage that ensues and such damage that has been caused as a consequence of the breach. Compensation can be awarded if negligence is proven.

The first two tenets are hardly medical matters, except in medicolegal negligence cases, and medical experts are usually asked to assess the third and fourth issues – has damage occurred, and if so, was it caused by the tort? The burden of proof lies with the claimant, who must prove his or her claim on a balance of probabilities – the 'standard of proof'. The claimant therefore needs to demonstrate first causation in fact, and then causation in law. The 'but for test' is the key to the former, remoteness of damage to the latter.

The system

Differences between civil and criminal law – two types of justice

The English legal system, which defies logical analysis, divides fundamentally into the civil and criminal divisions. This book is largely about cases which come before the former, but at the outset it must be noted that the standard of proof, and what has to be proved, is entirely different in the two courts. As will be noted, this leads to some strange anomalies in terms of expert evidence. While in criminal cases, conviction proceeds only if the case is 'beyond reasonable doubt', in a civil setting it is the 'balance of probabilities' which is required to establish liability.

In medical negligence cases, the balance between error of judgement and negligence can be a fine one, and attributing cause can be complicated. This is but one reason why such negligence claims have a far lower chance of success than most other personal injury claims (*Whitehouse* v. *Jordon*, [1981] 1 All ER 267: Jones, 2002).

The two types of justice are heard in different courts. Most civil negligence claims are dealt with through the county courts, but more complex and expensive cases go to the High Court, Queen's Bench division. There is a right of appeal, which is referred to the Court of Appeal, civil division, the head of which is the Master of the Rolls. The Court of Appeal does not hear witnesses (except in rare instances), and the final arbiter is of course the House of Lords, cases being heard by the Lords of Appeal. A more recent addition to this hierarchy is the European Court of Justice, which interprets community law. There is also the European Court of Human Rights, which is an organ of the Council of Europe, but since October 2000 the Human Rights Act (1998) has meant that much of the European Convention of

Human Rights has been a part of UK law, and decisions under it can now be made in the UK courts.

The reforms of Lord Woolf

The civil justice system underwent a radical reform in 1999. The ostensible reason was to bring a totally new perspective to civil litigation. This resulted in the Civil Procedure Rules (CPR). Lord Woolf, one of the Law Lords, later Lord Chief Justice, had some harsh things to say about experts and their role in the civil litigation process, effectively wishing that they could be dispensed with. He thought that the law had for too long been in the hands of the lawyers, rather than the courts, and that lawyers and their experts between them added delay, confusion and cost to the litigation process:

The subject of expert witnesses has figured prominently throughout the consultative process. Apart from discovery it was the subject which caused most concern . . . the need to engage experts was a source of excessive expense, delay and, in some cases, increased complexity through excessive or inappropriate use of experts (*Interim Report on Access to Justice*, Ch. 23, para 1).

The reforms meant that judges were to have greater control over the procedural conduct of the litigation, and a strict timetable would be set up for the running and completion of any individual case. Apart from abolishing the historically elegant word 'plaintiff' (as DSM has tried to abolish 'hysteria') and replacing it with 'claimant', he tried to minimise the role of experts and the impact of the adversarial system on the overall process.

There is now a supplemental hierarchical structure of the way that cases are handled, depending on the estimated settlement. Claims of less than £5000 are called small-track, and up to £15 000 are fast-track. The latter should be just that, speedy resolution with minimal cost. Multitrack claims are those over this figure.

Disclosure rather than secrecy has become the order of the day, both parties revealing to each other the totality of their evidence well before the trial. In theory there should be no last-minute revelations, no sudden exposés, no courtroom surprises. The new disclosure procedures are an enhanced form of the pre-existing discovery process, whereby parties are meant to disclose to each other documents they wish to rely on at a subsequent trial.

There is an alternative disputes procedure, in which the two parties can attempt a resolution of their differences with an intermediary mediator.

A payment into court, now referred to as the part 36 payment, may be made; this is an attempt to settle the case without a full trial. Literally, money is placed with the court, and the claimant may take it – or leave it. But, by opting for the latter, there may be later consequences. Thus, if, at the end of the trial the judge awards the claimant the same or less money, the claimant will be responsible not only for his or her own legal costs, but also the defendant's costs from the day of the court payment. Under the new CPR, the claimant can likewise make a formal offer of settlement, and if this is not accepted, the defendant suffers the same penalty, in reverse. This procedure (in which the facts are not disclosed to the judge) is a bit like Who Wants to be a Millionaire, where the prize money is on display, the questions are out, but the answer is unknown. This alone is only one twist of many, increasing the strains and tension of the legal screw, contributing to the claimant's lexigenic morbidity. The latter term derives from an understanding of the medical equivalent – iatrogenic morbidity. In the same way that doctors and medical treatments can be directly responsible for patients' symptoms, so can lawyers and the legal process. An alternative is juridogenic harm, introduced by Obomanu and Kennedy (2001), in the context of the dangers of extending the powers of tribunals under the proposed new Mental Health Act.

Try as hard as he could, however, Lord Woolf missed the point that the trial itself still remains adversarial in nature, and that the skills of the advocates and those instructing them are the only intoxicating ingredients of the otherwise bland cocktail that can spin the surest heads to distraction, confusing even the sharpest of expert witnesses. While experts are sworn to tell the truth, the whole truth and nothing but the truth, no such strictures are placed on the lawyers.

In routine clinical practice, it would be considered not only illogical, but also bad medical practice to withhold medical or other potentially useful information from a doctor assessing a case, but not so in legal practice. An expert may be denied access to vital medical documents (such as general practitioner (GP) notes, psychotherapy notes), and is expected none the less to formulate an opinion. In cases being considered in this book, such a practice is quite common, since claimants often express a wish for their preaccident medical, psychiatric and occupational history to be concealed. This is in marked contrast to criminal cases, in which every piece of medical evidence to support the defendant's invalid status is brought to the fore. As noted in earlier chapters, information on early upbringing, abuse, drug dependence and any forensic history is very relevant to understanding somatisation and related problems, and yet often deliberate attempts are made to hide such data; when it is disclosed, it is trivialised (Sim, 1992). Further, some medical reports which experts receive when evaluating a claimant are then removed from the trial documents, and the expert is unable to refer to them (being requested to change his or her report, and remove reference to such items – always a risky and somewhat dishonest exercise), even if the report supports the case, one way or another (the whole truth). Making medical diagnoses is a skilled clinical enterprise, and it is for the expert doctor, not someone trained entirely differently, to decide what is and what is not relevant to that exercise. Further, failure to note a document that the expert has seen in a report will constitute a breach of the expert's duty. Thus

Table 7.1 Some differences between civil and criminal medical evidence

	Criminal	Civil
Past history	Considered very important	Often concealed
More investigations	Considered valuable	Often refused
Hospital admission	Accepted	Often declined
Prognosis with treatment	Reported to be good	Reported to be poor
Unconscious motives	Not accepted	Acceptable
Nature of proof	Beyond reasonable doubt	Balance of probabilities
Single joint expert	Positively discouraged	Positively encouraged
Privilege of opinion	Allowed	Discouraged

all 'relevant' material considered and relied on in coming to an opinion must be disclosed. Again, civil and criminal law differ in this regard, since in the latter privileged information is sacrosanct, and an expert's opinion, based on privileged material, is itself privileged.

This issue of access to previous historical information is but one of several distinct differences between cases in the civil and criminal courts. A more complete list is given in Table 7.1. It is vehemently held in criminal cases that treatment will be effective, and the outlook will be good – offenders will be cured of their errant ways. In civil cases, medicolegal reports – at least from one side (for the claimant) – will often declare a grave prognosis, and then note the failure of treatments up to the time of the report as evidence that future treatments will be unsuccessful. In a criminal setting, any further medical investigations or offer of hospitalisation to help understand the case are seized on with alacrity, but in a civil setting are often declined, as patients with somatisation are notoriously reluctant to take up such suggestions. In terms of explanations for behaviour, the role of the unconscious is frequently invoked to explain away, for example, evidence of exaggeration of complaints in a civil setting, but criminal courts are notoriously reticent to entertain Freudian or neo-Freudian theories to forgive errant behaviour.

The Civil Procedure Rules

The relevant section for experts of the new Civil Procedure Rules is Part 35 (see also Appendix). As noted, Lord Woolf considered experts to be an unnecessary and expensive contaminant of the legal system, and sought to minimise their use, influence and fees. He opined that they could unduly affect the legal process through bias to one side of the case or another, and, as it was the prerogative of the legal teams themselves to decide on which expert evidence to rely, too many experts were being called, obscuring rather than clarifying the wood from the trees.

Three solutions to the problem were introduced. The first was that the courts rather than individual solicitors should have the power to direct how many experts there should be for any particular case, and who those experts may be, in terms of their disciplines. Further, the nature of expert evidence was to be directed, in terms of what expert evidence was required in a particular case, and the way it was to be presented to court (oral, written, etc.). All parties to the litigation are expected to work with the court to enhance the effective management of the case. Preaction protocols are laid down, and there are case management conferences in which a judge and the parties participate. This is when a timetable for the action is created, and experts are decided upon.

The second was the introduction of the single joint expert (SJE), appointed by the court to provide one report to be used by both parties. The third was the concept of experts talking to each other before a case comes to court, to produce a joint statement of points of agreement and disagreement upon which the court could rely.

These issues are discussed further below. However, it seems important first of all to note exactly what kind of creature Lord Woolf envisaged an expert to be.

Curiously enough, nowhere in Section 35 is a definition of an expert made explicit. Section 35.2 boldly declares that 'an "EXPERT" in this Part is a reference to an expert who has been instructed to give or prepare evidence for the purpose of court proceedings'. However, since it is the court that now directs which experts may be admissible, and the type of expert required, it is clear that such decisions must be made by the judge directing the case. In other words, previously it was up to individual solicitors and their advising barristers to have the expertise and possess their own expert knowledge of the intricacies of the type of cases they were dealing with to select the appropriate expert. Now it is the judges. This presumes that the judge responsible has considerable experience in the specific area of the case, and that he or she has received the relevant training necessary to understand the particular problems of the case. While this may often be a relatively simple matter, medicolegal, especially medical negligence cases, and several areas of medical practice such as psychiatry require considerable understanding before relevant decisions about experts can be made.

Within the directives there are some guides to an understanding of what an expert may be. We are given such helpful comments ranging from the quaint 1935 statement that: 'The opinion of scientific men upon proven facts may be given by men of science within their own science', to the equally unhelpful: 'any person who has such knowledge or experience of or in connection with that question that his opinion on it would be admissible in evidence'. No definition of what a scientific man may be is proffered, although the caveat that it shall be 'within their own science' seems clear enough and will be noted further later.

Halsbury's Laws of England takes the issue no further. 'Expert evidence may simply be described as the opinions of an expert on any question or issue on which he is qualified to express his opinions'. (Hailsham *et al.*, 1994). An expert is an expert!

However, it is clear in the new directives that the expert's duty is to help the court 'on the subject of his own expertise'. Oddly enough, there is no special requirement that the person is professionally qualified, although generally this is desirable. Also the expert should be 'to the forefront' of those practising in his or her area (CPR 29.2.3). The court however has the final decision as to whether a particular person has the necessary 'skill, experience and learning' to be considered an expert. This again requires the judge to have a considerable knowledge of the intricacies of the case presented and to be acquainted with the relevant skills and qualifications of the experts that may be used in any particular case.

A distinction that has been made, and is of further relevance to this issue, is between evidence based on fact, and that based on opinion. In the past, experts were employed to explain the technical aspects of their science, and later, in the eighteenth century, they were called upon to give evidence on opinion. Nowadays, experts are more often needed to provide the latter since, although facts may be in dispute, it is always the interpretation of the facts that becomes an opinion. Again, nowhere is this more relevant than in the medicolegal arena. It is the significance and the relevance of any observed facts that are important for the court, and this comes down to the matter of opinion. The opinion is the expertise but, in a legal system founded on adversarial dichotomy, it is not surprising that experts of differing opinions are found, both sides in a case wishing to give proper vent to the possible interpretation of the findings and facts of the individual case. As Nietzsche remarked, there are only atoms, air and opinions.

The expert's responsibility

This is covered in Part 35.3. 'It is the duty of an expert to help the court on the matters within his expertise. This duty overrides any obligation to the person from whom he has received instructions or by whom he is paid'. Again, this instruction seems based on the views of Lord Woolf that all experts are converts (to one side or another in a case), and that they are incapable of being unbiased in their opinions. No evidence incidentally was ever put forward to support this often-made allegation, and, in any case, such strictures on expert practice were laid down well before the CPR reforms. The statement of Judge Cresswell in *The Ikarian Reefer* ([1993], 2 Lloyd's Report 68 at 81) is given in Table 7.2, which provides a good summary of experts' duties, fully endorsed by Lord Woolf himself. However, this means that the report itself now has to be written in a more formal format than previously, being addressed to the court. Riders about the responsibility of experts need to be given in the report,

Table 7.2 Duties and functions of an expert witness

1. Expert evidence presented to the court should be and should be seen to be the independent product of the expert uninfluenced as to form or content by the exigencies of litigation

2. An expert witness should provide independent assistance to the court by way of objective unbiased opinion in relation to matters within his or her expertise. An expert witness in the High Court should never assume the role of an advocate

3. An expert witness should state the facts or assumptions on which his or her opinion is based. He or she should not omit to consider material facts which detract from his or her concluded opinion

4. An expert witness should make it clear when a particular question or issue falls outside his or her area of expertise

5. If an expert opinion is not properly researched because the expert considers that insufficient data are available, then this must be stated with an indication that the opinion is no more than a provisional one

6. If, after exchange of reports, an expert witness changes his or her view on a material matter . . . such change of view should be communicated to the other side without delay and when appropriate to the court

7. Where expert evidence refers to photographs, plans, calculations . . . or other similar documents, these must be provided to the opposite party at the same time as the exchange of reports

Judge Cresswell in *The Ikarian Reefer* (1993, 2 *Lloyd's Rep.* 68 at 81).

including the understanding that their responsibility is to the court, and verified with a statement of truth. The earlier simple: 'I believe that the facts I have stated in this report are true and that the opinions I have expressed are correct' has been amended to the tortuous: 'I confirm that insofar as the facts stated in my report are within my own knowledge I have made clear which they are and I believe them to be true, and that the opinions I have expressed represent my true and complete professional opinion'. The directives are that expert evidence must be restricted to 'that which is necessary to resolve the proceedings justly', and that 'no more than one expert in any one speciality' shall be used.

After the report is received, both parties have the right to put written questions about the report, whether acting for one party or as an SJE. However, such questions may be put only once, should be placed within 28 days of the service of the report, and must be only for clarification of the report. There then appears an innocent rider, namely that if the expert does not answer the questions, his or her report may be struck out of the proceedings. No timescale, incidentally, for the return of replies is stipulated, but in practice it is often requested by solicitors, and 28 days is considered reasonable.

This innovation has considerable relevance, and effectively can be a mini-cross-examination before a trial. In many cases it forms the basis for a settlement. In theory, the questions should not be so long and complex as to appear onerous, and if the expert feels this is the case he or she can ask for court directions.

At this point, the difficulties and conflicts that arise between being an adviser and an expert witness should be noted. Thus, a solicitor may seek advice from an expert about the feasibility of a case. At this point the expert has no responsibility to the court at all. The solicitor then requests the adviser to become the witness, namely to be the court's expert. There is a clear conflict here, especially since, as an adviser, the expert will be retained by the solicitor and legal team not only to have conference with counsel, but also, during the court proceedings, to sit behind counsel and provide guidance for that counsel only!

The single joint expert

Of all the Woolf directives, this may seem to be the most contentious, and the one most likely to subvert the legal process of seeking 'justice'. Section 35.7 directs that a single expert can be named by the instructing parties in agreement, or, if they cannot agree, then the court (judge) will select the expert for them. The instructions following this directive are however revealing. Thus, the SJE is to be appointed 'where it appears to the court, on the information then available, that the issue falls within a substantially established area of knowledge, and where it is not necessary for the court to sample a range of opinion'. In general, it is envisaged that the parties will come to an agreement over the SJE, but if this is not possible, the court may select an expert from the list prepared by the instructing parties, or the court (judge) may direct their own chosen expert, selected in 'some other manner'.

Both parties can put instructions to the SJE, and the judge may 'give directions about the payment of the expert's fees and expenses', seeking to limit the latter. Both parties are jointly responsible for the payment of these disbursements (although costs of subsequent questions are in the first instance borne by the questioning solicitors).

Discussions between experts

The court at any stage in the proceedings may instruct experts to discuss their respective reports, and to come to an agreed statement.

The experts are told to specify issues in the proceedings and to discuss them, and 'where possible, reach agreement on an issue'. In fact, provision is made for the court to direct the issues to be discussed, and the respective solicitors may be asked to draw up a list of relevant questions for discussion. The procedural judge can 'define . . . the subject matter to be covered' (35.12.1).

The joint statement must be prepared for the court, and address issues of agreement and disagreement, and a summary of the reasons for any disagreement outlayed. Interestingly, such joint discussions are not binding on the parties, and the content of the discussions is not to be referred to in court, unless both parties agree.

The directives are that experts have a discussion, so that a face-to-face meeting is not expected, and telephone or video interactions are accepted. 'The important point is that they should communicate effectively' (35.12 1.) Further, 'the meeting should cover only matters within the expert's professional competence'. The term is 'experts of like discipline'. There may be more than one discussion, as is deemed necessary. An unfortunate rider to this (clearly at odds with the last instruction) is that the court may direct a timetable for these discussions.

The problems

While, as so often on paper, many of these directives seem sensible, in practice they present experts with many problems that should have been envisaged. The following comments relate to medicolegal expert advice, especially in psychiatry and its borderlands, particularly in relation to somatoform disorders and related conditions, and may not be relevant to other disciplines. None the less, much of the publicity driving these reforms (other than financial considerations, which were paramount) related to delays in settlement of personal injury claims and medical negligence cases.

First, the definition of an expert is severely lacking. The direction is for experts of like disciplines to discuss cases together, experts themselves being 'within their own science', and 'qualified to express opinions'. Within medicine there are numerous specialities, and indeed subspecialities. There are also specialists in allied fields, such as physiotherapists, psychotherapists and psychologists, who may contribute to an understanding of a case, but who would not be in a position to provide a medical report *per se*, since they possess no medical qualifications. In other words, their science is different.

In many civil injury cases, combinations of physical and psychological injury have to be addressed, and often both problems are symptomatically intertwined. It is quite common, for example, for orthopaedic specialists to disagree with each other over the extent and reliability of a patient's orthopaedic complaints, and to seek clarification for an assessment of the claimant's mental health. In the latter field, psychiatrists may disagree over the extent of a patient's depression or anxiety, or, more often on the cause of any psychiatric disorder present. The diagnosis of posttraumatic stress disorder (PTSD) has created considerable problems in this regard (see Chapter 8); so much so that its overdiagnosis threatens the use and validity of the whole diagnostic concept. Accidents are often associated with bereavements, and bereavements are a part of life. The intermingling of symptoms of PTSD, bereavement and depression is a clear example of where clean and precise answers to questions of causation are unlikely to emerge through joint consultations between experts, or with SJEs.

This pessimistic conclusion emerges from the complications of psychiatry as a discipline (dealing with medical, sociobiological and psychological issues), the blurred boundary between diagnostic entities, and between psychiatric caseness (where psychiatric illness begins) and normal responses to stress, and the difficulties of establishing causation in medicolegal settings.

In the field of psychiatry, further confusion is brought to the court by the profusion of evidence deemed to be psychiatric. The term 'of like discipline' should, if anything, refer to the same level and kind of professional education and qualifications. Psychiatrists in the UK first qualify in medicine, then do postgraduate training in psychiatry, their specialist imprimatur coming from membership (later fellowship) of the Royal College of Psychiatrists. Under the CPR, it is not uncommon to be asked to confer with others who are *not* of a like discipline, but the joint consultation is requested seemingly simply because there is a doctor on the opposing side who seems the only one available to discuss the case with! 'Like discipline' has not been considered or thought through by the instructing judge (examples are psychiatrists being told to liaise with rheumatologists over issues such as fibromyalgia, or with orthopaedic surgeons over possible malingering).

A further error is investing paramedical specialists with the same 'science' as physicians and surgeons. An example here is the request to psychiatrists to confer with psychologists who are thought, mistakenly, to be medically qualified. Psychologists have their own training and diploma and degree structure, but they have no medical training, and the art of the differential diagnostic is not within their province. In the same way that an instructing solicitor would not seek a medical diagnosis of multiple sclerosis from a physiotherapist, it is inappropriate to seek a psychiatric opinion from a psychologist. The physiotherapist will give good advice about the level of functional impairment of a patient, and aid with issues of rehabilitation and management, but he or she cannot be a diagnostician. The same holds for psychologists and psychotherapists in the area of mental illness.

The British Psychological Society has offered instructions about this in its pamphlet *Psychologists as Expert Witnesses* (1999). They draw the distinction between psychiatry and psychology thus:

The evidence of psychologists and psychiatrists departs when the former begin to comment on the development and mental functioning of *ordinary individuals*. Psychologists do devote more of their training to the understanding of *normal human behaviour* than their psychiatrist colleagues, who *focus principally on the presence or absence of mental disorder* (authors' italics).

This implies that the evaluation of the absence or presence of psychiatric disorder, which after all is what the medical issues are about in these cases, is not in the province of non-medically qualified practitioners. The courts, in a medical report addressing psychiatric issues, require advice about 'recognisable psychiatric disorder' (see below), and this is strictly a medical matter.

Interestingly, the manual also states: 'Psychologists are not normally permitted to give evidence about how an ordinary person is likely to react to stressful situations'. This would seemingly exclude the use of psychologists in the evaluation of PTSD, and its variants.

The issue of the role of the expert also arises from another angle. It is not uncommon for solicitors to obtain expert advice from either the patient's treating doctor, or a specialist to whom the patient had been referred by the GP. In the pre-Woolf era this may have caused some difficulties, although, as noted, there a distinction has always been made between those providing evidence based on fact as opposed to those providing expert opinions. However, the CPR requirements are now that experts have a responsibility only to the court, hence the declaration that his 'duty is to the court, and that [he has] complied with that duty'. The dilemma is that if the patient has been referred to a specialist in his or her role as doctor, and not for any legal purpose, then the specialist's obligation is entirely to the patient. Although it is unfashionable to quote the Hippocratic oath these days, such obligations are made quite clear in the instructions to newly qualified doctors from the General Medical Council.

In other words, to comply with the CPR requirements, experts explicitly cannot be those who have seen the patient in the course of their non-legal work. Conflicts of opinion must arise since their duty is solely to the patient. There can be no more obvious cause of bias.

This problem has been recognised, but seems rarely to be acknowledged. The Court of Appeal made this explicit point in the case of *Vernon v. Bosley*, namely that using treating clinicians as experts makes it 'harder for them to be objective' ([1997] 1 All ER 577). In the more recent hearing of *Liverpool Roman Catholic Archdiocesan Trustees Inc. v. Goldberg*, Justice Neuberger opined that if an expert had a relationship with a claimant such that a reasonable observer might think it capable of influencing the expert's views, such evidence should not be admissible (*The Times*, 9 March 2001). The trial judge in considering the matter summed it up as follows: 'Where it is demonstrated that there exists a relationship between the proposed expert and the party calling him which a reasonable observer might think was capable of affecting the views of the expert so as to make them unduly favourable to that party, his evidence should not be admitted however unbiased the conclusions of the expert might probably be' (Evans-Lombe, 7 July 2001, New Law 2010712502). Further, all of this implies that no treating physician can be in a position to be an SJE!

Lord Woolf asks for experts to be at the 'forefront' of those in their area. This is very desirable, but the reforms actually act against those with such attributes. Thus, severe time constraints are now being placed upon experts, not only in respect of the time they are given to produce reports, but also with regards to answering questions put about their opinion. Such pressures are acting against the provision of expertise. Time is a commodity destroyed by others! Before an expert can produce a report, it is necessary to have other reports and notes available (for example, hospital and GP records). Collecting them, which is the responsibility of the claimant's solicitors, takes time, and can often be met with obstruction. Time is sometimes needed to review literature, and obtain relevant book chapters or academic papers. Artificially to demand time restraints is asking for reports to be prepared perhaps with incomplete information, which is bound to be contra-justice. Further, making the expert see a claimant within an unrealistically short time of referral means that experienced and effective experts are likely to be ruled out of the claim. In other words, experts are experts because of their reputation and knowledge. There are none who hang around waiting for a case to turn up! Any good expert will have a long waiting list. This is all the more so in medical work, since experts are likely also to have substantial hospital and academic appointments with a well-established institution from which, in part, their reputation arises. They cannot devote their whole time to medicolegal practice. Those who can are therefore likely to be the neophyte, the retired or the carpet-bagger – surely not what the courts want! Threatening to strike out reports simply because experts cannot be on hand to respond immediately to instructions again seems hardly tuned to the concept of justice! In fact, so specialised has medicolegal work become, with its own expertise, demands and intellectual horizons, that some specialists are none of the above, but have become specialists in medicolegal medicine, a discipline that they would argue should be recognised in its own right.

Further, the issue of failure to reply to a particular question may depend simply on an expert's inability to reply. For example, experts are often asked on findings of fact, which are entirely the province of the court. On issues of causality, the questions asked by one party may not be answerable in direct terms. In medicolegal practice this is quite common. Causality in the law and in medicine represent different concepts, as explored later, and while an expert may try to answer the unanswerable, the replies may unhappily fall on one side rather than the other in the conflict; the disgruntled party then tries to have the expert omitted from the trial. Another move hardly aimed at seeking 'justice'!

Single joint experts

This chimera seems to be the central showpiece of the reforms. It is supposed that life and law are so simple that, in reality, one person can satisfy the needs of both parties in a dispute that is quintessentially antagonistic in nature, and that the problems of bias, apparently brought into cases and sustained by experts, would be overcome. In fast-track cases an SJE is the rule; in multitrack cases their role is still being evaluated.

The SJE needs to be as unbiased as possible, and should copy to all parties any instruction-related correspondence. He or she should decline to attend any meeting or conference at which all the parties are not represented, and must send all parties copies of finished reports that must be addressed to the court.

There are several problems, especially in the field of psychiatry and related disciplines. First, as noted, facts are not opinions. The SJE is expected to receive instructions from both instructing parties which should set out the 'range of opinion on matters dealt with'. This often does not occur, and in many cases, only one letter of instruction is received, the alternative solicitor remaining anonymous. If the issue which requires the expertise is simple, and not central to the case, then the role of the SJE is clearer. The problem is that in so many cases the range of opinion is wide, especially in psychiatric medicolegal settings. A simple case of depression may be linked with genetics, traumatic upbringing, bereavement, past episodes of psychiatric illness and loss of a job. All of this needs to be put in the context of any accident. The range of opinion as to the relevance of the latter may be wide, and really should be for the courts to test, *by their criteria*. Often, then, if an SJE is doing his or her job properly, and casts the net widely over the sea of possibility, the report will of necessity fail to resolve the legal issues, any more than two experts did previously.

The CPR directions have allowed for this, by distinguishing between experts and expert witnesses: expert witnesses are those whose reports are for the court and can be used in court. But, if unsatisfied with the SJE's report, one or both parties are at liberty to hire their own advisors, who may assist in court, but may not give oral evidence. Instead of one expert, we may now have three!

Further, few accidents with neuropsychiatric consequences fall readily within the penumbra of one discipline. Assessment of head-injury claims may need a neurological, a neuropsychological, a neuroradiological and a psychiatric opinion. The balance of opinion of any one expert will relate to the other, and it may not be possible to reach a conclusion before all the reports are put in place. This requires time and the commissioning of the other experts' reports. There is a temptation to limit this, by refusing admission of one or other disciplines, but the reality is that all may be necessary, and would be used in reaching conclusions in a non-legal setting.

Recognising this, but seeking to limit advice, the court can insist on calling an SJE who is 'a leading expert in the dominant discipline' (35.7), who should prepare a general report incorporating the evidence of others. Again, this can only lead to an etiolated version of the clinical opinions being sought, and to limit the true scope of the probe.

In reality, the complexity of many cases is such that an SJE is simply inappropriate, since it will be obvious that a range of opinion will be expected, and should be tried by the due legal process. Indeed, this is recognised by the CPR where it states that an SJE is to be used when 'it is not necessary for the court to sample a range of opinion'. This should rule out the use of an SJE for all but the simplest psychiatric claims.

An SJE is very constrained on the advice that can be given to the parties. In a nutshell, if at one end of the range of the opinion given is that the claimant may be a malingerer, it is difficult to advise both solicitors to hire private surveillance agencies! Further, often the outcome of a case only becomes clear as the litigation proceeds, especially with complex neuropsychiatric problems. Sometimes it is only when conference with counsel is carried out that the full social complexity of the case is revealed, and clarity is achieved. Such in-house discussions are not readily available to the SJE, and this severely restricts the SJE's abilities to proffer effective advice.

Incidentally, there is no obligation on the parties to use the report of the SJE in a trial. If the parties do not agree, then presumably they must both be entitled to obtain their own reports, and again we are back with three experts! There are now several cases in which judgement in favour of parties wishing to retain their own experts after appointing an SJE has been given (*Daniels* v. *Walker* [2000] 1 WLR 1382; *Pattison* v. *Cosgrove*, *The Times*, 13 February 2001). Basically, if the case has any complexity, and the claim is substantial, as it is with many psychiatric cases, an SJE is unlikely to satisfy the needs of the case.

Such are the constraints placed upon an SJE, in terms of limiting the effect of a report on the legal process, that the concept has been challenged under Article 6 of the European Convention on Human Rights. Since the challenge was rejected by none other than Lord Woolf himself, this line has not yet gone further. It is yet another of the paradoxes of logic that, in contrast to the civil courts, an SJE is positively discouraged in criminal cases, because it might deny the rights to a fair trial under the Human Rights Act!

Discussion between experts

This seemingly sensible inclusion is ridden with problems, as should have been clear from the outset. The directive is that experts should communicate effectively, whatever that may mean. In practice, most discussions are conducted over the telephone, less frequently by teleconference of three or more experts. The court has the option to specify the issues to be discussed, but rarely seems to exercise this.

The discussions are to clarify, for the court, areas of agreement and disagreement between the experts, and to summarise reasons for disagreeing. The meeting is to be 'without prejudice'.

In practice, the discussions are (usually) politely conducted, and compromise is reached. There are however those who make this exercise very difficult, and sometimes frankly unpleasant. In such circumstances the expert can revert to the instructing solicitor and request that the court orders a face-to-face meeting. However, there is a main problem – agreement is reached if the two reports already reflect this; if there are areas of disagreement, apparent in the respective reports, these are reiterated. The disagreements are hedged with professional courtesy. In other words, little emerges that is not in the original documents, and a compromise is reached which, where there is disagreement, may be a totally different compromise to that which would be reached if the experts were subjected to the appropriate legal method, namely cross-examination. In summary, it is difficult to see how the case of one party could not be damaged by its own expert agreeing an issue in a manner inconsistent with the case as advanced by that party at trial (Kelly *et al.*, 2001).

Often the joint report evokes further questions from solicitors, because they think that the issues have not been resolved *from their point of view*, although usually this is because they have failed to put relevant questions to the experts earlier, as they can, before the joint consultation.

Often these discussions are held under unrealistic time restraints. Experts, as already noted, are not full-time servants of the court, and are not at hand to phone and find people for these consultations at the drop of a hat. The courts direct that the discussions must be held by certain dates, and reports produced shortly thereafter, but this hardly encourages effective communication.

It is not uncommon to be asked to discuss a case with another expert, only to find out that the other expert not only has not seen some or much of the relevant evidence (such as GP notes, or reports of other experts), but substantial evidence, such as video surveillance tapes, has not been made available to both sides. A further problem is that, after the discussion, a bundle of papers arrives, of importance to the case, which should have been available at the time of the joint conference, and further advice is sought.

These errors could be avoided if the judges involved gave due consideration to the time constraints of experts, set up sensible timetables, and directed solicitors to the effect that joint consultations should not take place until *all* the relevant material that will be considered in a trial has been made available to the experts in the case.

Although the directive for experts of a like discipline to discuss a case together seems straightforward, it is not, especially at the interface between neurology and psychiatry, and in the area of somatisation. The important issue of differences between psychiatrists and psychologists has already been noted. However, often at stake is whether or not a patient has 'organic' damage, and if so, how this is related to the patient's problems. In these cases, neurologists are asked to talk with neurologists, neuropsychologists with neuropsychologists, and so on. However, in reality all the experts are interdependent, and one set may find it difficult to reach conclusions of any validity alone. The joint consultation really needs to be arranged for all (four, six or eight) persons to be together at the same time – if the outcome is to have validity. This is rarely achieved, and if directed, is unsatisfactorily arranged. It cannot be up to the experts to organise these conferences, and this must remain the responsibility of the requesting solicitors. However, without such multidisciplinary discussions, the process of understanding these difficult cases is so fraught with hazards, and experts should advise their instructing solicitors that 'effective communication' is not possible if they believe that to be the case.

Claims for psychiatric injury

Claims for psychiatric injury have been awarded by the courts since at least the nineteenth century, but have grown considerably in magnitude and complexity over the past 25 years. The reasons for this include not only changes in law, but also in psychiatry with the advent of DSM-III (American Psychiatric Association, 1980) and succeeding editions, the reification of the concept of PTSD and related diagnoses, and a considerable public awareness of the possibilities of both litigation and psychiatric damage.

The term 'nervous shock' entered case law in the mid nineteenth century, and, judging by the speeches of the *Privy Council in Victorian Railway Commissioners v. Coltras* ([1883] 13 AC 222), it entered judicial language as a result of medical experts having used the expression when giving evidence.

The popular view is that it was actually Erichsen who first coined the phrase in relation to railway accidents. It has also been argued that the term had been the subject of earlier legal usage, in particular by the barrister Henry Godefroi, who referred to it in a paper he presented to the Judicial Society in 1870 (Mendelson, 1998,

p. 48). However, it is clearly entwined with medical concepts such as shellshock. The contemporary equivalent is psychiatric injury.

The law now treats nervous shock in a claim category of its own, especially when allegedly brought about by negligence. However, nervous shock does not equate with psychiatric illness, and before compensation ensues, the nervous shock has to be seen to have caused the subsequent psychiatric illness. In cases where there has been no physical injury, any emotional distress has to be beyond the normal human emotions, and must be a 'recognisable psychiatric disorder'. It must be further noted that the grief, sorrow or emotional hardship of caring for damaged loved ones is not included in the compensation package. Further, since the Hillsborough cases in relation to psychiatric injury, allegedly caused by negligence, certain limitations are placed on who can claim what, depending on such concepts as 'proximity', 'aftermath' and, most significantly, how the claimant has been categorised – as either a 'primary' or 'secondary' victim. Incidentally, the term 'victim' in this context is a legal term that emerged from the Hillsborough trial. Also, since Hillsborough, the law probably excludes compensation for possible shock involved in the postmortem identification of bodies (Pugh and Trimble, 1993).

Thus, ordinary mental distress is not compensated. If the claimant is physically injured, then there are damages awarded for pain and suffering, which fall under the category of mental distress, and for consequent psychiatric illness. However it is in the absence of physical injury that the law has special provisions to limit compensation, especially related to negligence.

The early line of relevant authorities for compensation for psychiatric injury is shown in Table 7.3. The courts have always adopted a cautious approach to opening the floodgates of compensation for nervous shock, initially accepting it only in association with physical injury (*Victorian Railway Commissioners* v. *Coultas* [1888] 12 App Cas 222). In the case of *Dulieu* v. *White* ([1901] 2 KB 669), the female plaintiff was awarded damages for fear of 'immediate personal injury' after a van and horses ran through the window of a public house where she was working. This principle was tested further in the Piper Alpha disaster (*McFarlane* v. *E. E. Caledonia* [1994] 2 All ER 1), following which the plaintiff claimed nervous shock after witnessing a fire on a drilling station on which 164 people were killed. However, the case failed as he was a bystander and had no proximate relationship to those killed and he was not in fear of his own safety.

Thus, two types of non-physically injured plaintiffs became defined (Table 7.4): those directly involved in accidents (so-called primary victims – in this text referred to as claimants) and those who are not directly involved, but have seen or heard or become involved in the consequences of an accident (the immediate aftermath), and have as a consequence suffered psychiatric injury (secondary claimants). The former

Table 7.3 Psychiatric injury

Date	Line of authorities
1886	*Victorian Railway Commissioners* v. *Coultas* (Australia) No damages for nervous shock unaccompanied by physical injury
1890	*Bell* v. *Great Northern Railway Co.* (Ireland) Damages awarded for nervous shock despite no physical injury
1901	*Dulieu* v. *White* Damages awarded for nervous shock limited to fear for oneself only
1925	*Hambrook* v. *Stokes* Damages awarded for nervous shock apprehending fear for safety of children
1932	*Donoghue* v. *Stevenson* Proximity does not merely mean physical proximity; it also extends to proximity of close relationships between people
1939	*Chester* v. *Waverely Corp.* (Australia) No damages for nervous shock on seeing corpse of 7-year-old son – no duty of care
1942	*Bourhill* v. *Young* No damages for nervous shock on witnessing accident involving a stranger – no duty of care
1953	*King* v. *Phillips* No damages for a mother who heard screams of son and ran to the scene – no duty of care
1964	*Boardman* v. *Sanderson* Damages awarded to father who heard screams of son and ran to scene
1967	*Abramzik* v. *Brenner* (Canada) No damages to mother told of death of two children – no duty of care
1968	*Dillon* v. *Legg* (California) Damages awarded to mother for emotional shock and physical injury from witnessing death of her child

are tested for by determining whether or not the claimant was *at risk* of physical injury, and therefore in the 'zone' of physical danger. They must therefore be exposed to the risk or reasonably think themselves at risk. Secondary claimants are those not categorised as primary. They essentially are the mere witnesses, and will not be in the zone of physical danger. A crucial point is that primary victims do not have to prove that the exposure was the cause, or that the harm was foreseeable. To be a primary claimant makes it therefore much easier to recover than being a secondary claimant because the latter, in addition to having to prove negligence and causation, must also satisfy other requirements.

Before summarising the current position on 'proximity' and the senses, it is necessary to examine three decisions of the House of Lords before the Hillsborough

Table 7.4 Recovery for psychiatric injury

1. Physical harm leading to psychiatric harm
2. Pure psychiatric harm
   (recognisable psychiatric disorder)

Gradual onset	Sudden events	
(occupational stress)	(e.g. PTSD)	
	Primary victims	Secondary victims

PTSD, posttraumatic stress disorder.

Table 7.5 The key House of Lords authorities containing the important principles for recovery of damage for psychiatric trauma

Bourhill v. *Young* [1943] AC 92
McLoughlin v. *O'Brien* [1983] 1 AC 410
Alcock v. *Chief Constable of South Yorkshire police* [1992] 1 AC 310
Page v. *Smith* [1996] 1 AC 155

case (Table 7.5). The case of *Hambrook* v. *Stokes Bros* ([1925] 1 KB 141) established that shock from what has been seen through the unaided senses is recoverable (the plaintiff saw an out-of-control lorry careering around a bend to the place she had just left her children. She did not see any collision, but feared for their safety, and was told that children had been injured). The case, the first successful secondary claimant, however, limited claims to those in close proximity of an accident and to information received through the 'unaided senses'.

The issue of the senses was further tested in the case of *Bourhill* v. *Young* ([1943] AC 92). A plaintiff heard a crash some 15 metres away, and some time later saw blood on the road. In fact, a cyclist was involved in an accident, and the plaintiff was not herself put in fear for her safety. She claimed nervous shock as the result of the noise of the collision and the visual aftermath. Her claim failed. She was in no physical danger, she was not in the immediate area of the impact, and she was a total stranger to the victim. An ordinary bystander was expected to withstand the sight and sound of road accidents. The claimant was pregnant at the time of the accident, and about a month later she gave birth to a stillborn child. It was thus further held that, as she was pregnant, she was not of 'reasonable fortitude'.

In the case of *McLoughlin* v. *O'Brien* ([1983] 1 AC 410), the plaintiff's daughter was killed and her husband and two other children suffered injuries in an accident which occurred 3 km from her home, where she was at the time of the accident.

About an hour after it happened she went to the hospital, where she was told that one of her children had been killed, and she witnessed her husband and the other two children very distressed, and saw them before they had been cleaned up. Her claim finally succeeded at the House of Lords, and in this case the nervous shock was held to be reasonably foreseeable. However, in addition the case examined the issue of close relatives, and the concept of the immediate aftermath. With regards to the latter, the 'proximity test' had to be satisfied. In his judgement of the case, Lord Wilberforce stated that: 'as regards proximity to the accident, it is obvious that this must be close in both time and space . . . The shock must come through sight or hearing of the event or of its immediate aftermath'. The House of Lords held that an 'hour or so' was the limit of the aftermath doctrine.

However, since then, the courts have sought to limit foreseeability. Foreseeability refers not to what a negligent party may have foreseen, but to what a 'reasonable hypothetical observer could reasonably have foreseen' (*Bourhill* v. *Young*). At the present time then, in order to recover, the secondary victim must pass the two tests, the 'proximity test' and the 'relationship test', and show that psychiatric injury was foreseeable, perceived through the claimant's own unaided senses, and that he or she is a person of so-called 'customary phlegm'.

The Hillsborough trial

A major disaster occurred at Hillsborough football stadium, in which 95 spectators were killed and 400 injured. Scenes from the ground were broadcast live on radio and television. Sixteen people, all but one being relatives of the dead or injured, brought claims for nervous shock resulting in psychiatric illness caused by hearing or seeing the news of the disaster.

The case had to do with defining the limitations of the secondary plaintiffs, the means by which nervous shock is caused, and again raised issues to do with the immediate aftermath. (*Alcock* v. *Chief Constable of South Yorkshire Police* [1992] 1 AC 310 HL).

With regards to the immediate aftermath, all were outside the above-quoted concept of the immediate aftermath, since the shortest time interval between the disaster and a relative seeing a body was 8 hours. The House of Lords placed considerable emphasis on the expression 'nervous shock' as connoting 'a reaction to an immediate and horrifying impact'. Since the bodies had been cleaned, the impact was not deemed horrifying!

The issue of 'within sight and sound' was also examined. The House of Lords found against the concept that those who heard or saw the events broadcast could succeed because they were not 'in proximity' to the events. Further, television was constrained by its own ethics against broadcasting pictures of recognisable suffering

Table 7.6 Primary and secondary claimants, recoverability for psychiatric damage

	Primary	Secondary
Physical injury	No	No
Foreseeability		
of physical injury	Yes	No
of psychiatric injury	No	Yes
Reasonable fortitude	No	Yes
Proximity tests	Not applicable	Yes

individuals. Thus, the secondary claimants at Hillsborough failed in their appeal on the grounds of proximity.

The 'relationship test' was also considered. In order to recover, the secondary claimant must have a close family relationship (a 'close tie of love and affection') with the victim, and this was upheld. This implied a spouse, parent or child (but not a brother!), but exceptionally it was accepted that there might be a relative or friend who had a loving relationship to the plaintiff, 'similar to a normal parent or spouse'.

Hillsborough thus limited the category of secondary claimants who may sue for psychiatric injury, clarified the means by which shock could be transmissible, and also restated the meaning of the immediate aftermath. Also distinctions between primary and secondary claimants became better defined. The distinctions between primary and secondary claimants are shown in Table 7.6.

The nature of foreseeablity is different for the two classes of claimant. For secondary claimants, a single test for foreseeability has not been adopted, and the restrictions of proximity (physical and familial) have been clarified. For primary claimants (within the scope of foreseeable physical harm, even if no tangible physical injury occurs), the situation has been defined by the case of *Page* v. *Smith*.

The eggshell skull

This case *Page* v. *Smith* [1996] AC 155, HL) has considerable notoriety, not only in relationship to the 'eggshell skull' principle, but also because it involved myalgic encephalomyelitis (ME), one of the somatisation variants.

It has long been the case in personal injury litigation that defendants take claimants as they find them, they are liable for the full extent of all the consequences of an injury, even if aggravated by pre-existing health problems: 'it is no answer to the sufferer's claim for damages that [the plaintiff] would have suffered less injury, or no injury at all, if he had not had an unusually thin skull or an unusually weak heart' (*Dulieu v. White and sons* [1901] 2 KB 669).

Mr Page, who for 20 years had suffered from ME, was involved in a road traffic accident, but was not physically damaged. In this case, the claimant was a primary claimant, and proximity was not an issue, but he suffered no physical injury, and a pre-existing medical disorder was reactivated – his ME became chronic. It was held that since personal injury of some kind (not necessarily psychiatric) was foreseeable, the defendant was liable. The Court of Appeal reversed the decision, but the House of Lords found for the claimant, and he recovered damages for the increased severity of his pre-existing syndrome, which included a considerable sum for loss of earnings. The case in part related to whether Mr Page was deemed to be of 'ordinary fortitude', and thus whether the injury was foreseeable or not. Persons of reasonable fortitude should be able to withstand life's slings and arrows, whereas with his pre-existing illness it was contended that Mr Smith was not of 'ordinary fortitude' and the injury was not foreseeable.

Thus, to quote Lord Lloyd in the above case:

1. In cases involving psychiatric damage, it is essential to distinguish the primary victim and the secondary victim.

2. In claims by secondary victims, the law insists on control mechanisms, in order as a matter of policy to limit the number of potential claimants. Thus, the defendant will not be liable unless psychiatric illness is foreseeable in a person of normal fortitude. These control mechanisms have no place where the claimant is the primary victim.

3. In claims by secondary victims, it may be legitimate to use hindsight in order to be able to apply the test of reasonable foreseeability. Hindsight, however, has no part to play where the claimant is a primary victim.

4. Subject to the above qualifications, the approach in all cases should be the same, namely, whether the defendant can reasonably foresee that his or her conduct will expose the claimant to the risk of personal injury, whether physical or psychiatric. If the answer is yes, then the duty of care is established, even though physical injury does not, in fact, occur. There is no justification for regarding physical and psychiatric injury as 'different kinds of damage'.

5. A defendant who is under a duty of care to the claimant, whether as a primary or a secondary victim, is not liable to damages for psychiatric damage unless the shock results in some recognised psychiatric illness. It is no answer that the claimant was predisposed to psychiatric illness. Nor is it relevant if it takes a rare form or is of unusual severity. Defendants must take their victims as they find them.

Thus, after *Page* v. *Smith*, primary claimants need not meet the proximity test, nor do they have to show that the psychiatric injury is foreseeable, as long as the physical harm is – which obviously is a formality as it was the foreseeability of such harm that led to the categorisation as a primary claimant in the first place.

Recognised psychiatric disorder

This term has been used with some frequency in this chapter, and is to be understood as a legal term requiring medical sanction. As it stands, the claimant must be shown to have suffered a recognisable psychiatric illness, and for both primary and secondary victims, it must be shock-induced (from 'a sudden shocking event'). The term became an alternative to nervous shock when used by Lord Denning in the case of *Hinz* v. *Berry* ([1970] 2 QB 40). In the trial *McLoughlin* v. *O'Brian*, Lord Bridge said: 'The first hurdle which a plaintiff must surmount . . . is to establish that he is suffering, not merely grief, distress or any other normal emotion, but a positive psychiatric illness'.

This stricture becomes relevant when thinking about who is the most appropriate person to provide expert evidence, discussed above, and reflects upon the issue as to what is a recognisable psychiatric disorder, and the value or otherwise of the use of diagnostic manuals.

In recent times, as discussed, the courts have placed more and more reliability on the recognised classification schemes. Much emphasis has been placed on the concept of PTSD, but in the context of this book, other posttraumatic disorders have been considered, especially in the area of somatisation. In Chapter 3, a number of conditions sitting at the borderland of psychiatry, neurology and rheumatology were discussed, and the validity or otherwise of diagnostic entities such as fibromyalgia, reflex sympathetic dystrophy and the like were considered. It was concluded that there was probably a core of patients who had the said condition, the borders of which were poorly defined, and some had tails like Halley's comet, extending into wide-open space.

The court is impressed with labels, and somehow naming is conceptualised as reifying. Many experts giving evidence in relationship to psychiatric illness seem to advise that their Platonic ideals have been enshrined in DSM-IV, and that once the criteria written down in the manual have been acknowledged, the diagnosis is secure and the thinking process is over. However, the pitfalls of this have already been discussed, especially in a medicolegal context. The issue is taken up again in Chapter 8 on causation and mechanisms.

Video evidence

Although viewed by some as an invasion of personal privacy, video evidence is often provided, revealing some aspects of a claimant's behaviour which may be of importance to an understanding of the case. More often than not, such evidence is brought forward to substantiate a claim of exaggeration of symptoms or malingering, and, as such it can be one of the most relevant pieces of *medical* evidence available to the trial. Such surveillance can be of particular value in cases of alleged somatoform disorder, essentially if establishing that the claimant can carry out physical acts that he or she claims not to be able to do. Care must be taken to acknowledge if a particular video has been edited, and that it does not present a distorted picture. In cases of physical injury, limited recordings are open to the rebuttal of 'good day, bad day' pronouncements by claimants.

At the moment there is no authority on how far enquiry agents may go to obtain video evidence, and at present the balance resides between Article 8 of the European Convention on Human Rights, namely that 'everyone has the right to respect for his private and family life, his home and his correspondence' and Article 6, which states that 'in the determination of his civil rights and obligations . . . everyone is entitled to a fair and public hearing'.

Compensation

Damages awarded are to place the claimant, as far as possible, in the position he or she would be in, had the breach of duty not occurred (*British Transport Commission v. Gourley* [1956] AC 185). Damages are payable if they are not too remote to be considered as either a direct consequence of the accident or an indirect but foreseeable consequence and if the claimant is left more vulnerable as a consequence of the accident to suffer further damage.

Compensation is for financial loss, but pain, suffering and impairment resulting from the injuries are also rewarded. Damages relating to financial loss, referred to as special damages, are easier to compute than 'pain and suffering' (general damages), and the nebulous predictions of 'future losses, including loss of earnings'. Suffering here refers to distress not directly related to any bodily condition, but includes 'fright', fear of future incapacity, humiliation, sadness and embarrassment (e.g. due to scars).

Sometimes damages are awarded for 'loss of amenity', such as failure to be able to do things previously enjoyable in life (such as sports), but include injuries to the senses, sexual dysfunction, loss of marriage prospects, and the like (Napier and Wheat, 1995). Aggravated damage refers to compensation for injuring a claimant's feelings. Often the amounts of compensation awarded are calculated purely on the basis of past cases, or by reference to books that quote damage figures. A list of some up-to-date figures is given in Table 7.7.

Bereavement damages, which can be claimed where death is caused as the result of another's wrongful act, are set by statutory instrument. It is payable to the deceased spouse or, if the deceased was under 18 and had never been married, to his or her parents. As of March 2002, the award was £10 000.

Table 7.7 Level of psychiatric damages

	PTSD	General psychiatric damages
Severe	£32 500–52 000	£28 500–60 000
Moderately severe	£12 000–30 000	£10 000–28 500
Moderate	£4250–12 000	£3000–10 000
Minor	£2000–4250	£750–3000

PTSD, posttraumatic stress disorder.
Reproduced from Bell *et al.* (2002), with permission.

Obviously damages may be tempered by factors such as pre-existing illnesses, contributory negligence, a *novus actus* (see Chapter 9), and, since the claimant is under a duty to mitigate any loss, refusal to accept treatment, which includes psychiatric care and taking psychotropic drugs, may also be taken into account.

Bryant *et al.* (1997) examined claimants' feelings about the legal process of compensations and their settlements. They followed 96 road traffic accident claimants up to 6 years; the claimants were identified as those seeking compensation from a total successive cohort of 172 people involved in accidents. Ten per cent of car accident and 16% of motorcycle claimants were rated as having PTSD. Respondents of unsettled claims reported being uncertain as to why their case had not been settled, or even at which stage of the legal process their claim had reached. Anger at their apparent losses and at the failure of others to recognise their suffering were prominent features of their mental states, and both anger and dissatisfaction distinguished the litigants from the non-litigants. Disappointment with the size of the final settlement was common, claimants often having been led to expect far more, or had not realised that such things as sick pay or legal fees would be taken from the final awards. Financial hardships during the long legal process were often clear, and one of the main criticisms was the failure of the legal process to provide money at the time it was really needed. Anger and dissatisfaction did not abate following settlement, and in some cases were made worse by the disappointment of the award.

In the past, many compensation claims were handled using state funding, the so-called legal aid system. Since 1995, lawyers have been allowed to use a variant of the American 'no-win, no-fee' basis, referred to as the conditional fee arrangement: their own fees only become payable if they win the case for the claimant. Their fees are set at some uplift value, usually around 25–50% of the damages won, and, in case the day is lost, an insurance premium will insure against having to pay the

Table 7.8 Summary of the current state of the art in case law

Rules for primary and secondary claimants/victims
1. Establish a duty of care
2. Establish that the damage is 'a recognised psychiatric disorder'
3. Establish that the psychiatric damage was caused by a 'shocking event'

Rules for secondary claimants/victims
1. Foreseeability, i.e. that psychiatric damage was foreseeable to someone of 'customary phlegm'
2. Proximity
   - Relationship between the accident and the accident victim
   - Proximity in time and space
   - The means by which the claimant received or perceived the information

Rules for primary claimants/victims
Proximity not needed
Foreseeability not needed

Adapted from Sprince (2002), with permission.

other side's losses. The effects of these new conditions on awards payable have not yet been fully appraised.

It is a general rule in the UK (but not in the USA) that the loser pays the costs of the winner, but under the legal aid system this does not apply. Thus, a legally aided claimant and legal advisers in theory have all to gain and little to lose by pursuing a claim to its limits. This has been referred to as 'legal aid blackmail' in Parliament, and, since legal aid is still available for many medical negligence cases, they are often relentlessly pursued, in spite of a 17% success rate, with considerable cost to the National Health Service. The inherent bias in this system may impinge on the right to a fair trial under the Human Rights Act (Barton, 2001).

Conclusions

This review has highlighted a number of significant issues, mainly to do with claims for compensation for psychiatric injury, and the influence of the new CPR on the role of the expert in such claims. The CPR have presented many challenges to the traditional court jousting that was the accepted way of settling civil disputes, and it seems that many fewer cases now end up in court than before. Whether they have rendered the whole process any less expensive has yet to be calculated.

Many problems in practice have been highlighted, which range from a lack of definition of what an expert is, through to the naivety of considering that an SJE can resolve the complexities of many cases, especially in the medicolegal domain, to the inadequacies of the instructions for joint reports. Most psychiatric cases are simply not appropriate for an SJE. The time restraints placed on experts means that solicitors are perhaps being denied access to experts of their choice – experienced people have waiting lists. Hurried joint reports are being prepared which may take the legal situation no further, and may not reflect an adequate summary of the medicolegal realities and complexities of the individual case. The joint reports, which are medical and not legal documents, are being used to settle cases, and important issues, which used to be threshed out in cross-examination, are left unexplored.

Case law has both extended the range of those compensated, but at the same time, largely for public policy reasons, has limited the claims of secondary claimants by means of foreseeability and issues of proximity and the aftermath: a summary of the current state of the art is given in Table 7.8. The stress of even embarking on litigation has been noted, and the term lexigenic used to emphasise the legal equivalent of iatrogenic illness.

Underlying all of this is the issue of causation, and the relationship of any accident to a claimant's psychiatric symptoms. These issues are discussed in the last chapter.

REFERENCES

American Psychiatric Association (1980). *Diagnostic and Statistical Manual of Mental Disorders* (DSM-III), 3rd edn. Washington, DC: American Psychiatric Association.

Barton, A. (2001). Medical litigation, who benefits? *British Medical Journal,* **322**, 1189.

Bell, J., Bruffell, M., Cherry, J. *et al.* (2002). *Guidelines for the Assessment of General Damages in Personal Injury Cases,* 6th edn. Oxford: Oxford University Press.

British Psychological Society (1999). *Psychologists as Expert Witnesses.* Leicester: British Psychological Society.

Bryant, B., Mayou, R. and Lloyd-Bostock, S. (1997). Compensation claims following road accidents: a six year follow-up study. *Medicine, Science and Law,* **37**, 326–36.

Hailsham, Lord, Hobbs, G., Hay, D. and Stickland, P. (1994). *Halsbury's Laws of England.* London: Butterworths.

Jones, M. A. (2002). *Text Book on Torts,* 8th edn. Oxford: Oxford University Press.

Kelly, M., Levene, S., Mead, P. and Langstaff, B. (2001). *Personal Injury Handbook.* London: Sweet and Maxwell.

Mendelson, D. (1998). The interfaces between law and medicine. Aldershot: Dartmouth.

Napier, M. and Wheat, K. (1995). *Recovering Damages for Psychiatric Injury.* London: Blackstone Press.

Obomanu, W. and Kennedy, H. G. (2001). "Juridogenic" harm: statutory principles for the new Mental Health Tribunals. *Psychiatric Bulletin*, **25**, 331–3.

Pugh, C. and Trimble, M. (1993). Psychiatric injury after Hillsborough. *British Journal of Psychiatry*, **163**, 425–9.

Sim, M. (1992). *Compensation Claims*. British Columbia, Canada: Emmes.

Sprince, A. (2002). *Text. Negligence: duty – psychiatric damage.* Cayman Islands: Cayman Island Law School.

Swift, J. (1998/1726). *Gulliver's Travels.* Oxford: Oxford University Press.

8

Mechanisms

Convictions are more dangerous enemies of truth than lies.

(Friedrich Nietzsche)

There is the world dimensional for
those untwisted by the love of things
irreconcilable.

(Hart Crane, *The Marriage of Faustus and Helen*)

Introduction

In the first chapter of this book, the historical underpinnings of today's theories were outlined. Hysteria, the paradigm of female illnesses, was genital, and remained so for some 2000 years. The wandering womb of the Greeks, *chorea lascivia*, Charcot's ovarian tenderness, and the theories of Breuer and Freud all echo ancient mythologies, of sexual energies released or denied, of *sparagmos*, of Kundrian capriciousness, of metamorphoses. These lingering ideas came up against the shift in localisation of the disorder from the abdomen to the brain in the seventeenth century, and the clear association of symptoms with the emotions. There then was an assimilation of the latter two ideas, especially with Briquet, that somehow intense emotional states acted through specific parts of the brain to provoke pathological symptoms.

With railway spine and shellshock came not only clarification of the concept of traumatic hysteria, but also a renewed organic wave of theories, up-to-date with concepts of molecular change, anaemia and concussion. However, it was never very clear how the nervous shock transmogrified into some pathological brain state, and even advocates of the neurological approach like Erichsen acknowledged in many cases the importance of the shock, of the emotional state aroused by the trauma.

The experiences of the First World War enlivened the debate on causation, removing a major platform from the then developing Freudian concepts of sexual conflict, and raising questions about the genuineness of the symptoms. This was paralleled by growing fears in civilian circles about the role of compensation in maintaining illness in patients with psychiatric symptoms, especially conversion disorders. However, these debates fell into relative silence for perhaps 50 years, only to be revived by several innovations.

One was a growing awareness of how the brain worked. A better understanding of neuroanatomy, experimentation and clinical observation led to the development of the concepts of the limbic system and the reticular activating system (RAS) as two cerebral modulators, of emotion and arousal respectively. Disturbance in such systems could lead to psychiatric illness, and they were affected by emotional events. Over this time there has been a growing psychiatric interest in the underlying neurobiology of neurotic as opposed to psychotic and major mental disorders. Treatments such as minor tranquillisers and antidepressants were developed, and tried, often successfully, in managing minor psychiatric morbidity. Anxiety, depression and associated conditions such as masked depression presenting with somatic symptoms became accepted in clinical practice.

Secondly, and undoubtedly most relevant, was the delineation of posttraumatic stress disorder (PTSD) in DSM-III (American Psychiatric Association, 1980); cause and effect rolled into one, and a guilty society with a multitude of post-Vietnam veterans to investigate and compensate. Shock echoed from the railways to the battlefront, rebounding back into the civilian afterlife of soldiers. Paradoxically, one fall-out was actually the concept of posttraumatic hysteria. The new terminologies of DSM and ICD (World Health Organization, 1993) conspired against the hysteria rubric; names changed, somatoform and somatisation appeared, but not in a traumatic context. Some opined that hysteria had disappeared, yet in specialist clinics the patients kept turning up and falling down. Often they were seen by neurologists, but a renewed awareness of the prevalence of sexual abuse and the appearance of so-called multiple personalities revived an interest in the concept of dissociation. Janet once again became popular, and theorising about hysteria is now again enjoying a renaissance.

In a legal setting, as noted, there is little reference to hysteria, and even less to malingering. Yet compensation for psychiatric injury has been accepted for years. Nervous shock became hijacked by PTSD, in spite of the many thousands of claimants who seek compensation after accidents for medically unexplained or incompletely explained symptoms. The real possibility that the legal process itself is related to the maintenance, or is even the cause of the clinical picture in some cases (referred to here as lexigenic morbidity) is acknowledged by practically anyone who knows about medicolegal practice, usually only to be dismissed. The law has yet to catch up with hysteria.

Issues of causation are discussed in the last chapter. First, medical and psychological theories of aetiology and pathogenesis are presented, picking up the history at the beginning of the twentieth century.

Freud, Breuer and Janet

It will be recalled that the term 'dissociation' comes to us from Janet, who proposed that extreme emotions interfere with information processing, which results in a failure to transform the mental imprints of an experience into what we now refer to as episodic or declarative memory. The uncontrolled emotions associated with the traumatic event prevent the mental integration or synthesis of experience and cause these memories to be split off or dissociated from ordinary consciousness. The memory traces of these traumas are then stored as unconscious, fixed liquidated ideas as long as they are not translated into the personal narrative. But as dissociated memories, they can intrude into the patient's life as preoccupations, perceptions but also as somatic complaints. Thus, according to Janet, *dédoublement* or double consciousness was the structure of the psyche in hysteria. Two or more discrete but potentially conscious modes of behaviour existed alongside one another, separated by amnesia. In summary, there was a degeneration of the normal singularity of consciousness.

Freud, after visiting the Salpêtrière, followed the ideas of both Charcot and Janet, and proposed that dissociation was the key to understanding hysteria. Splitting of consciousness was present to a rudimentary degree in every hysteria. This line of thinking influenced a generation of investigators, summed up by William James (1902) as follows:

in the wonderful explorations by Binet, Janet, Breuer, Freud, Mason, Prince and others, we have revealed to us a whole system of underground life, in the shape of memories of a painful sort which lead a parasitic existence, buried outside the primary field of consciousness, and making irruptions there into, with hallucinations, pains, convulsions, paralyses of feeling and of motion and the whole process of symptoms of hysteric disease of body and mind.

Both Janet and Freud were aware of the concept of degeneration, such an important part of nineteenth-century neuropsychiatric theory. For Janet, as for Charcot, not all people would succumb to hysterical symptoms but only those with predispositions, which were related to neuroinheritance and presumed neurophysiology. This was an embryonic version of an emerging concept of personality disorder, the basis of which for Janet was genetic, and for Freud was epigenetic. For the theories of both, people early in life developed integrated emotional–somatic structures, which remain in play for the rest of their lives.

Dissociation

This concept has evolved over time and, as the nosology of these conditions reveals, the term 'dissociation' remains influential today. For Janet dissociated memories become activated, involuntarily or through hypnosis, leading to the pathological phenomena. It was closely related to the concept of repression, introduced by Freud and Breuer, to explain conversion. Patients adopt the defence of repressing unpleasant memories. These, in vulnerable people, are dissociated from the psyche, but lurk beneath the conscious surface, envisaged as an energy force which can be 'converted' into somatic symptoms. It is well known that Freud in his original *Project* suggested a neurophysiological basis for these energies, but, as psychoanalytic theory developed, traumatogenic events gravitated from external happenings to inner efficient causation based on traumatic conflict arising from the patient's unacceptable desires and fantasies.

After half a century of the development of Freud's ideas, interest in dissociation was renewed by developments in neurophysiology, and the neodissociation theories of Hilgard (1977). Based on his own experimental work with hypnosis, Hilgard elaborated on Janet's theories, proposing a cognitive psychological model. In place of Janet's singularity of consciousness, he postulated separate cognitive structures that may succeed each other in dominance, and which are under the overall control of an executive ego. Cognitive structures segmented consciousness, but these were held in synthesis by an overarching control mechanism. Schemas related to specific tasks are selected by the executive, but once selected they can become autonomous, and thus dissociated. In other words, in this scheme, dissociation was seen as a part of the normal structure of the human psyche, and not, as for Janet and Freud, a pathological process.

Ludwig (1972), with an even more sociobiological perspective, suggested that dissociation is available as a defence mechanism of fright, and has both individual and species survival value. Dissociative disorders may evolve if this defence mechanism is persistently and inappropriately re-evoked, thereby promoting a partial or autonomous separation of subordinate cognitive structures from the executive control.

For Ludwig, the pathophysiology of dissociation involved the RAS, activity of which leads to an increase in corticofugal inhibition of sensory inputs, preventing the latter gaining access to and being integrated into subjective awareness.

Suggestion

The role of suggestion in the development of hysterical symptomatology has played a central part in the history of the disorder, and is also contemporary currency, especially in medicolegal practice. This has been a repeated theme throughout this book.

Charcot's detractors, especially those from the school at Nancy, such as Bernheim (1840–1919), denied any special mental state in hypnosis or hysteria, and implied that the phenomena observed by him were all the result of suggestion and expectation.

The concept that symptoms could arise from ideas in the patient's psyche had first been put forward by Sir John Russell Reynolds (1869), and as noted, was incorporated into the ideas of Charcot. However, Charcot refused to accept the idea that hysterical symptoms were nothing but those of suggestion. The theme of suggestion was taken up again after Charcot's death by his pupil Babinski, who renamed hysteria *pithiatisme*.

More recently, Merskey (1995) has revisited the whole controversy. In his view, hypnosis is a collusion between the patient and the hypnotist, an implicit agreement which leads to the desired effect for both. The phenomenon of epidemic or communicable hysteria, in which hysterical symptoms break out in a community, reflects on the importance of suggestion in the development of symptoms. To recap, certain people tend to be more affected, and current cultural beliefs are predominant, with the devils and witches of the medieval epidemics now being replaced by infections (myalgic encephalomyelitis) and chemical intoxications (as in the sick building syndrome, multiple chemical sensitivity). Sociological variables govern the spread of symptoms, which usually involve a person of high status with emotional problems, whose symptoms are replicated by those of lower status, in a closely knit group of often dissatisfied individuals. The significance of these hysteria epidemics is that they provide evidence of group effects leading to the development of somatoform symptoms which are psychologically induced, 'on a par with the individual hysterical symptom' (Merskey, 1995, p. 241).

It is acknowledged that people are suggestible, and that people vary with their degree of suggestibility. Advertising would not be successful without this human attribute, but perhaps suggestibility is an essential component of the development of the human psyche, with its own survival value. It is one component of learning. Parents suggest to their children how things are done, and how they should do things. All doctors are aware of the placebo response to medical intervention, but few contemplate the significance of suggestion in the development of their own patients' symptomatology.

W. H. R. Rivers (1864–1922), psychiatrist at the Craiglockhart Hospital, now famous because of his portrayal in Pat Barker's novel *Degeneration* about war neuroses, was an anthropologist and neuropsychiatrist, and he studied the power of suggestion in primitive cultures. For him, suggestion was an evolutionary form of instinctive behaviour, which originally developed in response to collective rather than individual human needs, but which in hysteria protects the individual. Hysterical symptoms become fixed through suggestion.

Thus, Janet, Ludwig, but also several contemporary theorists discuss the important role of suggestion in the development of hysterical symptomatology (Brown, 2002), but the tone of discussion has now shifted to emphasise normal rather than abnormal cognitive processes.

There is an association between conversion disorder and hypnotic suggestibility (Roelofs, 2002), but somatoform disorders are also reported to be associated with high levels of suggestibility (Janet, 1924; Ludwig, 1972; Brown, 2002). Thus, it is possible that patients with conversion disorders are also very suggestible to non-hypnotic influences. The links between suggestibility and personality have been noted in Chapter 2, especially with regard to histrionic and borderline varieties, and these personality anlages are linked to presentations with medically unexplained symptoms.

New hysteria studies

In spite of the theories that underlie the dissociation concept, there have been few empirical data to verify hypotheses and the older theories are difficult to reconcile with our modern conceptions of brain function. Further, much of the speculation has related to psychological models, rather than to underlying neurological processes, and could better account for negative phenomena (loss of function through inhibition) as opposed to positive symptoms (tremors, seizures and gait abnormalities).

Some early studies examined somatosensory evoked potentials in patients with hysterical anaesthesias, but the results were contradictory. Deficits in attention in patients with unexplained neurological symptoms have been reported (Bendefeldt et al., 1976), and more recently, changes of the later stages of sensory evoked potentials, referred to as the P300 wave (Fukada et al., 1996; Lorenz et al., 1998). Since the P300 component of the evoked response is related to the stage of conscious awareness, Sierra and Berrios (1999) interpret these data as suggesting implicit inhibition of sensory processing in hysterical anaesthesia. Some neurological data support this view. Thus, some patients with parietal lobe damage, notably on the right side, lose awareness of their sensory fields in relation to the left side of the body. This so-called hemineglect syndrome is also associated with changes in the later components of evoked responses (Lhermitte et al., 1985). Attentional mechanisms may well be associated with such symptomatology. However, there is no clue as to whether in conversion disorders this is state- or trait-related, and how this may relate to more complex clinical pictures, as seen in somatisation disorder.

The newer psychological theories adopt an information-processing approach to the problem. They assume that our perception and cognition and behaviour are governed initially by 'preconscious processes', over which we have no direct volitional control, and that our subjective experiences are interpretations of reality dependent not only on ongoing sensory experiences but also on our background memories and knowledge. The symptoms of hysteria are viewed as 'disturbances of consciousness and control arising from the chronic activation of learnt symptom representations in memory' (Brown, 2002, p. 229), which are related to underlying attentional mechanisms. Some symptoms are associated with non-volitional activation of stored behavioural representations, such as the convulsions of non-epileptic seizures.

This model allows for the direct influence of personal beliefs on the phenomenology such that 'rather than existing in isolation, therefore, symptom representations are inextricably linked to other aspects of knowledge, and may be activated indirectly by the spread of activation across the [memory] network' (Brown, 2002, p. 230). In other words, conceptual and linguistic representations are as relevant for symptom construction as are perceptions. In this theory, the primary problem in somatisation rests with cognition, rather than emotion, and the emphasis is on the use of normal rather than abnormal brain processing in symptom generation. The model allows for an important role of a person's beliefs in the development of symptoms, and explains the frequent occurrence of symptoms based on earlier physical illness, such as non-epileptic seizures in a patient with prior epilepsy, or unexplained orthopaedic symptoms occurring after an accident, on the background of an earlier whiplash injury or previous neck pains. It also explains the frequently documented association of somatoform disorders developing in paramedical personnel.

Directing attention to symptoms, by friends, doctors or lawyers, enhances their representation, perpetuating them, but also consolidating them into the cognitive mnestic structure. 'Chronicity develops from a self-perpetuating cycle driven by high level attention to the symptom representation. Deliberately checking to see if a symptom is still present increases the resting activation level of the underlying symptom's representation . . . [which] increases the likelihood of subsequent reselection, setting up a vicious cycle' (Brown, 2002, p. 231). Symptom representations eventually become autonomous, perpetuated by a continuous cycle of attention and representational activation and thus chronic.

The role of the medicolegal process in this chain of events is obviously suggestive, but the process is also one which is linked to the generation and persistence of symptoms outside legal circles. It explains how physicians can mould patients' symptoms to fit their own (the doctor's) cognitive representations of illness, and why the media can so easily feed the public with information about illness and disease, effectively false, but which provokes an epidemic. Negative affects (not especially depression) enhance the above events, providing heightened somatosensory sensitivity, and increase the tendency to rumination, and secondary gains, from extrinsic benefits, are as relevant as intrinsic emotional (primary gain) ones for symptom development.

In spite of these theories, the fundamental Cartesian dilemma remains exactly the same as it was for Freud and his followers, namely, how is the psychological 'converted' into the physical? By acknowledging the importance of representations of the external but also the internal world in the brain as the basis for our cognition, as opposed to asserting the dominance and reality of our everyday perceptions, the newer psychological theories take us further towards an integrative neurocognitive approach. Somatic structures are represented in the brain (body image), as are the perceptual representations of the world in which we live. We actually have privileged access to the former, but there is no a priori reason why they should not be integrated into our ongoing cognitive schemas, and subject to the same distortions that representational theory demands our everyday perceptions are subject to.

Since the work of Charcot, there has been little opportunity to examine brain function in patients with somatoform disorders. However, the advances in brain imaging that have occurred in the past decade have seen some studies emerging.

Recent neurological investigations – brain imaging

The availability of new brain imaging techniques such as magnetic resonance imaging (MRI) and positron emission tomography (PET), which can give an image of the structure or the functioning of the brain over a brief period of time, has allowed patients with conversion disorders to be compared with others, in an attempt to shed light on the underlying neurology of hysteria.

Marshall *et al.* (1997) investigated a female with left-sided paralysis diagnosed as conversion and reported with PET that when the patient was scanned trying to move the paralysed leg, the dorsolateral prefrontal cortex, the cerebellum and the anterior cingulate areas were all activated, but not the motor cortex opposite to the side of the paralysis. The main differences with activation of the contralateral normal side were in the cingulate and medial orbitofrontal cortex.

Spence *et al.* (2000) compared patients with conversion paralysis, with patients asked to feign paralysis, and controls, again using PET. The main difference between feigning and conversion was in the prefrontal cortex. The left prefrontal cortex was found to be underactive in the conversion patients, and the right side underactive in those feigning the paralysis.

These data are very limited, and obviously further studies are needed in this complex area. Marshall *et al.* concluded that the cingulate and orbitofrontal areas of the brain are involved in the neurology of hysteria, while for Spence *et al.* the prefrontal cortex was more relevant. These areas of the brain are known to be involved in regulating behaviour, especially in converting intention into action, and in inhibiting behavioural responses. For Spence *et al.*, hysterical paralyses are disorders of action, hence the involvement of the prefrontal areas.

Other theories

Aside from the psychological theories just discussed, other ideas about the development of medically unexplained symptoms, especially in a medicolegal context, based on clinical judgement and some common sense, have been suggested. Thus, in some patients, the preoccupation with bodily symptoms may be related to anxiety. In states of tension, muscle tone increases, heart rate increases, sweating occurs, all of which could be misinterpreted as suggestive of pathology by an already anxious patient. This is a poor explanation however of conversion disorders (in which anxiety is often not acknowledged), let alone somatisation disorder. However, the preoccupations of the anxious hypochondriac may well provide a seedbed for persistent misinterpreting of normal physiological processes.

Pilowsky (1995) noted that the ideas one has about one's body influence reactions to the body. Our body image is the sum of representations of the body in the brain, and is generally thought to be represented by schemata, especially in the temporal and parietal areas of the brain. It has been known for a long time that the body image as represented in the brain is totally different from the body image we see visually when we look at ourselves in a mirror, or the image that others see when they look at us. There are effectively gross distortions of the external body as represented in the brain (the homunculus), that relate in part to the importance of different body parts to our exploration of the world in which we live (more cortical space for the hands and lips, for example). These representations, like our others, are influenced by emotional and developmental experiences. Narcissistic people have overvalued ideas about their own body, and are preoccupied by appearance and pulchritude. While again not explaining somatisation, it is common clinical practice to find patients of the super-fit category who, after apparently trivial physical injury, decompensate into a dependent invalid role with multiple physical symptoms. More often than not this change occurs at a time in life when they are losing their physical prowess anyway, and, as keeping up with the training schedules becomes harder, muscles become softer.

There have been some studies of the links between personality and symptom perception. The trait negative affectivity, namely the tendency to view the self and life negatively, is associated with introspection and hypochondriasis (Pennebaker and Watson, 1991), and there is a relationship between somatosensory amplification and hypochondriasis (Barsky and Wyshak, 1990).

The association between disorders of affect and somatoform disorders is well established. Estimates of the frequency of depression in patients with hysteria range up to 50% (Klerman, 1982). However, it is often unclear if the depression is directly related to the aetiology of the somatisation (as in masked depression), or whether it is secondary to chronic invalidity. In general, studies emphasise the role of depression more in the acute syndromes, with a better prognosis as opposed to chronic disorders.

The importance of suggestion in modulating everyday human behaviour has been noted above. Pilowsky's ideas of abnormal illness behaviour (AIB) allow for a whole range of influences, cultural and familial, which may modify illness-related behaviour patterns, and perpetuate dependence.

Others have discussed the symptoms of hysteria as metaphors – illness has a meaning beyond the interpretation of a disease process, hence the clear distinctions between illness and disease, as already discussed. Engel (1962) developed this theme most effectively with his concept of the pain-prone patient, and this was taken up by Pilowsky (1995). These ideas are essentially a hangover from earlier psychoanalytic concepts. 'We see therefore that any aspect of body shape, function or appearance may have a special meaning for a person. The same applies to symptoms that they may develop. Such meanings are associated with emotions, which in turn have a physical component . . . When the meanings have become largely unconscious, the individual is left only with the somatic symptoms' (Pilowsky, 1995, p. 126). Engel noted, importantly, that the use of the body as a means of communication precedes in life other forms of communication, and that affects are attached to bodily movements very early on. Affective expression comes before cognitive development, and for him conversion symptoms corresponded to memory traces of previous bodily experiences.

Rebuttals

The above body of literature, on the mechanisms of conversion and somatisation, reveals a rich texture of often interwoven and overlapping ideas, but in practice there is always an undercurrent of concern about the veracity of the patient's symptoms, and about the clarity of diagnosis. This can be examined in relationship to today's counterpart of nervous shock, namely PTSD. When the diagnosis of PTSD was introduced into DSM-III, the concept seemed clear, and the underlying theories sound. However, gradually voices of discontent emerged. The discontent was, and is, a re-run of all the nineteenth-century arguments that have been discussed in Chapter 1. They revolve around the validity of the diagnosis, the relevance of the pretraumatic personality, the role of the trauma itself, and the reluctance to recognise the possibility of malingering. Again, policy issues are involved, to do with cost and compensation, as are politics.

These issues have been best revealed by Allan Young in his book, 'The Harmony of Illusions' (1995), and Tana Dineen in her 'Manufacturing Victims' (1999). Both have to do with the sociological creation of illness categories, and have considerable relevance for medicolegal practice. Although the discussions centre on PTSD, the relevance for a number of other syndromes outlined in this book must be obvious. The reader is referred for example to Malleson's deconstruction of whiplash in his book, *Whiplash and Other Useful Illnesses* (2002).

First, to return to the battlefield. As Ben Shephard (2000) noted, by the time of the Vietnam War, the concept of stress had become an acknowledged concept in military medicine, in part occasioned by the work of experimental physiologists such as Hans Selye, who outlined the body's physiological, especially hormonal, responses to stress. After the war, the post-Vietnam syndrome emerged, said to be an after-effect of the war trauma and a failure to adjust to civilian life. At the same time other 'syndromes' found their way into the literature, but also in the popular media. These included the post-Holocaust and post-Hiroshma variants; the idea of delayed stress reactions and related survivor guilt took hold.

Considerable pressure was placed upon the constructors of the developing DSM-III to include a category of illness such as 'catastrophic stress disorder'. In 1978 Mardi Horowitz, who had considerable influence on the construction of the final categories of the relevant section in DSM-III, published his very influential book, 'Stress Response Syndromes', which linked civilian and war-related trauma (shades of the debates about railway spine!). Thus PTSD emerged in DSM-III, a seemingly bright new star in a clouded sky, but actually one as old and controversial as the star of Bethlehem itself.

A new psychoscience was born, traumatology, a new clinical method evolved, namely checklist diagnosis (filling in rating scales), and we were all immersed in what Shephard referred to as the culture of trauma. At the forefront was the concept of the psychological trauma, especially the traumatic experience and memory. Dissociation theories re-emerged, and controversies, such as that about the false-memory syndrome, eventually flowered.

In recent times, the role of the patients' predisposition for the development of symptomatology has once again emerged as important. Failure to identify a general stress response syndrome, the variability of clinical pictures and rates of verifiable PTSD, and the general failure of treatment programmes, such as debriefing, has led to a reappraisal of the whole area. Further, there has been the shift away from analysing the traumatic memory to the personal experience, or meaning of the trauma. This, at a time when the law too is struggling with setting boundaries and guidelines for recovery for psychiatric injury!

Dineen (1999) mainly blamed the psychology industry for the creation of the victim culture. The very word 'victim' strikes awe and fear into the sufferer and the bystander-observer alike. Often medicolegal reports begin with the words: 'On such and such a day, Mr Smith was the victim of [an accident]'. Dineen noted that psychologising, pathologising and generalising are the three main techniques whereby the mundane is translated into exceptional, and illusion equated with reality. As already noted, there is no shortage of psychological theories throughout the last 120 years to bring to bear on the subject, all attempting to give explanations for the unexplainable. Even more ominous is the role of pathologising – the creating of pathological entities in which the normal is viewed as abnormal, and in which the abnormal establishes victim status.

While not denying that many people suffer from the effects of psychological trauma, the theory that many victims are manufactured by and for the (financial) benefit of the psychology industry is Dineen's main theme. False naming, interpreting and remembering are the main mechanisms in play, and the classic example is PTSD. However, some of the syndromes discussed in Chapter 2 clearly link with the first two. A combination of enthusiastic physicians, vulnerable patients and diagnostic criteria is all that is needed!

The subtitle to Young's *The Harmony of Illusions* is 'Inventing post-traumatic stress disorder'. Emphasising the traumatic memory as central to PTSD, he points out how difficult it is to distinguish in the biographies of patients the direction of time flow, from the past to the present, or from the present to the past. Perhaps in some patients the time flow is mainly backwards! He noted that Rivers had more or less stated the same: 'in most cases, it is not the traumatic memory that produces the physical and emotional symptoms of the war neuroses, rather the reverse: the symptoms account for the memory . . . the recalled memory is usually not the effective cause of the syndrome, but the patient's way of explaining it' (Young, 1995, p. 83). To quote Rivers (1920) directly: '[the patient] either consciously or more or less unconsciously looked for an explanation, and this tended to centre around some particular experience, in many cases a comparatively trivial experience' (p. 83). This echoes the problems revealed in Chapter 5, false-memory syndrome by another name, evoked not by the trauma, but by the trauma culture. PTSD placed memory at the centre of pathogenesis, but from Janet's 'fixed ideas' to Freud's 'reminiscences', Young points out that: 'the history of traumatic memory is a chain of analogies, between post-hypnotic suggestion and pathogenic secrets, between surgical shock and nervous shock . . . and so on. But analogy does a better job at proliferating meanings than containing them, and it introduces the problem of meaning variance' (p. 128). Young noted the huge discrepancies in the epidemiological data on the prevalence of PTSD, and the marked differences between the event criteria for diagnosis of the disorder between DSM-III and DSM-IV, the latter effectively enlarging the variety of experiences accepted from one 'outside the range of usual human experience' to 'events involving death (either actual or threatened) or serious injury (including threats to the physical integrity of onself or others)'.

... Words strain
Crack and sometimes break, under the burden,
Under the tension, slip, slide, perish,
Decay with imprecision, will not stay in place,
Will not stay still.

(T. S. Eliot, Burnt Norton)

Eliot puts it all so well. The fluidity of the concept of PTSD is central to Young's theme. The truth-value of a concept cannot be divorced 'from the social, cognitive, and technological conditions through which researchers and clinicians know their facts and the meaning of facticity' (Young, 1995, p. 10). As our history becomes the subject of our myths, our myths become the subject of our history. Man is his own hero; it is his myth that creates his history.

Concerns over the diagnostic validity and misuse of the concept of PTSD have come from several other authors. Stone (1985), taking a historical perspective, analysed the social construction of shellshock, noting how quickly the term became a buzz word among the soldiers at the front. The diagnosis, officially banned by the Army Medical Services in 1917, initially served as 'a makeshift umbrella' covering medical, administrative and disciplinary needs. It was a matter of labelling. The meaning of PTSD, its successor, has also migrated, being now seen not only as the only response to psychological trauma, but one which is not the fault of the sufferer, and is compensatable. Summerfield (2001) argued that the diagnosis is a direct legacy of the American war in Vietnam. It became an integral part of the propaganda of the antiwar movement, and the veterans became viewed not as the perpetrators of war but its victims. The diagnosis spread globally, and has become one means by which people achieve victim status, and compensation for that status. It is the one psychiatric diagnosis that people like to have! To quote at more length:

Originally framed as applying only to extreme experiences, that people would not expect to encounter everyday, it has come to be associated with relatively commonplace events; accidents, muggings, a difficult labour (with a healthy baby), verbal sexual harassment, or the shock of receiving (inaccurate) bad news from a doctor even in cases in which the incorrect diagnosis has been rescinded shortly afterwards. Increasingly the workplace in Britain is being portrayed as traumatogenic even for those just doing their jobs: paramedics attending road accidents, police constables on duty at disasters, and even employees caught up in what would once have been described as a straightforward dispute with management. All are seeking compensation for PTSD or for not being offered counselling ... an encounter between a sympathetic psychiatrist and a claimant is primed to produce a report of PTSD if that is what the lawyer says the rules require (Summerfield, 2001, p. 96).

Summerfield reinforced his arguments by noting the lack of specificity of the syndrome, and the failure of logic in linking cause and effect into a single diagnosis. It is effectively a 'pseudocondition'.

Others emphasise the 'normality' of PTSD, in other words it describes a normal human response to trauma, but by labelling it, reifying it and compensating for it, the reaction is transmogrified into a chronic psychiatric illness. No account is taken of epigenetic and genetic factors in its development; it is purely a categorical definition.

There are reports of factitious cases of PTSD, soldiers claiming all the symptoms and compensation when it can be shown that some were not even present at the supposed traumatic incident, others having no military service at all (Neal and Rose, 1995: Baggaley, 1998; Resnick, 1997). This is all a repeat of the shellshock experiences of nearly a century before.

In fact, the concept of the social construction of illness is well recognised in medical sociology, and has been a favourite theme of medical historians of psychiatric illness, especially with regards to schizophrenia. Smith, the editor of the *British Medical Journal*, ran a vote to identify the 'top ten non-diseases'. PTSD did not feature, but the journal produced an International Classification of Non-Diseases, which included among others: multiple chemical sensitivities, the total allergy syndrome, the false-memory syndrome, adjustment reaction, whiplash, chronic fatigue syndrome (CFS), fibromyalgia, stress and the Gulf War syndrome (GWS).

Smith (2002) quotes Illich (1976) with approval:

More and more people subconsciously know that they are sick and tired of their jobs, and of their leisure passivities, but they want to hear the lie that physical illness relieves them of social and political responsibilities. They want their doctor to act as lawyer and priest. As a lawyer, the doctor exempts the patient from his normal duties and enables him to cash in on the insurance fund he was forced to build. As a priest, he becomes the patient's accomplice in creating the myth that he is an innocent victim of biological mechanisms rather than lazy, greedy, or envious deserter of a social struggle (Smith, 2002, p. 884).

All these issues have come to the fore again with the GWS. Interestingly, the number of casualties with classical hysterical symptoms in that conflict seem to be low. However, in the aftermath, many personnel have reported symptoms, often with a somatic bias, now referred to as the GWS. There is doubt about its validity (Ishmail *et al.*, 1999), but over 17% of veterans believe they have the syndrome (Chalder *et al.*, 2001). The strongest association to having the syndrome is knowing another person who also has it! As with some of the other syndromes commented on in this book, the symptoms are non-specific and multiple (fatigue, joint and muscle aches, cognitive problems, headaches, affective problems, gastrointestinal and respiratory complaints and so on; Coker *et al.*, 1999), but they are also reported to a lesser frequency in non-deployed veterans. The current consensus of researchers seems to be that there is no GWS (Wessely, 2001; Lee *et al.*, 2002).

Wessely *et al.* (1998) have outlined the social, media and political pressures that have moulded the concept of CFS, these specifically emphasising the somatic rather than any psychiatric aspects of the syndrome. Classically described neurasthenia has been redefined as a new disease, in ignorance of history and philosophy. Patient organisations come in for particular criticism – thus, patients present to doctors not with symptoms but with diagnoses, which they wish to be verified, but the selection of which doctor to visit has to be taken with care! The label of CFS becomes part of a narrative, which 'allows the sufferer to make sense of his or her past, and to explain previous inabilities to meet expectation or fulfil cherished goals'. Wessely *et al.* opine, 'CFS is as much about protest as it is about illness' (pp. 339–40).

Another interesting example, with direct medicolegal intrusion, was the Camelford water pollution episode. In 1988, the domestic water supply to about 20 000 people in the Lowermoor area was contaminated with 20 tonnes of aluminium sulphate. The water became coloured, and tasted acidic. Some of the recipients reported immediate symptoms, such as nausea and vomiting, but soon there were rumours of more widespread complaints, and death or illness of animals in the locality.

An inquiry was set up, which eventually produced two reports, neither of which reached a conclusion that there was any evidence of long-term neurological or psychiatric damage that followed the pollution. However, David and Wessely (1995) opined, far from being the end of the matter, this was only the beginning. There was public outrage at the way the whole affair was handled, and it became known from other studies that aluminium might be related to the development of dementia, such as Alzheimer's disease.

Litigation was commenced, and information about possible adverse effects of the aluminium intoxication was obtained by self-report questionnaire. Cognitive complaints became central, and a group of self-selected litigants, who believed themselves to have been damaged, were tested neuropsychologically and electro-physiologically. Some of these claimants were reported to show abnormalities, but David and Wessely pointed out flaws in the design and methodology of these investigations (not least being the self-selection), and suggested an important influence of the litigation process itself on the data. They conclude: 'The need to demonstrate persistent disability, the experience of disbelief and the adversarial nature of the British legal process, all act to perpetuate disability' (p. 2). An incident had become a legend.

The legal impact on diagnosis was revealed by the disorder repetitive strain injury (RSI; Bell, 1989). Once diagnosed, discussed and compensated for, there was an epidemic of cases. The disorder lacked a clear diagnostic definition, a pathology and physical signs. Modern technology was to blame, committees, commissions and reports were produced, splints and slings marked out the office sufferer. However, following failures of compensation in legal cases, the epidemic withered.

The same happened with the false-memory syndrome. There was an explosion of cases, which rose to a peak in 1991–2, but, following failures in courts to establish the claims in many settings, there has been a dramatic fall in numbers, which now amounts to a trickle.

Other examples of doubt over the clinical validity of syndromes can be quoted from whiplash (Pearce, 1999; Malleson, 2002) to the sick building syndrome (Rothman and Weintraub, 1995). The criticisms are all in a similar vein, and have to do with the lack of clarification of diagnostic boundaries, the lack of any specificity of symptoms, the overlap of diagnoses, and the legal and political pressures that often lie behind their reification. Likewise, the concepts of dissociation and repression have received deconstruction and criticism, sometimes amounting to outright rejection. As noted, dissociation became so widely used that it became useless as a denotation of a discrete mechanism of psychopathology. It was used to refer to any incident of loss of awareness or control, even the ability to drive a car and talk at the same time. The original ideas of Freud and Janet, while undoubtedly influencing contemporary thought, were refuted, most ostensibly by the behaviourists, whose theories abandoned the very notion of the subjective mind. Lesser objections have to do with the lack of experimental evidence for the existence of repression (the foundation stone of psychoanalysis, as Freud put it) and dissociation, and a failure to understand the mechanisms whereby such processes could exert their influence over behaviour in terms of the language of current neuroscience. Even attempts to use evoked potential studies, and the new imaging studies discussed above, have really failed to solve the fundamental dilemma in relationship to the somatoform disorders, namely why and how the symptoms are originally manifest and then maintained.

Sociocultural influences

Thus, in spite of over 130 years of speculation about the mechanisms that underlie somatoform and related disorders, they remain elusive. It seems clear that, in some settings, such as with fibromyalgia or PTSD, there are a core of patients who, one day, may be identified by biological markers. The problems are, especially in the medicolegal setting, that the symptoms of the disorders reported are mainly subjective in nature, suggestibility seems a common human attribute, embedded as we are in our unique social matrix, and importantly, many of the so-called psychological defence mechanisms fundamentally relate to deception. Repression and dissociation conceal, from the self and from others. Deceit seems embedded in human communication – denial of this, our own deception, itself is therefore linked to the idea of repression. It is adaptive self-deception. An understanding of the somatoform disorders thus requires a multifactorial approach to aetiology and pathogenesis, but has to acknowledge the underlying important influence of deceit and pathoplastic social pressures.

Ford (1983) discussed the importance of the responses of significant others to a trauma that influenced the patient. He noted that the spouse and family may adopt appropriate or inappropriate actions, either leading to a quick return to full functional capacity, or encouraging guilt, regression, and dependence. The employer in an industrial accident may attempt to minimise liability, avoid responsibility and increase the financial consequences of an accident by laying an injured person off work. Antagonistic relationships can soon develop, that enhance the injured person's view of his or her 'victim' status. Physicians too bear a responsibility. By being oversolicitous about minor injuries, by conveying a poorer prognosis than justified, by emphasising the negative rather than the positive aspects of the situation, the doctor evaluating a patient can exacerbate the situation, and turn an opportunity for a return to health into a flight into illness. Union stewards and lawyers are also involved in the process: 'too often the interest expressed is to encourage the patient to maximize the injuries' (Ford, 1983, p. 183).

The role that compensation plays in sustaining symptoms has been constantly noted in this book, and the literature already reviewed. Ford summarises this thus: 'that the presence of secondary gain, at least in the form of disability payments, acts as a disincentive to rehabilitation, cannot be seriously challenged' (p. 185).

It is not unknown for litigants to be coached by lawyers or other advisers about how they should respond to a medicolegal examination, effectively to deceive. Shephard (2000) quotes the following from: *Post-traumatic Stress Disorder: How to apply for 100 Percent Total Disability:*

Tell them all about the symptoms you have that you have read about . . . Tell them about your anger and rage . . . tell them how screwed up life has been since you got back from Nam . . . [but] don't volunteer any information about your childhood, you had a normal childhood. Even if you didn't, for the purpose of the interviews you did (Shephard, 2000, p. 395).

Early life experiences are known to relate to the later development of somatoform disorders. This in part may come from inappropriate use of medical facilities early in the index patient's life by his or her parents, a form of Münchausen-by-proxy, whereby children are repeatedly taken to their general practitioners, but for the parents' gratification, not because of any infantile illness. Pasquini *et al.* (2002) reported that mothers' losses and other severe life events within 2 years of the patients' birth were risk factors for the development of dissociative disorders. Early hospitalisation and parental separation may also be relevant, with the development of anxious and maladaptive attachment behaviour, leading to inappropriate care-seeking.

There has been a growing interest in sexual abuse as an antecedent to somatoform disorders, taking up where the early views of Freud left off. Much of the literature is flawed by the one factor that is often difficult to overcome, namely verification of the abuse, and the extent of the abuse. None the less, it seems accepted that sexual abuse is commonly reported in patients with psychiatric illness, but this is by no means specific for dissociative or somatoform disorders. Morrison (1989) noted a history of sexual abuse in 55% of women with somatisation disorder as opposed to 16% in affective disorder. This may apply in particular to women with chronic pelvic and abdominal pains (Leserman *et al.*, 1998), although such histories have also been noted in patients with non-epileptic seizures and irritable bowel syndrome, in comparison to patients with epilepsy and Crohn's disease (Reilly *et al.*, 1999). Higher scores on the Dissociative Experiences Scale are noted in people reporting early childhood abuse than in those with no abuse (Chu and Dill, 1990).

There are numerous problems interpreting this literature (Tillman *et al.*, 1994). There is a high frequency of reporting of abuse, physical and sexual in the general population, and defining what abuse may be, as opposed to sexual contact, is a slippery boundary. The studies at best show only a weak statistical association, and do not take into account the fact that those who claim abuse often come from dysfunctional families, with the genetic and pathological environmental (epigenetic) implications of that. The abuse may be more a marker of the dysfunctional environment, rather than being causative of any specific psychopathology. In the study of Nash *et al.* (1993), although patients who were sexually traumatised in childhood reported more dissociative symptoms than those not abused, the significance disappeared when family environment was taken into account.

The literature on the association between personality disorders and somatisation has been reviewed in Chapter 2. It was noted that certain personalities, especially antisocial, borderline, histrionic and dependent people, are overrepresented in populations that somatise, and possible mechanisms for this include the cognitive style of such personalities. However, since abnormal personal development and personality disorders link to both genetic and epigenetic environmental factors, the multilayered complexity underlying the development of somatoform and dissociative disorders must be clear. There is no single pathway, but a veritable *olla podrida*. Celani (1976) advocated an entirely culturosocial theory of conversion disorders, in which patients 'learned to communicate helplessness, thereby facilitating an environment in which attention and support are gained and aggressive impulses avoided'. Patients' symptoms are reinforced by those around them, and by any

Table 8.1 Theories of conversion

Author	Historical date	Theory
Briquet	1859	Stress affecting brain
Reynolds	1869	Dependent on an idea
Bertheim	1890	Suggestion
Charcot	1892	Degeneration theories
Freud	1893	Repression
Janet	1907	Dissociation
Ludwig	1972	Centrifugal inhibition of afferent stimuli
Celani	1976	Cultural and social
Hilgard	1977	Neodissociation
Brown	2002	Information processing

associated secondary gains. The paper from Tarsh and Royston (1985) emphasised the role of the family in medicolegal claimants with chronic psychiatric symptoms, which was paramount. 'The more that relatives believed totally that a claimant is physically ill and took over helping that person, the more that person relapsed into chronic illness, which becomes a way of life' (p. 24).

This brings the argument back to malingering. Even the great Charcot suggested that 'malingering is to be found in every phase of hysteria', and many clinical opinions are to be found echoing this with various degrees of conviction. Some have referred to 'honest liars' (Spiegel, 1980), people who create false stories under hypnosis, which they believe to be true – liars who do not know they are lying. In general, there are those who think that there is much more malingering around than meets the eye; the literature has been discussed in Chapter 4.

There are many entrances to the sick role, and there are several forms of AIB. However, a medical system that is somatically bound, a compensation system that is collusive and a sociocultural system that helps shape the experience and presentation of illness all contribute to the final clinical picture in patients with somatisation, and this is all the more relevant in medicolegal settings.

Conclusions

This chapter has attempted to review the various theories of symptom generation and maintenance in hysteria, somatisation and related disorders (Table 8.1). The pendulum has swung, once again, from the organic to the psychological, although newer methods of studying brain function may well provoke a return to the somatic. No theory stands out as either easily verifiable or satisfactory when applying it to all the various guises of the somatising disorders. Newer psychological theories emphasising normal as opposed to abnormal information processing may be one way forward, but no theory will succeed unless personality variables and sociological influences are also taken into account. Suggestibility is one theme that has echoed down the ages, and seems very relevant to cases in a medicolegal context, embedded as they are in a peculiar matrix of competing, often bewildering forces.

Failure to appreciate the fragility of our diagnostic constructs, by physicians, experts, patients and lawyers, often lies at the heart of conflicts in the court setting, and as some suggest, has led to the creation of illnesses which possess about as much substance as the Emperor's new clothes. This is not to take away the fact that many people suffer considerably from accidents, and that posttraumatic psychological syndromes have been recognised for centuries. However, overdiagnosis, oversolicitous behaviour, excessive dependence and inappropriate prognostication contaminate the waters of the healing well, which is often made out to be deeper than it need be.

REFERENCES

American Psychiatric Association (1980). *Diagnostic and Statistical Manual of Mental Disorders* (DSM-III), 3rd edn. Washington, DC: American Psychiatric Association.

Baggaley, M. (1998). Military Munchausen's: assessment of factitious claims of military service in psychiatric patients. *Psychiatric Bulletin*, **22**, 153–4.

Barsky, A. J. and Wyshak, G. (1990). Hypochondriasis and somatosensory amplification. *British Journal of Psychiatry*, **157**, 404–9.

Bell, D. S. (1989). "Repetitive strain injury"; an iatrogenic epidemic of simulated injury. *Medical Journal of Australia*, **151**, 281–4.

Bendefeldt, F., Miller, L. L. and Ludwig, A. M. (1976). Cognitive performance in conversion hysteria. *Archives of Psychiatry*, **33**, 1250–4.

Brown, R. J. (2002). The cognitive psychology of dissociative states. *Cognitive Neuropsychiatry*, **7**, 221–36.

Celani, D. (1976). An interpersonal approach to hysteria. *American Journal of Psychiatry*, **133**, 1414–18.

Chalder, T., Hotopf, M., Unwin, C. *et al.* (2001). Prevalence of Gulf War veterans who believe they have Gulf War syndrome: a questionnaire study. *British Medical Journal*, **323**, 473–6.

Chu, J. A. and Dill, D. L. (1990). Dissociative symptoms in relation to childhood physical and sexual abuse. *American Journal of Psychiatry*, **147**, 887–92.

Coker, W. J., Bhatt, B. M., Blatchley, N. F. and Graham, J. T. (1999). Clinical findings for the first 1000 Gulf war veterans in the Ministry of Defence's medical assessment programme. *British Medical Journal*, **318**, 290–4.

David, A. S. and Wessely, S. C. (1995). The legend of Camelford. *Journal of Psychosomatic Research*, **39**, 1–9.

Dineen, T. (1999). *Manufacturing Victims*. London: Constable.

Engel, G. (1962). *Psychological Development in Health and Disease*. Philadelphia: WB Saunders.

Ford, C. V. (1983). *The Somatising Disorders; illness as a way of life*. New York: Elsevier Biomedical.

Fukada, M., Hata, A., Niwa, S. *et al.* (1996). Event related potential correlates of functional hearing loss: reduced P3 amplitude preserved N1 and N2 components in a unilateral case. *Neuropsychiatry and Clinical Neurosciences*, **50**, 85–7.

Hilgard, E. R. (1977). *Divided Consciousness: multiple controls in human thought and action*. New York: Wiley.

Horowitz, M. (1978). *Stress Response Syndromes*. New York: Jason Aronson.

Ishmail, K., Everitt, B., Blatchley, N. *et al.* (1999). Is there a gulf war syndrome? *Lancet*, **353**, 179–82.

James, W. (1902). *Varieties of Religious Experiences*. New York: Longmans Green.

Janet, P. (1924). *The Major Symptoms of Hysteria*, 2nd edn. New York: Macmillan.

Klerman, G. L. (1982). Hysteria and depression. In: *Hysteria*, ed. A. Roy, pp. 211–28. Chichester: John Wiley.

Lee, H. A., Gabriel, R., Bolton, J. P. G., Bale, A. and Jackson, M. (2002). Health status and clinical diagnosis of 3000 UK Gulf veterans. *Journal of the Royal Society of Medicine*, **95**, 491–7.

Leserman, J., Li, Z., Drossman, D. A. *et al.* (1998). Selected symptoms associated with sexual and physical abuse history among female patients with gastrointestinal disorders: the impact on subsequent health care visits. *Psychological Medicine*, **28**, 417–25.

Lhermitte, F., Turell, E., LeBrigand, D. and Chain, F. (1985). Unilateral visual neglect and wave P300. *Archives of Neurology*, **42**, 567–73.

Lorenz, J., Kunze, K. and Bromm, B. (1998). Differentiation of conversive sensory loss and malingering by P 300 in a modified odd-ball task. *Neuroreport*, **9**, 187–91.

Ludwig, A. M. (1972). Hysteria – a neurobiological theory. *Archives of General Psychiatry*, **27**, 771–7.

Malleson, A. (2002). *Whiplash and Other Useful Illnesses*. Toronto: McGill-Queens University Press.

Marshall, J. C., Halligan, P. W., Fink, G. R. *et al.* (1997). The functional anatomy of hysterical paralysis. *Cognition*, **64**, B1–8.

Merskey, H. (1995). *The Analysis of Hysteria*, 2nd edn. London: Gaskell Press.

Morrison, J. (1989). Childhood molestation reported by women with somatisation disorder. *Annals of Clinical Psychiatry*, **1**, 25–32.

Nash, M. R., Hulsey, T. L., Sexton, M. C., Harralson, T. L. and Lambert, W. (1993). Long-term sequelae of childhood sexual abuse; perceived family environment, psychopathology and dissociation. *Journal of Clinical and Consulting Psychology*, **61**, 276–83.

Neal, L. A. and Rose, M. C. (1995). Factitious post-traumatic stress disorder. *Medicine, Science and Law*, **35**, 352–4.

Pasquini, P., Liotto, G., Mazzotti, E., Fassone, G. and Picardi, A. (2002). The Italian group for the study of dissociation. Risk factors in the early family life of patients suffering from dissociative disorders. *Acta Psychiatrica Scandinavica*, **105**, 110–16.

Pearce, J. M. S. (1999). A critical appraisal of the chronic whiplash syndrome. *Journal of Neurology, Neurosurgery and Psychiatry*, **66**, 273–6.

Pennebaker, J. W. and Watson, D. (1991). The psychology of somatic symptoms. In *Current Concepts of Somatisation, Research and Clinical Perspectives*, eds. L. J. Kirmayer and J. M. Robbins, pp. 21–35. Washington, DC: American Psychiatric Press.

Pilowsky, I. (1995). *Abnormal Illness Behaviour*. Chichester: John Wiley.

Reilly, J., Baker, G. A., Rhodes, J. *et al.* (1999). The association of sexual and physical abuse with somatisation: characteristics of patients presenting with irritable bowel syndrome and non-epileptic attack disorder. *Psychological Medicine*, **29**, 399–406.

Resnick, P. J. (1997). *Malingering of Post-traumatic Disorders*. In: *Clinical Assessment of Malingering and Deception*, ed. R. Rogers, pp. 130–52. New York: Guilford Press.

Reynolds, J. R. (1869). Remarks on paralysis and other disorders of motion and sensation, dependent on idea. *British Medical Journal*, **ii**, 48–485.

Rivers, W. H. R. (1920). *Instinct and the Unconscious*. Cambridge: Cambridge University Press.

Roelofs, K. (2002). *Disturbed Information Processing in Conversion Disorder*. Nijmegen: Drukkerij Quickprint.

Rothman, A. L. and Weintraub, M. I. (1995). The sick building syndrome and mass hysteria. In *Malingering and Conversion Disorders*, ed. M. I. Weintraub, pp. 405–12. Philadelphia: WB Saunders.

Shephard B. (2000). *A War of Nerves*. London: Jonathan Cape.

Sierra, M. H. and Berrios, G. (1999). Towards a neuropsychiatry of conversion hysteria. *Cognitive Neuropsychiatry*, **4**, 267–88.

Smith, R. (2002). In search of "non-disease". *British Medical Journal*, **324**, 883–5.

Spence, S. A., Crimlisk, H. L., Cope, H. *et al.* (2000). Evidence for discrete neurophysiological correlates in prefrontal cortex during hysterical and feigned disorder of movement. *Lancet*, **355**, 1243–4.

Spiegel, H. (1980). Hypnosis and evidence; help or hindrance? *Annals of the New York Academy of Science*, **347**, 78.

Stone, M. (1985). Shellshock and the psychologists. In *The Anatomy of Madness*, vol. 2, ed. W. F. Bynum, R. Porter and M. Shepherd, pp. 242–71. London: Tavistock.

Summerfield, D. (2001). The invention of post-traumatic stress disorder and the social usefulness of a psychiatric category. *British Medical Journal*, **322**, 95–8.

Tarsh, M. J. and Royston, C. (1985). A follow-up study of accident neurosis. *British Journal of Psychiatry*, **146**, 18–25.

Tillman, J. G., Nash, M. R. and Lerner, P. M. (1994). Does trauma cause dissociative pathology? In *Dissociation; Clinical and Theoretical Perspectives*, eds S. J. Lynn and J. W. Rhue, pp. 395–414. New York: Guilford Press.

Wessely, S. (2001). Ten years on: what do we know about the Gulf War syndrome? *Clinical Medicine*, **1**, 28–37.

Wessely, S., Hotopf, M. and Sharpe, M. (1998). *Chronic Fatigue and its Syndromes.* Oxford: Oxford University Press.

World Health Organization (1993). *The ICD-10 Classification of Mental and Behavioural Disorders.* Geneva: World Health Organization.

Young, A. (1995). *The Harmony of Illusions. Inventing Post-traumatic Stress Disorder.* Princeton: Princeton University Press.

9

Causation and the question of consciousness

It is incident to physicians, beyond all other men, to mistake subsequence for consequence.

(Samuel Johnson, 1734)

The desire to take medicine is one of the greatest differences between man and animals.

(Orson Welles)

Causation

The last chapter was concerned with the mechanisms, the aetiology and patho-genesis of conversion disorders and somatisation. It is clear that aetiology and pathogenesis are not the same, that pathogenesis (a process) is subject to patho-plastic influences, and that, at the end of the day, the cause (aetiology) of these disorders is inevitably multifactorial. In psychiatric practice generally, causation is an elusive spectre, which looms large in medicolegal circles, but like that of the Brocken, remains a shadowy projection in the mist.

As this chapter will demonstrate, there are considerable differences between the legal and medical concepts of causation, and neither of them copes well with the two millennia of philosophical writings on the subject. As Jolowicz *et al.* (1971) comment:

To a certain point the common law does touch on metaphysics. But no test of remoteness of causation put forward by Anglo-American courts would satisfy any metaphysician. On the other hand, no test suggested by metaphysicians would be of any practical use to lawyers.

In other words, a trial for damages is a practical, not a theoretical inquiry. Causation is to be understood as the person in the street and not as either the scientist or the metaphysician would understand it. This is all very well, but the person in the street, bound down and educated only to subscribe to folk psychology, believes in all kinds of things that are manifestly incorrect, if not positively misleading. This is no better illustrated than by the person in the street's conception of causality. Some of these fallacies with regards to illness have already been noted in earlier chapters. However, from the point of view of clinical psychiatry, logical relations are usually only those of weak implication, and at the philosophical level, the proposition that all events have causes, referred to as the principle of sufficient reason, is neither provable nor refutable (Bebbington, 1980). If the law is interested in seeking truth, these fundamental principles have to be acknowledged. They also need to be embraced by any expert offering advice to the courts on matters of causation of psychiatric injury.

In general, the law seeks to assess the straw that breaks the camel's back; medicine and psychiatry recognise the polyphonic nature of pathogenesis. When it comes to straws, different doctors may differ considerably in their interpretation, which may depend on their theoretical orientations and biases, as much as on which of two sides in a medicolegal case they may be advising. In essence, the courts are involved in allocating responsibility, which means choosing from amongst several potential claims.

Causation – general comments

The philosophical revolution of the seventeenth century accompanied the contemporaneous scientific revolution, that of Copernicus (1473–1543), Kepler (1571–1630), Galileo (1564–1642), and Newton (1643–1727). Philosophy allied with science rather than religion and with the Enlightenment came an unprecedented but unfounded confidence in human reason. Descartes (1596–1650) believed that, after doubting everything, except himself as a thinking being, it was possible to establish the triumph of human reason and infallibility over the irrational, and reason, once the attribute of the creator, was transferred to the human faculties. *Res cogitans* was distinguished from *res extensa*, and a mind–body dualism was established which became enshrined in philosophical and lay thinking for the succeeding centuries. These philosophical legacies remain with us today, especially in folk psychology. They distinguish mind from body, but, perhaps because of the nature of the human mind, with its myth-loving metaphysical intuitions, or perhaps due to the overriding power and influence of the church, there also developed a dual-truth universe, one which embraced reason but also faith.

Hume (1711–76) attacked the basis for both. His thesis, in brief, was that our knowledge of causality could not be based on reason alone, but was dependent only on our experience that particular things are constantly 'conjoined' to each other. Effect and cause are different, and the former cannot be found in the latter. Cause and effect are determined by the mind of the observer, and are entirely subjective. Reason is easily deceived, cause was linked to effect through an association of ideas, through custom and habit; instinct and feeling were therefore predominant in determining causality.

It was Immanuel Kant (1724–1804) who literally turned philosophy around, a revolution in thinking about thinking as profound as the later revolutions of Darwin or Freud. Aroused from his dogmatic slumbers by Hume's treatise and scepticism, he argued that all knowledge had an a priori component, independent of experience (in contrast to a posteriori knowledge, which is acquired from experience). Our cognitive apparatus, our brains, constitute, construct and contribute to the formal aspects of our knowable world; we do not simply passively receive sensory information. Our claims about reality are only valid as claims about reality as experienced by an individual; we deal with phenomena (things as they appear) as opposed to noumena (things in themselves). Claims about the world cannot be made independently of our cognitive structures, our brains contribute causality to experience, and one cannot assume that causality exists as an independent feature of the world outside our experiences. His category of causation is thus independent of experience, causality is built into our cognitive framework, things conform to the mind – the mind became seen as creative!

A consequence of Kant's revolution was that science could never produce knowledge that was certain, reaffirmed by the much later twentieth-century philosophy of Karl Popper, since every observed fact presupposes representations and interpretations. As Nietzsche (1880) opined; 'Against positivism, which halts at phenomena – "there are only facts" – I would say: No, facts are precisely what there are not, only interpretations' (p. 481). Nietzsche realised the fallibility of all knowledge, and his near-contemporary Freud emphasised the significance of symbolic representation in our synthesis of reality. Interpretation is overdetermined, there are no single sovereign constructions of the mind, only sensations and theory-soaked solipsistic souvenirs for our contemplation.

A different line of argument about causation was taken by J. S. Mill (1886). A lot of philosophical and legal discussion of cause is based on an assumption that causes are individual events, and causal relationships exist between events (Davidson, 1993). For Mill, cause is 'the sum total of the conditions positive and negative taken together . . . which being realised, the consequent invariably follows' (s.3). In other words, any cause must include all antecedent conditions. Mill's doctrine of the plurality of causes requires a set of conditions, insisting on complexity and plurality. This leads on to the important distinction between necessary and sufficient conditions. A is the cause of B only if A is *sufficient* for B (other things being equal), as opposed to A is the cause of B only if A is *necessary* for B (other things being equal). The third alternative is of course that A is the cause of B only if A is *sufficient* and *necessary* for B (other things being equal). Where there are two or more minimally sufficient conditions, which is so often the case with historical events, which is one way to view a medicolegal inquiry of the outcome of accidents, several causes may be ascribed to the same event, and historical arguments revolve around the priority of different causes.

Historians select facts that are significant for their purpose, and which fit their patterns of rational explanation and interpretation (Carr, 1961). The historian has some end focus, and will select explanations that serve this purpose. Hence the importance of another type of cause, which has also been discussed from time to time, namely that of final causes, which was introduced to philosophical thought by Aristotle (384–322 BC). It was one of four types of causation, but was of considerable significance in Aristotle's scheme. Cause was found in the ends of things (*telos* – hence teleological), rather than the beginnings. History through the selective gathering of information acquires meaning and a purpose, beyond the secular nature of any facts, and the historian cannot separate fact from interpretation. Facts do not speak for themselves: historians, claimants, doctors and lawyers speak for them!

Some argue, and this comes nearer to the legal approach, that probability rather than conditionality is an appropriate way of reaching at causality. Quantum physics has radically altered our view of the world and also of causality by acknowledging that A may cause B on some occasions but not others. Causation in these terms becomes only an increase in probability, a stochastic process. Again the problem of overdetermination comes into the equation since probability theory allows for the possibility of other probable causal factors, perhaps incompatible with the given suggested causal factor and more efficacious than it.

Causation in medicine

The rules of science are not those of the courtroom, and this dictum is relevant for the whole issue of causality in medicolegal practice. In medical science, and especially in psychiatry, causality is no longer linked to deterministic bonds between cause and effect. Instead statements are made about necessary and sufficient causes. Distinctions are made between meaning and causality, and understanding and explaining. Statistics reveal only probabilities, possibilities and uncertainties.

Analogies abound in folk psychology explanations. The brain works like a clock (being 'wound-up', or 'regular as clockwork'), or with electricity ('run down', or 'loss of sparkle'), or as a cybernetic system, with feedbacks, goal-seeking behaviours and circuits which become disrupted and have to be corrected. Computer analogies are now popular, with talk of the brain's hardware and software, of systems that need rebooting, of failures due to information overload. The idea of a person with a thin skull is a favourite courtroom analogy, which has popular appeal, but is deeply flawed as a concept of cause in psychiatry (Sim, 1992). Application of concepts in physical science (a particular strain on a certain material of a fixed strength causes bending of that material to such and such a degree, and at a certain strain it will certainly break) is not applicable to mental science, and even hard-line materialists accept a discordance between events of the mind and events of the brain – the psychological and the physical. While every mental state must have an accompanying brain state, direct mind–brain identity is far from being established, and is not currently the fashionable interpretation.

Sim (1992), a long-standing advocate of seeking logic in courtroom practice, put it thus:

> severe stress is not usually followed by psychiatric illness and when it does it bears no relation to the severity of the stress and that, generally, the outcome is very good and in quick time. In compensation cases there seems to be current belief that all accidents, whether resulting in physical injury or not must result in psychiatric disability. There is no evidence to support such a view. It seems to be peculiar to compensation cases . . . the causes of breakdown are . . . as one would expect, varied and complex (p. 47).

Yet not everyone understands this, or apparently is aware of this. Often it is possible to read in an expert report 'I have no doubt that the [psychiatric] illness in this case was caused by the accident'. This can rarely be the case. Such naivety bedevils logic, seeks solution through simplicity and betrays an ignorance of a basic understanding of the psyche. This is the more so with cases of severe psychiatric disorders, including somatisation.

Shock is another of these analogies which strikes at the heart of the patient and the court alike. The concept of shock had a reasonable and interesting history (shell-shock), but the physical transmogrified into the psychological, and the term took off on its own. Nervous shock, as Sim noted, is the expected outcome of every accident. The very term 'posttraumatic stress disorder' (PTSD) implies within it cause and effect! As Winn noted in the trial of *James* v. *Woodall Duckham Construction* ([1969] 1 WLR 903):

> I would have ventured to think that no neurosis can properly be called a 'traumatic' neurosis unless there is a continuous chain of causation between the trauma and the neurosis. The fact that a neurosis has occurred *post* an accident certainly does not prove that it has occurred *propter* the accident . . . one feels, very much to one's embarrassment, that psychiatrists appear to talk of 'traumatic' neurosis, and 'post-traumatic' neurosis virtually as though those two terms were synonymous.

Legal practitioners, with many shortcomings in respect to an understanding of psychiatric principles and practice, which after all is why experts are required, do appear to seek an understanding of causation from a medical view when instructing medical experts. The problems are that in psychiatry, causation generally is simply not understood, even by psychiatrists, and strictures, such as asking questions in terms of the equally flawed *but for* test, are often laid down.

The role of intrinsic as opposed to extrinsic factors in the development of psychopathology has been poorly represented in legal settings, having been undermined by the thin-skull analogy, and such terms as posttraumatic whatever. As noted above, conditions such as PTSD and the somatoform disorders are heavily dependent on genetic, epigenetic and constitutional factors, and simple explanations of causation reliant solely on the extrinsic are intellectually dishonest. The overemphasis on the 'thin skull' means that it is often difficult to balance a discussion on causation in medicolegal settings, and a neglect of consideration of trajectories of illness and the influences of personality on causation. As one observer commented: 'there is all the difference in the world between a thin skull shattering and a thin mind doing the same thing. A thin skull straightforwardly breaks into pieces, but a thin mind goes to pieces in a way that suits its owner' (Malleson, 2002, p. 302).

In theory the law requires everything that is given in evidence to be proven, but a truism is the exception *res ipsa loquitur* – the thing speaks for itself. In legal terms this maxim is not used in the context of causation, but only in relation to proving breach of duty. However, the belief that being involved in an accident invariably causes mental illness seems so heavily ingrained in the legal and lay mind that it seems to be treated as such a truism, subsequence being totally confused with consequence.

There have been many theories of the cause of illness. In the past sin was often invoked, supernatural agents visiting the healthy and causing morbidity. Punishment was part of this equation, causality was capricious. With medical progress, disease was either viewed ontologically (some noxious agent invading the body or a part of the body), or as a 'reaction' by the body to the noxious agent. The ontological view initially held that individual diseases, which could be distinguished and classified, had some kind of independent existence, like a Platonic archetype, and the art of clinical medicine was to discern and understand them. This kind of thinking received considerable support from those like Rudolf Virchow (1821–1902), a distinguished pathological anatomist, who defined a disease as a living entity which affected a part of the body, and was reflected in the visible pathology. By this time (late nineteenth century), the disease entity however was not thought of as an alien invader, but rather as an intrinsic component of the patient's body. Cause was related to explaining the patients' symptoms, but causality was seen only from a pathological level, and it became assumed, for a while, that diseases were monogenic. Scientific determinism then allows the obvious causal chain to be established – every event is a 'sufficient' cause of its effect, and every effect has as its antecedent a 'necessary' cause. As Kräupl Taylor (1979) went on to explain:

[This] plausibility diminishes, when a wider context is considered. Causal chains cannot be viewed in isolation then, but as individual elements in a welter of constantly interacting causal chains. As a result, no single event can be regarded as the sufficient cause of an effect. An event A is the cause of the immediate effect B only in conjunction with favourable adjuvant circumstances whose composition may be, and often is, largely unknown . . . each effect in the possible range will have its own probability of occurring, depending on the frequency with which its favourable adjuvant circumstances are present (p. 24).

Reaction as a concept contains within it a more obvious causality, namely event B being a reaction to event A. The reactions were viewed as bodily processes that were evoked by a noxious agent, the pus for example from an infection. The reaction was seen as part of the body's defence against a pathogen, but it could contribute to morbidity.

The problem with these theories is that, while they may apply to physical conditions that affect the body, they have been taken over to psychiatry and applied to psychological mechanisms, on the naive assumption that causality in the psychological realm is no different from the physical. Reactive theories impregnate a lot of psychiatric thinking (e.g. inherent in terms such as reactive depression or PTSD), but in reality most clinical pictures are overdetermined, causation is heterogeneous and the final presentation is determined pathoplastically. Disease is not the same as disorder, and illness, that with which the patient presents to doctors, is the outcome of variant states, predispositions, predestinations and processes.

Causation in psychiatry

Karl Jaspers (1883–1969), philosopher and psychiatrist, introduced the distinction between causal and understandable connections in psychopathology (*Kausale und verständliche Zusammenhänge*; Jaspers, 1963). The background to this distinction emerged from the social sciences, especially the theories of Weber, which posited that causality in the social sciences functioned differently than in the physical sciences (Cutting, 1997). Psychological explanation (*psychologisches Erklären*) is different from rational understanding (*rationalen Verstehen*). Thus, there are explanations in terms of beliefs, desires and so forth, and there are causal explanations of the natural sciences and physics. In the psychological realm, connections are not contingent, but based on individual meaning, but meaningful connections are not causal in the usual meaning of the word, that is, covered by a natural law. To state one reviewer: 'meanings are not causes . . . and hence the turn-of-the-century dichotomies between meaning and causality, understanding and [causal] explanation' (Bolton and Hill, 1996, p. 177).

For Jaspers, *Verstehen* and *Erklären*, empathetic and causal reasoning respectively, reflect different layers of interpreting phenomena, but only the latter belongs to the realm of natural science. *Verstehen* presents an Aristotelian view of causality. Humans as symbolic animals, and living in a world of meaning, beliefs and intentions, are both agents and organisms, a mind and a brain (Slavney and McHugh, 1987). We can understand (*verstehen*) the anger of someone who is attacked, the sadness of one bereaved. However, truly causal connections (*erklären*), are established empirically by the scientific method. *Verstehen* accords to the meaning of mental events, that which is largely self-evident from a human point of view; it relies on interpretation. But Jaspers (1913/1963) acknowledged that: 'another possible way of understanding is always at hand' (p. 356). This leads to collisions of understanding: 'the most radical mistakes spring from conclusions drawn as to the reality of what has been understood, whenever these conclusions have been based on the self evidence of some one-sided understanding. The exclusion of the opposite, without any attempt to follow it up and understand it, means that we manipulate reality in favour of an "*a priori*" understanding that makes an arbitrary selection of the facts' (Jaspers, 1913/1963, p. 357). Such understanding must be inconclusive,

in part because [it] rests on interpretations, which may never acquire enough empirical support to convince us that all which could be known is known, and in part because they are rooted in biological mechanisms (such as instinctual drives), which cannot themselves be grasped through understanding. But meaningful connections are also inconclusive because life is happening as we observe and interpret it, and because the final chapter cannot be written for someone who has both choice and a future (Slavney and McHugh, 1987, p. 38).

Thus in psychiatric practice when analysing phenomena, *verstehen* and *eklären* must always be distinguished, but often are not, and in medicolegal practice this fundamental is usually ignored. Interpretations are taken as explanations, understanding is conflated with causation, what may be meaningful is taken as causal. The dilemma was summed up by Himsworth (1986) as follows:

the progress towards solving the problem of whether two things were causally related depends on asking if something else was present which, if it were, would go at least some way towards explaining what happened. But, how could anybody have any inkling of what might be present, if what happened in between the first and second events noted is outside their experience? The answer is, of course, that they do what people always do in such circumstances. They call upon their imagination to fill in the gaps in their factual information and thus enable them to construct a hypothetical sequence to account for the association in question . . . On the face of it, this is a hazardous procedure. We should do well to ask, therefore, to what extent, if any, do the fabrications of the imagination have any foundation in fact? (p. 47).

Causation in law

What might have been is an abstraction
Remaining a perpetual possibility
Only in a world of speculation.

(T. S. Eliot, *Burnt Norton*)

Eliot (*Burnt Norton*) sums up crisply the quotidian situation of the civil legal enquiry, and hits at the heart of the beloved *but for* test, which has become central to causation in the law.

In tort, either in relationship to the breach of duty and the injury or the injury and any loss, the sine qua non test has become the cardinal principle, the one which the claimant must demonstrate to hold. At all times the burden of proof rests with the claimant and it is never for the defendant to establish that some other cause or combination of causes may be responsible for the situation. However, in settings of overdetermined causality, where a claimant has established, on the balance of probabilities that a given operative cause or agent led to his or her injuries, the claimant only has to show that the tortious element of the exposure materially contributed to the injury (*Bonnington Castings Ltd* v. *Wardlaw* [1956] 1 All ER 615). This idea, of a material contribution arose out of a case of industrial disease, but it appears to have been adapted for psychiatric damage on the assumption that causality in the physical and psychological realms can be logically equated. Unfortunately 'the law cannot take account of everything that follows a wrongful act; it regards some subsequent matters as outside the scope of its selection . . . In the varied web of affairs, the law must abstract some consequences as relevant, not perhaps on grounds of pure logic but simply for practical reasons' (Lord Wright *Liesbosch Dredger* v. *S. S. Edison* [1933] AC 449).

Thus, the law, for purely policy and practical reasons, has a tendency to ignore logic, and its sister discipline philosophy. 'Common-sense principles' are evoked (Lord Dunedin *Haber* v. *Walker* [1963] VR 339, 357–8), akin in neuroscience to folk psychology, and in terms of the above discussion, explanations assume the status of causal statements.

There are various expressions used by the law to refer to cause. One of these relates to proximate cause and another addresses the issue of remoteness (*in jure non remota causa sed proxima spectatur*). Remoteness must be seen as distinct from causation, and although this hints at the principle of proximity of events in space and time to an accident (the aftermath), this interpretation is quite misleading in terms of establishing *the* cause of causes (*causa causans*). Further, to complicate the matter, as noted in Chapter 7, reference to aftermath and physical proximity is only relevant in the context of secondary claimants who suffer psychiatric harm, and even then, this is linked to the duty of care. In fact, the doctrine of remoteness again has to do with setting limitations on liability, and these limitations are set as a matter of legal policy, and are not based on any logic to do with understanding causation. Remoteness tests whether or not the consequences of a tort are too remote from an initial potential cause to be considered. A much-quoted example (which does not apply in English law) is the fact that it has been held in New York state since 1866 that if a fire, which has been started negligently, spreads to another building, recovery can only be for damage to the first. The law does not trace a series of events beyond a certain limit, reinforcing the point that cause in law is a blend of both fact and policy. Liability is limited to what is then referred to as *foreseeable*. The idea of establishing a proximate cause, and the limits of foreseeability are, as discussed, a practical legal device to set limits on who may recover what, but are quite intellectually removed from the considerations of logic and philosophy.

A reasonably foreseeable intervening cause is accepted in the chain of causation, but not unforeseeable or abnormal intervening causes. The latter are referred to under the phrase *novus actus interveniens*.

The well-known legal maxim was given in *The Wagon Mound* ([1961] AC 388, p. 426): 'the essential factor in determining liability is whether the damage is of such a kind as the reasonable man should have foreseen'. There is however an interesting catch to this seemingly straightforward statement, namely that foreseeability applies only to liability, and not to damages, at least as far as physical injuries are concerned. The case often cited is *Smith* v. *Leech Brain* ([1962] 2 QB 405). A plaintiff, as a consequence of negligence, burned his lip, and then developed cancer at the site of the burn, from which illness he died. The widow succeeded in a claim for damages, even though the development of the cancer could not have been foreseen.

It has already been noted in Chapter 7 that, where no physical injury has occurred, the law adopts a different policy in relation to psychiatric injury depending on whether the claimant is a primary or secondary victim. This relates to a distinction between consequential and pure psychiatric harm (Jones and Sprince, 2001). If the psychiatric illness is consequential on physical injury, or if the claimant is a primary plaintiff (in the danger zone), the foreseeability test does not apply. If the defendant injures someone directly, harm may be envisaged, and if caused by the injury, then the cost of any harm may be recovered. In the case of secondary claimants, to recover, they must show not only that the harm was foreseeable, but also that it was foreseeable in a person of reasonable fortitude. In other words, primary claimants may recover for completely unforeseen consequences of injury, but not secondary claimants.

Establishing cause in law generally relies on the sine qua non. Would *B* have occurred if *A* had not occurred? This question sets up the sine qua non (cause in fact or material cause) of *B* and seems or should be independent from the consequential question, 'Is there any principle which precludes the treatment of *B* as the consequence of *A* for legal purposes'? This second question is practically very much again a matter of legal limitation.

The *sine qua non* test relies on a principle that the cause of an event is one (out of a set), which is sufficient to be invariably and unconditionally followed by it. In Mill's (1886) analysis, the other members of the set are necessary and subsequently linked. This sets up the necessary and sufficient conditions and the sine qua non. However, in the legal context, especially in psychiatric cases, applying this maxim is fraught with hazards. If one and only one sufficient cause is established, the *sine qua non* is clear. In medicolegal psychiatric settings, this is rarely achievable. It is usually either the case that not every relevant factor which might contribute to the clinical picture is a sine qua non, or that not every supposed sine qua non is *the* causally relevant factor. Any factor can only be one of a set, and therefore there is always more than one, which may act as a sufficient cause in addition to any accident. A most obvious example is the contribution of bereavement, which may have been occasioned by an accident, in which a loved one is killed, or independently, when a parent, spouse or child dies around the time of the accident or subsequent to it. Loss of an occupation, failure of a marriage or other significant relationships, and the use of alcohol or illicit drugs are other examples often met with in psychiatric practice, which may or may not themselves be indirectly or directly related to the accident and the injuries in question.

The lawyers' formulation of the sine qua non is the *but for* test. Would the loss have occurred *but for* the breach or injury? However, this test is clearly inappropriate in complex situations, which psychiatric cases are by their very nature, and is confounded by such issues as noted above and by legal considerations, which the law refers to as concurrent and contributory causes. These are purely legal matters, such as when there is more than one wrong-doer that simultaneously injure the claimant, or when the claimants' acts are contributory to the outcome, for example in not wearing a seat belt while driving. An issue in many of the cases touched upon in this book relates to the issue of the free will of the claimant as an intervening force in determining symptoms, in other words exaggeration of complaints for the purposes of compensation. If the claimant freely chooses, for example, not to return to work, then the causal connection between the injury and loss of earnings is negated.

The classic case of consecutive causes is that of *Baker* v. *Willoughby* ([1970] AC 467). The claimant suffered a leg injury, and was forced to take up a new job. In his new position he became the victim of an armed robbery; the already-injured leg was further damaged and had to be amputated. The *but for* test here would suggest that the liability of the defendant who caused the first injury was limited to the loss suffered before the second injury, which was the decision of the Court of Appeal. This is shown diagramatically in Figure 9.1. The original accident occurred

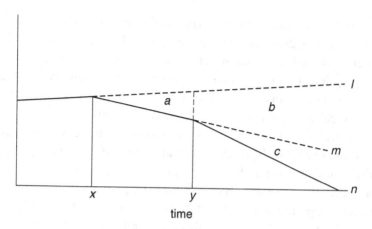

Figure 9.1   Causation and remoteness. Reproduced from Ogus (1973), with permission.

at point *x*, and the claimant's assets are represented by the unbroken line. His losses are therefore *a*, until the second accident at *y* when *n* represents his actual position after the second injury, and *m* the expected position if he had only one injury. Thus *a* + *b* are the losses he would have sustained following only one injury. The argument is over who should be liable for *b*, the perpetrator of the first or second injury (Ogus, 1973)? Lord Pearson, in the House of Lords, observed that the Court of Appeal argument led to manifest injustice, especially as it was not possible to sue the robbers. Accordingly the defendant was liable for the full extent of the injury (*a* + *b*), without reduction or limitation on account of the subsequent injury.

In the case of *Jobling* v. *Associate Dairies Ltd* ([1982] AC 794), the claimant injured his back as a consequence of the defendant's negligence. It was discovered that the patient developed severe back disease, unrelated to the accident, but which came on before the trial, which precluded him from working. The House of Lords opined that this illness had to be taken into account in assessing liability, the so-called 'vicissitudes argument'. Thus, assessment of damages reflects the possibility of other contingencies that might reduce a claimant's earning capacity or working life. If the claimant would have been in that state in any event, then the defendants are not responsible for it. Of course, if the symptoms are worse than they would have been, then the claimant is entitled to claim for the difference.

Another often-quoted case, that relates to the failure of the *but for* test, is that of *Cutler* v. *Vauxhall Motors Ltd* ([1971] 1 QB 418). The plaintiff grazed his right ankle in an accident, but subsequently developed a varicose ulcer at the site of the graze. Varicosities had been present prior to the injury, but the ulcer emerged after the accident. There followed an operation, and a claim for damages for loss of earnings, and pain and suffering due to the operation. The trial judge, and the Court of Appeal, disallowed this on account of the fact that the varicosity *per se* would have worsened anyway, and would have needed an operation at some time. One judge at the appeal dissented on the grounds that what was essentially a probability had been converted into a certainty, but the appeal was disallowed, on the basis of the *but for* principle. There are clear parallels with this case and the development of somatised symptoms in patients with somatoform disorders, where the vicissitudes of life's varicosities have unveiled inevitable vulnerabilities.

The principle of the eggshell skull means that it is irrelevant that a defendant does not know about such predispositions at the time of the tort, and, in psychiatric practice, emotional susceptibilities and pre-existing psychiatric vulnerability are not regarded as intervening events. The general principle here is that abnormal circumstances existing at the time of the tort will not negate a causal connection (Hart and Honore, 1985). However, there are clearly exceptions, and in practice, as revealed by the cases quoted, the courts actually do take into account pre-existing liabilities and past medical events when assessing damages, especially if there is a 'real possibility that the plaintiff would anyway have been affected' (*Wilson* v. *Peisley* [1975] 7 ALR 571). To quote Hart and Honore (1985):

It has been argued that a distinction should be drawn between a pre-existing condition which in its natural progression would have affected the victim and one which required an external trigger such as the defendant's conduct to set it off. But this distinction appears unsound. At most it may be said that the chance of an external trigger is sometimes slight, so that the reduction of damages on its account will not be great. Though the defendant has the burden of adducing evidence of the possibility of harm triggered by a later event, he need not show that there was more than an even chance of its occurrence (p. 180).

Thus, the claimant's pre-existing psychiatric vulnerability is relevant to liability but not compensation. The claimant's unforeseeable vulnerability cannot convert a trivial event into a compensatable loss. This is very relevant to cases of somatisation, but also to the assessment of many cases in which the pretraumatic personality is such a significant factor in the patient's presentation. It is only by taking into account the life history of the claimant that one may come to appreciate that the apparent injury was but one of numerous sufficient causes for the clinical presentation, and that the vulnerability to breakdown was so great, the propensity to sink into a state of dependence so well ingrained into the injured personality, that the accident has hardy altered the prognosis of the patient at all. As Robert Graves wrote:

Lest men suspect your tale to be untrue
Keep probability – some say in view . . .
Sigh then, or frown, but leave (as in despair)
Motive and end and moral, in the air;
Nice contradiction between fact and fact
Will make the whole read human and exact. (Dineen p. 76).

Consciousness

The plaintiff appeal of lawyers over the years, since the introduction of the Workmen's Compensation Acts and related compensation schemes, in civilian life and in the forces, is to ask of symptoms the question: 'but doctor, are they conscious or unconscious?' This seemingly simple question, repeated over and over again in the court setting, has an innocence, which, like Faust's poodle, harbours the most diabolical complexity.

A number of years ago it was easier. As a generalisation, neuroscientists were not interested in the subject of consciousness, and most of the literature revolved around Freudian psychoanalytic speculation, which had more to do with the unconscious than the conscious mind. For Freud our innermost nature was as hidden to us, as was the reality of the external world, all we know of the latter being filtered and limited by the screen of our sense organs. However, the developing idea that much of our behaviour is driven by unconscious forces was of no interest to legal minds. The very concept of the *mens rea* implied an outdated Cartesian mind–body split, and the idea that an act did not imply a conscious derivative was quickly removed from appeals of the criminal court, but then paradoxically assumed exaggerated importance in civil settings, especially as it is a concept only applied to criminal law! If in the matter of medically unexplained symptoms, behaviour was deemed conscious, there was no compensation, but if it was unconscious then from such depths gold could be mined.

In recent years things have changed. Consciousness has become a very respectable topic for neuroscience, and a multitude of books and theories have emerged that relate to two main issues. The first is the question of what is consciousness, and does it exist as an entity? The second line of investigation is neurobiological; where in the brain is consciousness located? How does the brain actually do it? The former enterprise has been the province more of philosophy, the latter of the newly rediscovered discipline of cognitive neuroscience. Neither of these areas may seem of relevance to the law and its practitioners, but it is simply not possible to dwell among the sustaining corn without becoming entangled with the furrowed weeds. If the first questions put above are to be posed, how may they be answered from a contemporary perspective that is relevant to an understanding of hysteria?

Consciousness is an accepted feature of the function of the brain. However, at the outset it must be recognised that it is an emergent property. It does not exist as some independent metaphysical Cartesian ego, separate from the brain in location and substance. It prospers from a multitude of brain processes, based on distributed neural networks and interactions between multiple representations, which are dynamic and not static, and which precede outside awareness, and are hidden from us. Thus, most of what we do and the vast majority of our psychological

Figure 9.2   The unity of conscious experience. This celebrated picture, first published by Edgar Rubin, in 1921, can be interpreted in two ways. It shows either a white vase against a black background or two black counterdisposed faces against a white background. It is impossible to perceive both alternatives simultaneously, but switching from one interpretation to the other can be achieved in as little as about half a second. From Cotterill (1998).

processes in fact occur non-consciously. Consciousness seems necessary to allow for a coherent structure of our ongoing behaviour, and serves as a monitor for some of our ongoing behaviour. In phylogenetic terms, the evolution of the unity of consciousness must have had considerable survival value, enhancing the moment of existence into a coherent whole to enable effective spontaneous and rapid action.

Consciousness therefore is intolerant of ambiguity, unlike extraconscious processing which allows for a multitude of contrasting representations, out of which the unified conscious process must emerge. It is well known for example that certain patterns, which we can see and which could be either one thing or another (either a duck or a rabbit; or either an old man's face or a beautiful girl: Figure 9.2), can only be seen as either one or the other, and not both at the same time. Once a gestalt, hidden within a jumbled picture is revealed to us, it is difficult not to continue seeing it again and again on re-exposure.

Human consciousness, our self-consciousness, is closely linked to language, to the availability of words, themselves symbols, one thing standing for another, an indirect representation of the world and its contents, which they represent. Language is mainly the prerogative of the left hemisphere of the brain which, over generations of evolution, has shifted the balance of the bicameral brain's equality, suppressing the right hemisphere's non-verbal prosodic elegance of expression. Two sets of experiments of considerable importance have been carried out in recent years that have radically altered our understanding of ourselves and our relationship to our own conscious experiences, in many ways as shattering to our preconceptions of our nature as the Darwinian revelations of the nineteenth century.

Conscious intention has been shown to be a post-hoc event. Libet (1993) conducted a series of investigations related to a subject's awareness of sensory stimuli, and the timing of that awareness. In these experiments, the activity of the brain was monitored by measuring electrical potentials from the surface of the brain, so-called cortical evoked potentials. If for example the skin is stimulated, a signal is seen at the cortex some 20 ms later, lasting some 50–100 ms, but the subject is unaware of the event – it is subliminal. Trains of stimuli of about 500 ms duration are needed to elicit a conscious report of the stimulus. In other words, we do not experience the world in real time, there is a 'neural delay' before consciousness of an event occurs and we then retrospectively refer backwards in time to the moment of the sensory experience.

Even more astonishing is the similar neuronal delay that occurs before we gain the conscious experience of our intention to act. It has been known for some time that recording electrodes from the brain will detect a wave of activity that precedes a motor act, the so-called readiness potential (RP). Subjects are placed in an experimental set-up in which they are primed to expect a second stimulus by a first stimulus, and upon receipt of the former they have to respond with a motor task. The timing of the latter is monitored by an electromyogram. The RP is recorded as a negative scalp potential some 800 ms before the actual motor act. Libet established that a similar potential could be recorded about 550 ms before a self-paced spontaneous motor act, but astonishingly, by asking subjects to note the time point when they became aware of their intention to act, he found that the potential appeared some 350 ms before the awareness of conscious intention. Intentional, 'voluntary' acts are thus initiated by the brain without awareness, they are unconscious in intention, and begin about half a second before the act itself!

The second group of experiments related to the so-called split-brain subjects. The two sides of the brain are strongly interconnected by white-matter fibres running in the various commissures and the corpus callosum. The corpus callosum is a huge structure, which straddles the two halves of the brain and connects large parts of the two hemispheres. In some neurological conditions, the corpus callosum is surgically divided, for example for the control of difficult epilepsy, leading effectively to hemispheric disconnection. It is then possible, using specialised stereoscopic tachistoscopic presentations of stimuli, to present pictures or visual commands to each hemisphere selectively. Gazzaniga (1993) used these split-brain patients to explore the cerebral basis of consciousness. He showed that there is a 'left-brain interpreter' which rationalises behavioural inconsistencies. Thus, as one example, he projected a picture of a chicken claw to the left hemisphere, and a snow scene to the right. He then asked subjects to choose from an array of items in front of them a relevant associated item, in this case the correct ones being a shovel for the right side and a chicken for the left. The subject chose the opposite, but when asked to explain the choices replied that the chicken claw went with the chicken and one needed a shovel to clean out the chicken shed! The left brain thus provided a coherent explanation for the anomalous response, which had failed to include the visual information from the right hemisphere. Further, the subject was conscious of his responses, but unaware of the incorrectness or the origin of them.

The experiments of Libet have occasioned much debate, and vigorous defences of the position of those who subscribe to the Cartesian concept of free will have been penned. However, they raise important issues about the relationship between conscious intention and behaviour, and question the role of consciousness itself in so-called voluntary behaviour. The experiments led to similar conclusions, namely that intentions to act arise unconsciously, but the split-brain investigations demonstrate the other remarkable conclusion, namely that our verbal left hemispheres rationalise our behaviour, which can even be referred backwards in time! As one group of researchers puts it in respect of our conscious behaviours, 'we are all spin doctors' (Grigsby and Stevens, 2000, p. 272). We all have to provide a coherent explanation for our behaviour, consistent with our own image of ourselves, these attributions being non-consciously generated from our flawed lopsided brain. Flawed in the sense of our inability to have much insight into the origin of our behaviours, which are predominantly if not exclusively unavailable to consciousness, lopsided in the sense of the overriding dominance of the verbal control over our conscious experience. Control over and insight into what we do and how we do it are effectively extremely – some would say totally – limited. 'All our so-called consciousness is a more or less fanciful commentary on an unknown, perhaps unknowable, but felt text' (Nietzsche, quoted by Safranski, 2002, p. 208)

These important experiments into the neurophysiological and neuroanatomical basis of consciousness are startling in their implications for the concept of free will, and the agency of a subject over so-called voluntary behaviour. Of course we all think we have free will, we all feel subjectively consciously in control of our actions, but the illusion has been revealed. As Einstein remarked:

If the moon, in the act of completing its eternal way around the earth, were gifted with self consciousness, it would feel thoroughly convinced that it was travelling its way of its own accord on the strength of a resolution taken once and for all. So would a Being, endowed with higher insight and more perfect intelligence, watching man and his doings, smile about man's illusion that he was acting according to his own free will (quoted by Libet *et al.*, 1999, p. xii).

As one researcher put it: 'it is the result of thinking, not the process of thinking, that appears spontaneously in consciousness' (Miller, 1962, p. 56). The brain produces post-hoc rationalistion of our behaviour; accuracy and logic are simply not key components. Language allows for this rationalisation, which produces non-consciously constructed explanations. Grigsby and Stevens (2000) explain it thus: 'At bottom is a cooking up of reasons for what one does, spontaneously, not necessarily based on any awareness of the real causes of one's activity, but often involving recognition of patterns learned in association with past experience' (p. 244).

One current neuroscience view is therefore that most of our behaviour is generated by non-conscious brain processing. Our control and our insight into that control are astonishingly limited, and rationalisations abound, skilfully but deceptively given by our verbal left hemisphere. All we really know about are representations of our environment and ourselves, generated by our brains, and influenced by our past, our present environment and our future expectations. We give our own interpretations of our behaviour, and the tendency is to gloss and polish; these attributions however themselves also arise from non-conscious brain processes.

Behaviours that are learned become automatic, they shift in locus from being explicit to implicit, and to act against such ingrained propensities becomes very difficult. Character is a product of genetics and procedural learning, the acquisition is one of a process rather than a fact.

> The automatic, unconscious, repeated performance of routine behaviours is the essence of character. Activities that once may have been performed voluntarily become so ingrained over time that it is hard to imagine that they might be done differently. The individual tends to forget the circumstances under which a behaviour was learned (if they were ever known), and the schema, mediated by a relatively specific neural network, acquires a functional autonomy independent of the original learning (Grigsby and Stevens, 2000, p. 311).

People simply do not know how they became the way they are or why they have various behavioural dispositions, and it is likely the case that consciousness is not just so involved in decision-making as we like to think. Once the gestalt has formed, once closure of the cognitive construct has occurred, it is very difficult to see an alternative, that is the nature of the human mind.

In the same context, antisocial behaviour, mendacity and dishonesty can become habitual and rationalised. The power of language is that it lifts us out of the current moment, yet it is tied to symbolism. It is through language and related memory systems that experiences are stored, integrated, revived and re-evaluated, but also representations are re-represented with subsequent distortions, myths emerge as dominant social and personal constructs, the narrative of our individual lives is sculpted. 'The inner world is full of phantoms and will-o'-the wisps; the will is one of them' (Nietzsche, 1976, p. 494).

We have seen how certain personality predispositions are a central feature of many somatoform presentations, especially with chronic invalidism and somatisation disorder. Personality emerges as a feature of brain organisation, and there is every reason to believe that neural processes vary between individuals to explain individual differences in behaviour but also in potential for behaviour. The accessibility or otherwise of individuals to conscious insight of their behaviour will therefore also vary with their personality. However, since so much is simply not available to consciousness, it is logical to stop asking the question whether individuals are conscious of their behaviour or not, or what may be the role of consciousness, and ask how may the behaviour have arisen and what may be done to modify the behaviour and change it?

The answer to the first question has already been given. Even if consciousness for a certain behaviour can be implied (e.g. a patient claims a paralysed hand, but can be shown to be using it when observed discreetly), it does not mean that consciousness of the act is actually relevant for the expression of the behaviour, i.e. that the behaviour is consciously generated. There can be no implied causality, yet causality is central to the legal dilemma.

In most instances we do not know how the behaviours have arisen, we only have conjecture and a body of evidence, weak though it is, as has been presented in this book. Some people long for dependence more than others. They seek to extend neotony, the very delayed period of postnatal dependence that alone characterises human development. Personality variables and early environmental events are all relevant; these have been discussed in Chapter 2. People become what they are by developing their dispositional anlage, encouraged by those significant around them. A potential golfer, with a famous sporting father, at a young age has his recognised talents honed; he then adopts the paraphernalia of the apprentice, eventually becoming the man the childhood fathered. His neuromuscular system behaves that way, his character emerges that way, and then his lifestyle becomes embellished by his ongoing social matrix. Suggestion has played an important part in the moulding of the superstar image, yet all becomes neurobiogically ingrained. Nietzsche referred to this process of transformation as that of developing a second nature. The foot soldier fears that he will forget how to walk if he is taught consciously how to lift up his feet, but once marching has been incorporated into his body schema, it becomes second nature. However, as he opined about this process: 'true as it may be second nature . . . I have only now taken true possession of my first nature with this second nature' (Nietzsche, quoted by Safranski, 2002, p. 55). Consciousness, with language, are a part of the system of communication between people, between doctors and patients, and between lawyers and their clients. Memories, through the tricky, sticky medium of language, become contaminated by suggestion: autosuggestion is only a part. In the act of becoming we become who we want to be, but the act comes first (*in Anfang war die Tat!*).

If it is then not helpful to ask if symptoms are consciously derived or not, how should these medically unexplained symptoms be dealt with from a legal perspective? If conscious or unconscious causation cannot be proven, who should be compensated and for what? In fact this must be purely a legal matter, and, as outlined in Chapter 7, the law sets limits on compensation for psychiatric injury usually based on matters of policy and not on grounds of logic, and not much in alignment with contemporary medical thought. If someone can be shown to be doing something they adamantly refuse to accept they can do, this must be taken at face value. In the same way, someone who has opted for the life of an invalid, with the predispositions and preoccupations that go with that, must also be taken at face value. It is up to the law to decide if it wishes to compensate people with certain lifestyles, or who seem to be deceiving those advising them. If the somatoform symptoms are secondary to or coexist with a psychiatric disorder, and the latter can be shown to be an injury in tort, then the law can deal with that.

The second issue relates to what may be done to ameliorate the behaviour. If the answer is very little, then this needs to be stated. If the chances of rehabilitation are low, there is little point in suggesting prolonged periods of rehabilitation, since nothing will shift the patients' adoption of the sick role, except perhaps temporarily. Some people have taken the path of illness (Freud referred to this as a flight into illness), but have travelled too far for a return ticket to be of any value.

If the person manifestly can do something which they claim they can't, and if there is good reason to believe that the outcome will be favourable after the court case is settled, this needs to be expressed. The role of lexigenic factors here must be acknowledged, and taken into account when expressing a prognosis.

If some treatable psychiatric disorder is manifest, then the appropriate agencies need to be engaged, and aggressive treatment given. Time and time again in legal cases it is possible to read an expert report, done several years previously, advocating for example cognitive-behavioural therapy or antidepressant treatments which have never been instigated. The solicitor who receives such advice about a client but then fails to act on it, is compounding the lexigenic injury. A copy of the report to the patient's general practitioner with a suggestive letter is probably all that is needed. Several years later, when treatment may be offered, it is too late. Behaviours have become ingrained, and treatments rendered far less effective.

Claimants themselves often reject treatments, such as antidepressants, usually on very weak grounds, such as a fear of addiction with the drugs. Psychotropic drugs are very effective in patients with recognisable psychiatric disorders, from schizophrenia to PTSD, and to decline treatment during the course of a medicolegal inquiry must be seen as a failure to mitigate losses on behalf of the claimant.

Conclusions

This book has been about hysteria and its variants, with a particular emphasis on somatisation disorder, chronic or Briquet's hysteria, and their presentations in a medicolegal context. Hysteria has been shown to be as old as medicine itself, and there is little point in abolishing the term, or in pretending that disorders such as somatisation disorder are new conditions, discovered by the inventors of DSM and other committee-driven classifications. It is also clear that the these disorders are much commoner than recognised, but appear in various clinics under a multitude of terms, some with a core of credibility, such as irritable bowel syndrome, others fabulous, such as multiple chemical sensitivity and the like. All specialists view their symptom of interest through their own telescope, often picking up the wrong end, and the vision shrinks further.

Considerable emphasis has been placed on the differences between ordinary medical practice and the role of the expert in medicolegal cases. Some routines, such as the use of rating scales to assess symptoms, are not only unhelpful, but can be positively misleading. Relying on classification schemes such as the DSM and ICD often distorts not only clinical sense, but the whole of the patient–physician interaction. The latter is further influenced by the intrusion of the law, and the necessity to leap certain hurdles before a case can be considered for compensation. It has been shown how the limits are set, mainly as judgements of policy, and issues of medical importance have little to do with such decisions.

The underlying theories of the aetiology and pathogenesis of various forms of hysteria have been discussed, and the pendulum swings noted: the organic to the psychological, to the organic and back to the psychological. At present there is a swing back to the neurophysiological, with attempts to show changes in brain function, using imaging techniques. However, all of this is undermined unless the human situation is considered, and the ever-present human disposition to incorporate familial and social pressures into ongoing behaviour. Calamity, conflict and constitution all impinge on human consciousness and have a bearing on causality.

A considerable dispute in medicolegal practice often revolves around issues of exaggeration and malingering, but this, as the literature has revealed, is an age-old dilemma, catalysed by issues of financial compensation. There is some evidence, reviewed herein, that directly implicates compensation in the maintenance of symptoms. This should not divert attention away from the very real symptoms and suffering that many patients develop as a consequence of accidents, but it does raise fascinating questions about the development of symptoms in medical practice, outside the legal forum. Suggestion, a favourite psychological shibboleth, has a larger part to play in all of this than is often revealed!

The importance of personality and disorders of personality has been noted, again an aspect of this area, so often ignored or understated. It is rare to read in medicolegal reports that claimants are examples of a personality disorder, and yet some personality variants are not only overrepresented in patients presenting with somatisation, but they are also susceptible to the very mechanisms that interlink with somatisation – suggestibility, exaggeration, imprecision, poor reality testing and the like. The developing symptom history itself often reflects the personality disorder, and the abnormal illness behaviour is a diagnostic aid. Illness is simply a way of life for some people, irrespective of any disease process. Failure to understand the differences between illness and disease, between symptoms and signs, and between claimants and patients, is at the heart of the intellectual failures in this area.

The patient seen in medicolegal practice is not the same as the patient seen in ordinary medical consultation. Failure to appreciate this leads to many deceptive errors. The doctor–patient relationship is different, the expectations are different (notably that in ordinary practice patients come for reassurance that they do not have a disorder, and/or for treatment; in medicolegal practice claimants come for confirmation that they *do* have a condition and, often, that they will not get better), the very consultation practice is different. Experts cannot be or become treating agents without abandoning their impartiality to the courts.

This final chapter has attempted to examine causality and consciousness, central to the hysteria story, but has no ready solutions to the simple question about the role of consciousness in the aetiology and pathogenesis of symptoms. Certainly we are all unconscious of so much of our behaviour and the derivation of it, that it is hardly surprising that the genesis of the symptoms of hysteria will remain, for the individual patient, a mystery. As Kant revealed, what the mind seeks is not intellectual understanding (*Verstand*), but meaning (*Vernunft*) – truth and meaning are different concepts for the human mind, and meaning always takes precedence over truth. Mythical and logical thought are not the same since many aspects of myth are inaccessible to logic and the truths of logic are without precedent in myth. Whether pattents have conscious insight into the fact that things could be different is a separate matter, but even if they do, whether or not they can then do anything about it is still a further question. Those neurophilosophers who are interested in the question of consciousness could be well advised to study hysteria as a paradigm of a disorder of conscious experience. It seems to have been ignored by nearly all commentators in this otherwise lively intellectual area.

Hysteria, a medical chimera with centuries of tradition, cannot be abolished by mere committee. It is a diagnosis of the fascinating by the fascinated. It straddles myth, personal and societal, and reality; it demands notice of the extrinsic and the intrinsic in human motivation, it challenges the central foundations of medical diagnoses and practice. Hysteria *hysteron proteron*.

REFERENCES

Bebbington, P. (1980). Causal models and logical inference in epidemiological psychiatry. *British Journal of Psychiatry*, **136**, 317.

Bolton, D. and Hill, J. (1996). *Mind, Meaning and Mental Disorder*. Oxford: Oxford University Press.

Carr, E. H. (1961/1990). *What is History?* London: Penguin Books.

Cotterill, R. (1998). *Enchanted Looms.* Cambridge: Cambridge University Press.

Cutting, J. (1997). *Principles of Psychopathology. Two Worlds, Two Minds, Two Hemispheres.* Oxford: Oxford Medical Publications.

Davidson, D. (1993). *Causal relations.* In *Causation,* eds. E. Sosa and M. Tooley, pp. 75–88. Oxford: Oxford University Press.

Gazzaniga, M. S. (1993). Brain mechanisms and conscious experience. In *Experimental and Theoretical Studies of Consciousness,* pp. 247–62. Chichester: Wiley.

Grigsby, J. and Stevens, D. (2000). *Neurodynamics of Personality.* New York: Guilford Press.

Hart, H. L. A. and Honore T. (1985). *Causation in the Law,* 2nd edn. Oxford: Oxford University Press.

Himsworth, H. (1986). *Scientific Knowledge and Philosophic Thought.* Baltimore: Johns Hopkins University Press.

Hume, D. (1777/1995). *Enquiries Concerning Human Understanding and Concerning the Principles of Morals.* Oxford: Oxford University Press.

Jaspers, K. (1913/1963). *General Psychopathology.* Translated by: J. Hoenig and M. W. Hamilton. Manchester: Manchester University Press.

Jolowicz, J. A., Lewis, T. A. and Harris, D. M. (1971). *Winifield and Jolowicz on Tort,* 9th edn. London: Sweet & Maxwell.

Jones, M. A. and Sprince, A. (2001). Conversion disorder: a legal diagnosis. In: Contemporary Approaches to the Study of Hysteria ed. P. W. Hallegan, C. Bass and J. C. Marshall, pp. 155–170. Oxford: Oxford University Press.

Kräupl Taylor, F. (1979). *The Concepts of Illness, Disease and Morbus.* Cambridge: Cambridge University Press.

Libet, B. (1993). The neural time factor in conscious and unconscious events. In *Experimental and Theoretical Studies of Consciousness,* ed. B. Libet, A. Freeman and K. Sutherland, pp. 123–46. Chichester: Wiley.

Libet, B., Freeman, A. and Sutherland, K. (1999). *The Volitional Brain.* Thorverton: Imprint Academic.

Malleson, A. (2002). *Whiplash and other Useful Illness.* Toronto: McGill-Queens University Press.

Mill, J. S. (1886). *A System of Logic Ratiocinative and Inductive,* 8th edn. London: self-published.

Miller, G. A. (1962). *Psychology, The Science of Mental Life.* New York: Harper and Row.

Nietzsche, F. (1880/1968). *The Will to Power.* New York: Viking.

Nietzsche, F. (1976). *The Portable Nietzsche.* New York: Penguin.

Ogus, A. I. (1973). *The Law of Damages.* London: Butterworths.

Safranski, R. (2002). *Nietzsche, A Philosophical Biography.* New York: W. W. Norton.

Sim, M. (1992). *Compensation Claims.* Victoria, BC: Emmes.

Slavney, P. R. and McHugh, P. R. (1987). *Psychiatric Polarities.* Baltimore: Johns Hopkins University Press.

Appendix: Civil Procedure Rules Part 35

www.lcd.gov.uk/civil/procrules

WHAT'S	UPDATES	CURRENT	STATUTORY		CONSULTATION	COMMENTARIES	CONTACT	SEARCH
NEW?	& ZIPS	VERSIONS	INSTRUMENTS					
	Rules & Practice	Schedule 1 –	Schedule 2 –		Pre-Action	Glossary	Court	Index
	Directions	Rsc	Ccr		Protocols	Forms	Guides	

Part 35 is intended to limit the use of oral expert evidence to that which is reasonably required. In addition, where possible, matters requiring expert evidence should be dealt with by a single expert. Permission of the court is always required either to call an expert or to put an expert's report in evidence.

Expert evidence – general requirements

1.1 It is the duty of an expert to help the court on matters within his own expertise: rule 35.3(1). This duty is paramount and overrides any obligation to the person from whom the expert has received instructions or by whom he is paid: rule 35.3(2).

1.2 Expert evidence should be the independent product of the expert uninfluenced by the pressures of litigation.

1.3 An expert should assist the court by providing objective, unbiased opinion on matters within his expertise, and should not assume the role of an advocate.

1.4 An expert should consider all material facts, including those which might detract from his opinion.

1.5 An expert should make it clear:

(a) when a question or issue falls outside his expertise; and

(b) when he is not able to reach a definite opinion, for example because he has insufficient information.

243

1.6 If, after producing a report, an expert changes his view on any material matter, such change of view should be communicated to all the parties without delay, and when appropriate to the court.

Form and content of expert's reports

2.1 An expert's report should be addressed to the court and not to the party from whom the expert has received his instructions.

2.2 An expert's report must:
   (1) give details of the expert's qualifications;
   (2) give details of any literature or other material which the expert has relied on in making the report;
   (3) contain a statement setting out the substance of all facts and instructions given to the expert which are material to the opinions expressed in the report or upon which those opinions are based;
   (4) make clear which of the facts stated in the report are within the expert's own knowledge;
   (5) say who carried out any examination, measurement, test or experiment which the expert has used for the report, give the qualifications of that person, and say whether or not the test or experiment has been carried out under the expert's supervision;
   (6) where there is a range of opinion on the matters dealt with in the report-
      (a) summarise the range of opinion, and
      (b) give reasons for his own opinion;
   (7) contain a summary of the conclusions reached;
   (8) if the expert is not able to give his opinion without qualification, state the qualification; and
   (9) contain a statement that the expert understands his duty to the court, and has complied and will continue to comply with that duty.

2.3 An expert's report must be verified by a statement of truth as well as containing the statements required in paragraph 2.2(8) and (9) above.

2.4 The form of the statement of truth is as follows:

> I confirm that insofar as the facts stated in my report are within my own knowledge I have made clear which they are and I believe them to be true, and that the opinions I have expressed represent my true and complete professional opinion.

2.5 Attention is drawn to rule 32.14 which sets out the consequences of verifying a document containing a false statement without an honest belief in its truth.
   (For information about statements of truth see Part 22 and the practice direction which supplements it.)

2.6 In addition, an expert's report should comply with the requirements of any approved expert's protocol.

Information

3 Under Rule 35.9 the court may direct a party with access to information which is not reasonably available to another party to serve on that other party a document which records the information. The document served must include sufficient details of all the facts, tests, experiments and assumptions which underlie any part of the information to enable the party on whom it is served to make, or to obtain, a proper interpretation of the information and an assessment of its significance.

Instructions

4 The instructions referred to in paragraph 1.2(8) will not be protected by privilege (see rule 35.10(4)). But cross-examination of the expert on the contents of his instructions will not be allowed unless the court permits it (or unless the party who gave the instructions consents to it). Before it gives permission the court must be satisfied that there are reasonable grounds to consider that the statement in the report of the substance of the instructions is inaccurate or incomplete. If the court is so satisfied, it will allow the cross-examination where it appears to be in the interests of justice to do so.

Questions to experts

5.1 Questions asked for the purpose of clarifying the expert's report (see rule 35.6) should be put, in writing, to the expert not later than 28 days after receipt of the expert's report (see paragraphs 1.2 to 1.5 above as to verification).

5.2 Where a party sends a written question or questions direct to an expert, a copy of the questions should, at the same time, be sent to the other party or parties.

5.3 The party or parties instructing the expert must pay any fees charged by that expert for answering questions put under rule 35.6. This does not affect any decision of the court as to the party who is ultimately to bear the expert's costs.

Single expert

6 Where the court has directed that the evidence on a particular issue is to be given by one expert only (rule 35.7) but there are a number of disciplines relevant to that issue, a leading expert in the dominant discipline should be identified as the

single expert. He should prepare the general part of the report and be responsible for annexing or incorporating the contents of any reports from experts in other disciplines.

Assessors

7.1 An assessor may be appointed to assist the court under rule 35.15. Not less than 21 days before making any such appointment, the court will notify each party in writing of the name of the proposed assessor, of the matter in respect of which the assistance of the assessor will be sought and of the qualifications of the assessor to give that assistance.

7.2 Where any person has been proposed for appointment as an assessor, objection to him, either personally or in respect of his qualification, may be taken by any party.

7.3 Any such objection must be made in writing and filed with the court within 7 days of receipt of the notification referred to in paragraph 6.1 and will be taken into account by the court in deciding whether or not to make the appointment (section 63(5) of the County Courts Act 1984).

7.4 Copies of any report prepared by the assessor will be sent to each of the parties but the assessor will not give oral evidence or be open to cross-examination or questioning.

Index

Numbers in *italics* refer to tables and figures.

abnormal illness behaviour (AIB) *37*, 36–8, 39,
    48–50, *71*
  see also illness
abreaction 151–2
abulia 132
accident neurosis 100–1
accident-related amnesia
  assessment problems 112–13
  duration 113
  and head injury assessment 112
  ongoing 113
  posttraumatic 112–13
  psychogenic 113
  relevance to somatisation 112
  retrograde 112
accidents
  hysteria provoked by 8, 12–14
  see also accident-related amnesia; claims for
    psychiatric injury
aggravated damage 192
AIB *see* abnormal illness behaviour (AIB)
Alcock v. *Chief Constable of South Yorkshire Police*
  [1992] 188–9
alexithymia 58
Alzheimer's disease *117*
amitriyptyline 148
amnesia
  of criminal offences 124
  feigned, tests for *126*, *129*, 127–9
  see also accident-related amnesia; psychogenic
    amnesia
Amsterdam Short Term Memory Test 128–9
anaesthetic patches 1, 7, *51*
anterior cingulate syndrome *131*
antidepressants 148, 150–1
antisocial personality disorders 34, 92
anxiety 24, 205
apathetico-akinetico-abulic syndrome
  131–2
assessment 140
  see also clinical presentations: history-taking;
    rating scales

attitude pathosis 88–9
Auditory-Verbal Learning Task 126

back/neck injuries, follow-up of litigants 161–2
Baglivi, Georgio 3
Baker v. *Willoughby* [1970] *231*, 230–31
belle indifférence 47–8
bereavement damages 192
Blackmore, Sir Richard 6
blindsight 120–21
body dysmorphic disorder 58
body image 205
borderline personality disorder
  features 34–5
  neuropsychological deficits
    executive function 135–6
    memory 134
    summarised *136*
    visual discrimination/filtering 134–5
Bourhill v. *Young* [1943] 187
brain
  imaging studies 204
  left hemisphere rationalisation of
    behaviour 235, 236–7
  processing models 110–11
  see also frontal lobe syndromes
Breuer, Joseph 10
Briquet, Pierre 6–7
Briquet's syndrome *see* somatisation disorder
  (Briquet's syndrome)
Brodie, Sir Benjamin 8
but for/*sine qua non* test 228, *231*, 229–32

California Verbal Learning Test *126*, 128
Camelford water pollution episode 211
carpal tunnel syndrome 76
Carter, Robert Brudenell 5
causalgia–dystonia syndrome 66, 69–70
causation 220–32
  general ideas
    causality built into cognitive framework
      (Kant) 222

causation (*cont.*)
  final causes (Aristotle) 223
  human reason and mind–body dualism
      (Descartes) 221
  increase in probability 223
  necessary and sufficient conditions 222
  plurality of causes (Mill) 222
  representation and interpretation 222
  role of instinct and feeling (Hume) 221
  in law 228–32
    foreseeable 229
    material contribution to 228
    pre-existing vulnerability and 231–2
    remoteness and 228–9
    sine qua non/but for test 228, *231,*
        229–32
  in medicine 223
    accidents and psychiatric illness 224
    analogies in folk psychology 223
    legal views of 224–5
    physical concepts 223–4
    theories of 225–6
    understandable connections (Jaspers)
        226–7
character 237
Charcot, J-M 7–8
Cheyne, George 4
children, somatoform disorders in 157
chorea lascivia 2
chronic fatigue syndrome (CFS) 60–3
  clinical presentation 62
  course 62
  fatigue 60–1, 62
  mass hysteria hypothesis 61–2
  myalgic encephalomyelitis (ME) 61
  neurasthenia 60–1, 62
  overlap with other syndromes 77
  personality profiles of patients 63
  prognosis *158,* 157–8
  psychiatric co-morbidity 63
  social construction of 79, 211
  somatisation rates 77
  treatment 148, 149
  and virus infections 62–3
civil justice system
  courts 169–70
  issue of expert access to histories 171
  medical evidence, differences from criminal
      system *172,* 172
  reforms of Lord Woolf 170–71
    case hierarchy 170
    disclosure procedures 170
    payment into court 170–71
    role of experts 170, 172
    see also Civil Procedure Rules regarding
        experts; claims for psychiatric injury
Civil Procedure Rules regarding experts 172–84,
    246
  discussion of issues
    discussions between experts 176–7
    experts' responsibilities 174–6
    matters of opinion 174

selection of experts 173, 174
single joint experts 176
practice direction
  assessors 246
  form and content of reports 244–5
  general requirements of experts 244
  information availability 245
  instructions 245
  questions to experts 245
  single experts 245–6
problems in medicolegal practice 177, 194–5
  definition of expert 177
  discussions between experts 183–4
  experts of 'like discipline' 178
  psychiatry/psychology distinctions 178–9
  questions of causation 178, 180–1
  single joint expert roles 181–2
  time constraints 180, 183
  treating clinicians as experts 179–80
claims for psychiatric injury 184–94
  in absence of physical injury 185
  authorities *186, 187*
  caution of courts 185
  claimants; views of process 193
  compensation *see* compensation
  key decisions
    Hillsborough trial 188–9
    Page v. *Smith* [1996] 189–91
  key decisions (pre-Hillsborough)
    Bourhill v. *Young* [1943] 187
    Hambrook v. *Stokes Bros* [1925] 187
    McLoughlin v. *O'Brien* [1983] 187–8
  nervous shock 184–5
  primary and secondary claimants 185–6, *189,*
      194
  recognised psychiatric disorder 191
  recoverability criteria *187, 188, 189, 194*
    foreseeability 188, 189
    proximity test 188
    reasonable fortitude 187, 190
    relationship test 189
    unaided senses 187
  rules for claimants, summarised *194*
  video evidence 191–2
classification 21–40
  manuals 22
    DSM-IV *see* DSM-IV
    ICD-10 *see* ICD-10
    medicolegal aspects of use 29–31, 191
  modern concepts
    development of 22–3
    symptoms, signs and diseases 23
  of neuroses 24
  of somatoform disorders
    development 24–6
    in DSM-IV and ICD-10 *28,* 26–9
clinical presentations 45–83
  disorders
    chronic fatigue syndrome *see* chronic fatigue
        syndrome
    dystonia 48–50, *69, 70, 71,* 68–71
    fibromyalgia *64,* 63–5

hypochondriasis 57–8
occupational 75–6
pain *see* pain, hysterical
reflex sympathetic dystrophy 66–8
somatisation 26, 29, 54, 55, 52–7
spectrum of 76–8
whiplash *see* whiplash injury
functional somatic syndromes 46–7, 76, 77
history-taking 46–7, 77
illness history 48
onset of disorder 47–8
patient personality 47
presence of AIB 48–50, 71
physical examination 46, 51, 50–2, 52, 56
range of symptoms 46, 45–6
surgical procedures, frequencies of 53–4, 55, 56
symptom frequencies 54
cognitive-behaviour therapy 148–50
cognitive styles 38
hysterical 32–3
impulsive 33
cognitive tests 132–3
coin-in-the-hand test 126
communicable hysteria *see* mass hysteria
compensation
Conditional Fee Arrangement 193–4
damages 193, 192–3
'legal aid blackmail' 194
and traumatic neuroses 153
and whiplash injury 73–5
of workers and malingering 86–7
see also litigants: follow-up studies of
compensation neurosis 85, 88, 153
complex regional pain syndrome 66, 67, 68
concussion of the spine 12–13, 86
Conditional Fee Arrangement 193–4
confabulation 120–21
consciousness 234, 233–9
current main issues 233
important experiments
neural time factor (Libet) 234–5
in split-brain subjects 235
implications of results 235–7
and language 234, 237
legal aspects 233, 238–9
and second nature development
(Nietzsche) 238
in somatoform presentations 237–8, 241
see also dissociation
construct validity 141
content validity 141
conversion 10–11
conversion disorders
brain-imaging studies 204
classification 24, 25, 26
differentiation from malingering 101
epidemiology 44, 43–5
features of 105
pain in 59–60
personality styles 32

prognosis 156
in children 157
treatment 162–3
see also treatment
corpus callosum 235
cortical evoked potentials 234–5
courts of law 169–70
CPR *see* Civil Procedure Rules regarding experts
criminal medical evidence, differences from
civil 172, 172
criterion validity 141
Cutler v. Vauxhall Motors Ltd [1971] 231–2
cyberchondria 57

damages 193, 192–3
degenerative dementia 117
Demara, Ferdinand Walter 95
dementias *see* degenerative dementia;
pseudodementia
dependency, encouragement of 55–6
depression
and chronic pain 60
reactive 24
and somatoform disorders 205–6
depressive dementia 117, 116–17, 118, 134
Descartes, René 221
diagnostic manuals 22
medicolegal aspects of use 29–31, 191
see also DSM-IV; ICD-10
Diagnostic and Statistical Manual, IVth edition
(DSM-IV) *see* DSM-IV
disease 23
causality theories 225–6
dissocial (antisocial) personality disorders 34, 92
dissociation 119–20, 199–200
classification of disorders 25, 28–9
doubts about the concept 212
Janet's concept of 9, 28, 199
as part of normal psyche 200
physiological 120
rating scales 120, 144, 146–7
use of the term 120
Dissociation Experiences Scale (DES) 146–7
dissociative amnesia *see* psychogenic amnesia
dissociative (multiple) identity disorder 123
dopamine, and dystonia development 68
DSM-IV 22
categorisation of somatoform disorders 28
malingering in 87–8, 90–2
multiaxial approach 23
proper use of 30–1
somatisation disorder, diagnostic criteria 26, 27
see also diagnostic manuals: medicolegal
aspects of use
Dulieu v. White [1901] 185
dysmorphophobia 58
dysthymia 24
dystonia 48–50, 69, 70, 71, 68–71

effort syndrome 15
'eggshell skull' trial 189–91

Employers' Liability Acts (1880, 1906) 86–7
Engel, George 59
epidemic hysteria *see* mass hysteria
epidemiology 41–5
    conversion disorders *44*, 43–5
    hypochondriasis 45
    importance of GP records 42
    problem with frequency estimation 42
    sex differences 45
    somatisation disorder 45
Epstein–Barr virus 62–3
Erichsen, John Eric 12–14
erklären and *verstehen* 226–7
executive function
    deficits in borderline personality
        disorder 135–6
    tests of *125*, 125, *132*, 132–3
    see also frontal lobe syndromes
exercise 149
expert witnesses
    access to historical information 171, *172*
    duties and functions (pre-CPR reforms) *175*
    views of Lord Woolf 170, 172
    see also Civil Procedure Rules regarding experts
explicit memory 111

face validity 141
factitious disorders 92–3, *105*
    see also Münchausen's syndrome
Falret, Jean Pierre 6
false memories
    confabulation 120–21
    creation of 123
    false confessions 121
    flashbulb memories 122
    lobby groups 123
    medicolegal importance 123
    memory amplification in PTSD 123
    recovered memories controversy 121–2
    suggestibility to 122–3
false-memory syndrome 49, 122, 212
fatigue 60–1, 62
    postviral 62–3
    rating scales *144*
    see also chronic fatigue syndrome
feminism and hysteria 17–18
fibromyalgia
    antidepressant treatment 148
    clinical presentation 63–5
    cognitive-behaviour therapy 149
    diagnostic criteria *64*
    graded exercise 149
    prognosis 158
flashbulb memories 122
follow-up studies *see* prognosis
forced choice tests 126–7, 128
foreseeability 188, 189, 229
free will 235–6
Freud, Sigmund 10–11, 122, 199, 233
frontal convexity syndrome *131*
frontal lobe syndromes 129–30

clinical features *131*, 130–2
detection *125*, 125, *132*, 132–3
problems with assessment 133–4
    see also executive function: deficits in borderline
        personality disorder
fugue *see* postictal fugue; psychogenic fugue

Ganser syndrome 28, 119
general practitioners (GPs)
    role in treatment 152
    usefulness of notes 42
generative organs and hysteria 1, 4–5
geste antagoniste 71
glandular fever 62–3
Glasgow Coma Scale 112
globus hystericus 1
grand chorea epidemics 2
Griesinger, Wilhelm 4–5
Gulf War Syndrome (GWS) 210–11

Hambrook v. *Stokes Bros* [1925] 187
head-injury assessment 112
    see also frontal lobe syndromes
Health Attitude Survey 146
Hillsborough trial 188–9
historical overview of hysteria 1–20
    dissociation 9
    French work 6–7
        Charcot 7–8
        Janet *see* Janet, Pierre
    Freud's work *see* Freud, Sigmund
    hysteria in men 3, 6, 10
    involvement of the brain 2–3
    involvement of the emotions 3
    involvement of the generative organs 1, 4–5
    mass hysteria 2
    nervous disorders 3–4
    new hysteria studies 17–18, 21
    personality structure 4, 6
    posttraumatic neuroses
        civilian accidents 8, 12–14
        war neuroses 11–12, 14–17
    role of consciousness 5
    sexual repression 5
    suggestion 9–10
    wandering womb 1
    witchcraft 1–2
    see also mechanisms of symptom generation and
        maintenance: evolution of theories
histrionic personality disorder *see* hysterical
    personalities
Hoover's sign 50
Human Rights Act (1998) 169
Hume, David 221
hypnosis 151–2, 201
    use by Charcot 7–8
hypochondriasis
    body dysmorphic disorder 58
    classification *28*
    clinical features 50, 57–8, *105*
    defined 57

historical ideas 3–4, 6
monosymptomatic 57
prevalence 45
rating scales 143, 144
hysteria 241
issues about the term 31–2
loss of the term 21
mass 2, 61–2, 201
see also historical overview of hysteria; men:
hysteria in
hysterical amnesia 119
hysterical dementia 118, 117–9
hysterical gaits 52
hysterical personalities 31–4
cognitive style 32–3
features 32, 33
historical descriptions 4, 6
hysteria and 31–2
medicolegal dilemmas 33–4

ICD-10
dissociative disorders in 28–9
malingering in 88
somatoform disorders in 28, 29
see also diagnostic manuals: medicolegal aspects
of use
illness
causality theories 225–6
and disease 23
illness behaviour 35–6
abnormal 37, 36–8, 39, 48–50, 71
normal 36
models of progression to 36
social construction of 210
social and cultural aspects 35–6
Illness Behaviour Questionnaire (IBQ) 145, 144–6
implicit memory 111
impulsive personalities 33
incidence 43
see also epidemiology
infectious mononucleosis 62–3
International Classification of Diseases, 10th edition
(ICD-10) see ICD-10
interobserver reliability 141
interviews, semistructured 142, 146
irritable bowel syndrome (IBS) 77

Janet, Pierre 8–9, 28, 199
Jaspers, Karl 226, 227
Jobling v. Associate Dairies Ltd [1982] 231
Jorden, Edward 2
juridogenic harm 171

Kant, Immanuel 222, 241
Kardiner, Abraham 15, 17

Laycock, Thomas 5
learning 111
see also memory
left hemisphere rationalisation of behaviour 235,
236–7

'legal aid blackmail' 194
lexigenic morbidity 171
limbic system 198
litigants, follow-up studies of 159
neck and back injuries 161–2
posttraumatic neuroses 159–61
litigation, costs of 84
Liverpool Roman Catholic Archdiocesan Trustees
Inc. v. Goldberg 179–80
long-term memory 111
Lordat, Count de 86
lying
in children 97–8
classification of 97
detection of 102
general consideration of 96, 104
neuroanatomy of 97
self-deceit 96–7
simulation/deceit in animals 97
see also pseudologia fantastica

McFarlane v. E. E. Caledonia [1994] 185
McLoughlin v. O'Brien [1983] 187–8
malingering 84–108, 215
attitude pathosis and 88–9
conscious and unconscious aspects 98
definitions of 88, 89, 89
detection 98–103, 104
attitude and behaviour 100–2
caught in flagrante delicto 98–100, 191–2
confession/betrayal 100
differentiation from conversion disorder 101
memory tests 126, 127–9, 129
miscellaneous techniques 102
observation of claimants 102–3, 191–2
orthopaedic patients 101–2
in the diagnostic manuals 87–8, 90–2
distinctions from conversion 89, 89
early examples 1, 85–7
features of 105
medical/psychiatric interpretations 89
medicolegal aspects 90–1, 103–4, 106
memory complaints 124
military setting 90
overlapping conditions 92–8
as a social concept 88
subdivisions of 90
suspicion-arousing features 88, 90–2
mass hysteria 2, 61–2, 201
mechanisms of symptom generation and
maintenance 215–6, 240
anxiety 205
attentional 202
disorders of affect 205–6
dissociation see dissociation
evolution of theories 197–8
see also historical overview of hysteria
hysteria symptoms as metaphors 206
influence of body image 205
insights from brain-imaging studies 204
newer psychological theories 202–4

mechanisms of symptom generation and
    maintenance (*cont.*)
  personality and symptom perception 205
  repression 5, 200, 212
  sociocultural 214–5
    see also sociocultural influences and
      somatoform disorders
  suggestion 9–10, 122–3, 200–2
  summarised 215
medicolegal aspects
  claims *see* claims for psychiatric injury
  cost of litigation 84
  doctor–patient relationship 241
  malingering 90–1, 103–4, 106
  medical negligence 169
  use of diagnostic manuals 29–31
  use of rating scales 142–3
  see also causation; Civil Procedure Rules
    regarding experts; litigants, follow-up
    studies of
memory
  classification 111
  deficits in borderline personality disorder 134
  false *see* false memories
  malingering and 124
  neurological damage and 124–5
  past notions of 109–10
  processes 110, 111
  tests 125, 125–7
    development of 124
    executive function 125, 125, 132, 132–3
    interpretation of 124, 127
    for malingering 126, 129, 127–9
    unreliability of 109, 120–1, 136–7
    see also accident-related amnesia; frontal lobe
      syndromes; psychogenic amnesia
memory distrust syndrome 121
men, hysteria in 3, 6, 10, 45
  pain syndromes 59–60
  see also war neuroses
Mill, JS 222
Minnesota Multiphasic Personality Inventory
  (MMPI) 143
motor symptoms, tests of 50, 133
Mott, Sir Frederick 14
Münchausen's syndrome 93–4, 105
  by proxy 94
myalgic encephalomyelitis (ME) 61
Myers, Charles 15
myofascial pain syndrome 65

narcissistic personalities 60, 205
National Adult Reading Test 126
neck/back injuries, follow-up of litigants 161–2
negligence 169
nervous disorder, hysteria as 3–4
nervous shock 184–5
neurasthenia 60–61, 62
neuralgodystrophy 66
neuropsychological tests *see* memory: tests
neuroses, classification of 24

'non-diseases' 210
  see also specific conditions
non-epileptic seizures *see* pseudoseizures

occupational disorders of upper limbs 75–6
On Concussion of the Spine (Erichsen) 12–13
orbitofrontal syndrome *131*
orthopaedic patients, signs of malingering
  in 101–2

Page, Herbert 86
Page v. *Smith* [1996] 189–91
pain 58
pain, hysterical 58–9
  depression and 60
  diagnostic criteria 59
  location of 60
  'pain-prone' people 59–60
Paracelsus 2
passive-dependent personalities 34
pathologising 208
perseveration 130, 133
personality
  CSF patients 63
  and history-taking 47
  and somatisation 25, 38, 214, 240
    see also personality disorders
  and symptom perception 205
personality disorders
  antisocial/dissocial 34, 92
  borderline *see* borderline personality disorder
  histrionic *see* hysterical personalities
  memory impairment and 119, 134
  relationship with neuroses 24
physical examination *46, 51, 52,* 50–2, *56*
physiological dissociation 120
Piper Alpha disaster 185
positron emission tomography (PET) studies
  204
postictal fugue 116, *116*
posttraumatic amnesia (PTA) 112–13
  see also situational amnesia
posttraumatic neuroses
  and compensation 153
  follow-up of litigants 159–61
posttraumatic stress disorder (PTSD)
  concerns about the diagnosis 206–10
  establishment as a diagnostic category 207
  factitious cases 210
  memory amplification in 123
  traumatic memory 208
postviral fatigue 62–3
precedent 168
pretraumatic amnesia *see* retrograde amnesia
  (RA)
prevalence 42
  see also epidemiology
primary care 42
Primary Care Evaluation of Mental Disorders
  (PRIME-MD) 146
principle of sufficient reason 221

prognosis 163
  children 157
  chronic fatigue syndrome *158*, 157–8
  fibromyalgia 158
  follow-up studies
    early *154*, 153–6
    recent *155*, 156–7
  litigants 159
    neck and back injuries 161–2
    posttraumatic neuroses 159–61
  predictors *159*, 159
  pseudoseizures 158
pseudodementia 116
  depressive *117*, 116–7, *118*, 134
  hysterical *118*, 117–9
pseudologia fantastica 94–5
pseudoseizures 18, 43, 45, 158
psychasthenia 60
psychiatric injury, claims for *see* claims for
    psychiatric injury
psychical paralysis 8
psychogenic amnesia
  accident-related 113
  features 113–15
  personality disorders and 119
  syndromes
    hysterical amnesia 119
    listed *114*
    pseudodementia *see* pseudodementia
    psychogenic fugue 114, 115–16, *116*
    situational amnesia 115
psychogenic dystonia *see* dystonia
psychogenic fugue 114, 115–16, *116*
psychogenic movement disorders,
    prognosis 156–7
psychogenic seizures *see* pseudoseizures
psychologists and psychiatrists, as expert
    witnesses 178–9
psychopaths 34
psychoses
  discovery of underlying pathologies 23
  frontal lobe deficits in 134
  pseudologia fantastica in 94–5
PTSD *see* posttraumatic stress disorder
    (PTSD)

railway accidents 12
  concussion of the spine 12–13, 86
  related hysteria 13
railway spine (Erichsen's disease) 13
rating scales
  how used 140–41
  issues about use 141–2
    in medicolegal practice 142–3
  reliability 141
  response sets 142
  semistructured interviews 142, 146
  sensitivity 142
  somatoform disorder assessment *144*, *145*,
    143–7
  validity 141

Raven's Progressive Matrices 128
reaction 226
readiness potentials 235
recovered memories controversy 121–2
reflex sympathetic dystrophy (RSD) 66–8
reliability of rating scales 141
remoteness, in law 228–9
repetitive strain injury (RSI) 75, 211–2
repression 5, 200, 212
reticular activating system (RAS) 198, 200
retrograde amnesia (RA) 112
revenge and the law 168
Rey 15-item Memory Test 128
Reynolds, Russell 8
Rivers, WHR 201, 208
Ross, TA 15, 16, 17, 153
Royal Free Disease (myalgic encephalomyelitis;
    ME) 61
RSD (reflex sympathetic dystrophy) 66–8

Sargant, William 17
schizophrenia, frontal deficits in 134
selective serotonin reuptake inhibitors (SSRIs) 148
semantic memory 111
semistructured interviews 142, 146
sexual abuse
  and recovered memories 121–2
  and somatoform disorders 214
shellshock 14–15, 16, 209
  see also war neuroses
Shorter, Edward 18
short-term memory 111
shoulder–hand syndrome 66
Showalter, Elaine 17–18
signs (term) 23
sine qua non/but for test 228, *231*, 229–32
single joint experts (SJEs) 176, 181–2, 245–6
situational amnesia 115
Slater, Eliot 17, 153
Smith v. *Leech Brain* [1962] 229
social construction of illness 210
sociocultural influences and somatoform
    disorders
  deceit 212–13
  early life experiences 213–14
  personality style 214
  responses of others 213, 215
  sexual abuse 214
  see also compensation
sociopathy 34
sodium amytal abreaction 151–2
somatic delusional disorder *105*
Somatic Symptom Index (SSI) of the Diagnostic
    Interview Scale (DIS) 146
somatisation
  definitions 25
  introduction of term 24–25
  rating scales *144*
somatisation disorder (Briquet's syndrome) *105*
  clinical presentation 26, 29, *54*, *55*, 52–7
  diagnostic criteria 26, *27*, 29

somatisation disorder (Briquet's
    syndrome) (*cont.*)
  early research 25
  epidemiology 45
  prognosis 155–6
  symptoms *46*
somatoform autonomic dysfunction 29
somatoform pain disorder 29, 59
Somatosensory Amplification Scale 146
'split-brain' subjects, experiments in 235
splitting, in borderline personalities 35
standard of proof 169
Stekel, Wilhelm 25
stem completion tasks *126*
Structured Clinical Interview for
    DSM–Dissociative Disorders
    (SCID-D) 146
Sudeck's atrophy 66
suggestion 9–10, 122–3, 200–2
  see also abreaction; hypnosis
surgery, in somatisation patients 53–4, *56*
Sydenham, Thomas 3
sympathetic nervous system and RSD 66, 67–8
Symptom Check List 90 (SCL-90) 143
symptoms (term) 23
syndromes (term) 23

tender points *64*, 64, 65
tennis elbow 76
tenosynovitis 75
test–retest reliability 141
therapists, desirable attitudes *151*
torts 169
Tower of London task 133
treatment 147–53
  abreaction 151–2
  antidepressant 148, 150–1
  cognitive-behaviour therapy 148–50
  diversity of remedies 147
  exercise 149
  follow-up studies *see* prognosis
  general guidelines 150
  GP role 152

  helpful therapist attitudes *151*
  hypnosis 151–2, 201
  lack of studies on 147
  and legal claimants 239
  problems of diagnosis 147–8
  setting 152
  specialist 152–3
  targets for *151*
Trials test 128
tricyclic antidepressants 148

undifferentiated somatoform disorder 29

validity of rating scales 141
Vernon v. Bosley [1997] 179
verstehen and *erklären* 226–7
victim culture, creation by psychology
    industry 207–8
video evidence 191–2

Waddell's signs *52*, 52, 145
wandering womb 1
war neuroses 11–12, 14–17
  see also malingering: military setting
Wechsler Memory Scale 126, 128
whiplash injury 71–2
  chronic 72–5
    attributable pathology 72–3
    pre-accident pain 74
    prognostic factors 72
    psychiatric aspects 73, 74
    role of compensation 73–5
    symptoms 72
  follow-up of litigants 161–2
Whiteley Index of Hypochondriasis 144
Whytt, Sir Robert 3–4
Willis, Thomas 3
Wisconsin Card Sorting Task (WCST) 133
witchcraft 1–2
women, pain-prone 59
Woolf, Lord *see* civil justice system: reforms of
    Lord Woolf
workers' compensation and malingering 86–7